On Niebuhr

On Niebuhr

A Theological Study

Langdon Gilkey

The University of Chicago Press
Chicago and London

LANGDON GILKEY has taught most recently at Georgetown University, the University of Virginia, and the University of Chicago Divinity School, where he is the Shailer Mathews Professor of Theology (emeritus). He is the author of a number of books, including *Shantung Compound, Gilkey on Tillich,* and *Nature, Reality, and the Sacred.*

The University of Chicago Press, Chicago 60637
The University of Chicago Press, Ltd., London
© 2001 by The University of Chicago
All rights reserved. Published 2001
Printed in the United States of America
10 09 08 07 06 05 04 03 02 01   5 4 3 2 1

ISBN (cloth): 0-226-29341-6

Library of Congress Cataloging-in-Publication Data

Gilkey, Langdon Brown, 1919–
      On Niebuhr : a theological study / Langdon Gilkey.
          p.   cm.
      Includes bibliographical references and index.
      ISBN 0-226-29341-6 (alk. paper)
      1. Niebuhr, Reinhold, 1892–1971.   2. Theology—History—20th century.   I. Title.
   BX4827.N5 G55   2001
   230′.092—dc21   00-060728

♾The paper used in this publication meets the minimum requirements of the American National Standard for Information Sciences—Permanence of Paper for Printed Library Materials, ANSI Z39.48-1992.

Dedicated with love to my family

Sonja
Frouwkje and Stephane
Amos Welcome
Whitney, Laura, and Sofia

Contents

Abbreviations

Niebuhr's works directly cited in this book are indicated as follows:

BT   *Beyond Tragedy*
FH   *Faith and History*
MM   *Moral Man and Immoral Society*
ND   *The Nature and Destiny of Man*
RE   *Reflections on the End of an Era*

Preface

The central intent of Niebuhr's theology, and so of this volume, is the understanding of society, especially political society, and the understanding of history and of the human nature that in part creates and in part disturbs society and history. Let us note that in Niebuhr's theology it is our common social and historical world that is understood or made intelligible, not some transcendent 'theological' realm. However, it is also true that in Niebuhr's case the understanding of our social world is a theological understanding—that is, one accomplished by viewing human being in its deeper, religious dimension, in its relation to God as well as in its political and economic relations. To present this theological way of understanding our social and individual existence is the central purpose of this volume.

For many people in the 1930s and 1940s, through the devastation of the Depression, of social and racial unrest, and of two world wars ending in the Holocaust, the meaning and direction of history, and so the nature of the humans who helped create it, became utterly central questions. The optimism and the extravagant confidence in progress characteristic of the early part of the century had now vanished, and a deeply felt spiritual void remained. Hence Niebuhr's realistic yet hopeful interpretation of our common life held great power and authenticity. In a turbulent epoch when evil often appeared to be dominant, Niebuhr's theology seemed to present the possibility of a social realism that maintained its moral nerve and did not become either cynical or despairing, even when self-interest appeared to rule everywhere. Since the optimistic base for creative work for justice was now gone, the question was: How is it possible to have hope and to maintain the struggle for justice in a world so filled with self-interest? Niebuhr provided a very persuasive answer; he did not so much destroy the reasons for social action as reground them in a much soberer social epoch. This certainly is one of the reasons that his thought, from 1932 through 1960, had such a very great impact on American secular as well as religious social understanding.

Our problems are now, in many ways, different; but the question of moral integrity, amid a very ambiguous and precarious political and historical scene, remains. Every new freedom from tyranny seems to end in corruption, and even the new problem of the preservation of nature discloses itself in the end as a political and so a moral problem. Thus I find Niebuhr's thought still remarkably relevant at the end of the century. To present it to our time as a real possibility for contemporary understanding appears to me, therefore, an important venture. Also from this vantage point, half a century later, the question of Niebuhr's relation to "modernity" is a newly fascinating one. He saw himself to be in major conflict with modernity; yet from our perspective, he seems to have absorbed, and reinterpreted theologically, many of the most important assumptions of modern culture—as have perhaps the postmodernists themselves. Niebuhr may not persuade a young mind today that there is a God who gives meaning to our history—as Niebuhr himself certainly believed—but he will persuade that mind that history so understood is very close to the history we all continue to experience each day.

Much that Niebuhr wrote is here omitted from consideration. I will not examine his veritable library of commentaries, articles, and essays. For the purpose of presenting the core of his thought, two elements of this corpus are essential: his early political writings and his mature theology. This volume concerns itself with these materials only: his view of social and political behavior, of human nature as the source of that behavior, and all this in relation to God, the ground of the hope for and confidence in history's meaning. As I noted above, these were reflections that fitted well the crises of the turbulent times in which they were formed. Hence they had a great impact on American intellectual and religious life—and they significantly shaped my own life and experience, as the book will also seek to show. These various themes are, therefore, woven in and through the book: an analysis of Niebuhr's thought as it develops through political commentary to theology; the relevance of this analysis to the crises of the 1930s and 1940s; and the role that his thought played in my experience during the Second World War and in my subsequent life's work.

One further point. There is a very great deal that has been written about Niebuhr's thought, both in the recent past and in the present. Most of this has, for very good reasons, concentrated on his political and ethical understanding, which remains for us today both relevant and interesting. These are excellent works; I shall omit consideration of them only to limit the length of this otherwise unwieldy volume. In any case, to my knowledge, no one has tried to present Niebuhr's political and ethical views in the light of his entire theological viewpoint—which was, I believe, the way that he always saw those views. That is to say, he understood politics and ethics *theologically*, in relation to what he regarded as the Christian understanding of human being, of the creativity and the ambiguity of freedom, and of the course of history under God. As he argued repeatedly, this theological framework is essential for any valid comprehension of the puzzles and paradoxes of our ordinary experience. Thus to present the whole Niebuhr, as I think he saw his own thought, is the other main purpose of the volume.

∞

There are several persons whom I wish to thank for their help in the making of this volume. First of all, the administration and the faculty of theology, especially its chair, Tony Tambusco, of Georgetown University, generously provided support for the preparation of the manuscript through the Landegger Theology Department Fund. And my longtime friend and colleague at Georgetown, Joan Reuss, patiently, and with amazing accuracy, typed the manuscript from my illegible script and inaudible dictation. I am grateful for many reasons, some of them nostalgic, to the University of Chicago Press for agreeing to publish this volume. And, above all, I wish to reexpress my gratitude to Sonja, especially, and to my enlarging family—to whom this book is dedicated—for bearing with me so lovingly, not only during the preparation of the book, but all through these many wonderful years of love, of caring, of play, of work—in short, of vivid and lively life together.

Langdon Gilkey

PART 1

First Encounters and Early Political Writings

CHAPTER 1

Early Encounters

It may be well to begin this volume on the theology of Reinhold Niebuhr with a brief account of my own relation to him. Although never intimate, that relation spanned many years of my early life, and, more important, it was of the most crucial significance in the direction that my own existence and my life's work have taken. Contact with his extraordinary intellectual power and insight effected a transformation simultaneously of my self-understanding and my understanding of the world, a transformation that has remained central to my subsequent experience. Hence this volume is a most grateful tribute to his person and also an exposition and analysis of his thought.

This relation to Niebuhr began, as far as I can remember, toward the end of my boyhood when I was probably twelve or so years old. My father, Charles W. Gilkey, was the dean of the chapel of the University of Chicago, a liberal, social gospel minister of some repute, and a friend for many years of Reinhold Niebuhr, a decade his junior. Later, when I was vividly aware of who Niebuhr was, I noted that he had come each year as visiting preacher in the chapel, and, as was the custom, he must have stayed many times in the guest room of the dean's home. So I must have seen him often as a boy, but no memories accompany this realization.

What I do remember clearly were two bizarre scenes in our house when I was twelve and thirteen, scenes I have later recalled, many, many times, with some amusement. Father's office at home was on the first floor, adjacent to the living room and also to the dining room. I remember sitting with my mother at the table having lunch (this was 1931) when Father suddenly burst out of his office in his shirtsleeves, waving a letter and shouting in rollicking good humor: "Reinnie's gone and done it!"

"Gone and done what?" asked Mother.

"Gone and gotten married! Can you believe it? What a relief for the rest of us!"

"What do you mean, Charley?"

"I mean that Reinnie's such an ascetic, and a self-sacrificing one at that, that he made all the rest of us feel like half-hearted, slack Christians. He gave away most of his small salary to help friends and colleagues in need [this in the desperate Depression years], and, as a bachelor, he never went home until all hours but stayed up endlessly talking with students. And he always said he knew *we* couldn't do those things because we have families. So it's a great relief to hear of his descent to becoming one of us. Bless him!"

The second scene, almost a repetition of the first, came probably a year later. Father burst out of his office, this time waving a book and saying with dumbfounded consternation: "Reinnie's gone crazy"—again I had no idea of whom he was speaking.

"Why, Charley, what makes you say that?" asked Mother.

"He's written this book, and I don't understand at all why he has done it or what he's saying—and neither does Harry [Fosdick]!"

The book, of course, was *Moral Man and Immoral Society* (1932). My father's amazed and shocked assessment was, as we shall see, typical of the response of liberal Protestants, and in fact of most of Niebuhr's friends, to this explosive volume. I should at once add, however, that it was less than a decade later that both Father and Harry Fosdick came to find a vast amount of wisdom—as well as political and theological truth—in what had first appeared to them a radical volume.

∞

The next scene represents my first direct contact with Reinhold Niebuhr. It came much further along in my own development, though in fact only some eight years later. It was spring 1940, and I was about to graduate from Harvard College. As we shall see, I was then one of many very confused young people, increasingly distraught by the grim sequence of events taking place across the Atlantic as Western Europe steadily succumbed to the might of the Nazi armies. We were horrified at what was happening to Europe; also we felt involved in these very real crises, which were crises for each of us personally, for our class, and for our whole generation. And of course, we were quite right. This was a crisis less of the mind than of the spirit, one of bewilderment, of fear, and of the beginnings of our first taste of the despair of meaninglessness. Into this crisis Niebuhr's voice brought for me a genuine word of renewal. This "word" effected a disclosure of something quite new and quite steadying, a quite unexpected slant on things that made possible once more a realistic political understanding on the one hand and a moral commitment and confidence on the other; in short, a saving grace. For this event to become at all clear to present readers, it is necessary to convey some sense of the situation all of us faced in that graduating spring of 1940.

Many, many college students in the 1930s had been brought up in the spiritual aftermath of World War I. This was a period in which to academics, church folk, schoolteachers, and secular liberals alike—at least in the middle-class North—war, any war, was a useless, wasteful, bloody affair, with little if any moral or valid political justification. War represented for us a purely destructive turmoil caused solely by the ambitions of imperialists and the greed of armament makers. This was a viewpoint that grew out of the widespread assessment, common in the 1920s and 1930s, of the causes of the First World War. For us there could be—and so we were told by sermons, in school, via the theater, and even some films—no evil comparable to war. Hence there could be no moral or even practical justification of armed conflict; peace, so we repeated endlessly, was the prior concern of anyone with political interests, the major moral obligation of any reflective person, and the central message of the Christian gospel.

As a result of this mind-set, the more idealistic of my generation were, almost without thinking, inclined toward pacifism, and, at the least, devoted to the work for peace—devoted, to be sure, if a bit unprincipled and unreflective in this allegiance. Those less inclined to idealistic sentiments were, nonetheless, ardently noninterventionist. War was a European problem, generated by a now-irrelevant imperial lust for colonies and empire; America, which wanted neither, had no business taking part again in such sordid and destructive matters. That this viewpoint about participation in war was not confined to local American liberals is shown by the Oxford Oath of 1938 ("I will never again fight for king or country") and the fact that three out of the four class orators at our Harvard graduation in June 1940 passionately rejected any involvement at all in the present war against Hitler. (Needless to say, and ironically, these were the classmates who two years later fought and perhaps died in that war and collectively helped to win it.) In our consciousness, then, there was this powerful background of moral commitment to peace at all costs combined with a revulsion at the uselessness, greed, and idiocy of war, and a quite personal (but not publicly mentioned) fear of death—for without purpose or point to it, such a prospect as war contains nothing but fear.

There was, however, also in our consciousness another element of equal, if growing, moral weight. In the 1930s our generation had come to awareness of public events. Certainly the Depression was all around us; as a privileged group, however—and we would not have been at Harvard had we been otherwise—that did not weigh as heavily on our minds or on the minds of our parents as it did on many others. But we were increasingly aware of an ever-darker and more ominous historical reality growing in the wider world. When I was twelve, Japan attacked and overran Manchuria; five years later Japan engulfed (and "raped") the eastern half of China; that same year Mussolini bombed, strafed, and dismembered Ethiopia. Above all, in 1933, Hitler came to power in a renascent and angry Germany: the ruthless programs against the Jews began, civil freedoms were universally eliminated, Hitler uttered threats at all the rest of Europe and began inexorably after 1936 to gobble up lands around Germany and to lay claim to others. In 1938 the Western world was terrified at the prospect of another war over Czechoslovakia. Finally the nightmare came true, as war in Europe began on September 1, 1939.

We all reacted to this grim event as we had long before decided to react—we refused, we would not go. In that fall of 1939, I helped form with Avery Dulles the Keep America Out of the War Committee and ran it avidly until about January. Then one guest speaker, Senator Walsh of Massachusetts, argued against any intervention because, as he put it, "Britain's empire, which we would be supporting, was fully as oppressive and evil as Hitler's, which we would be opposing." Common in those isolationist days, this argument seemed to me far too askew to consider seriously. Yet was not Walsh right? Britain too was guilty of a host of imperialist sins. Nevertheless, disgusted with this reading of present affairs and so with isolationism, I resigned from the committee.

What this resignation signaled was the growing force of the other horn of our dilemma: the outrage at the manifest injustice of Hitler's steadily expanding Reich. There was as yet little clear sense among us that this conquest would ultimately pose a serious threat to our own security, though a dim awareness of danger was beginning to balance the aversion to, even the fear of, conflict. (Evidently President Roosevelt had long been thoroughly aware of this point.) With the fall of France in spring 1940, however, this balance began to shift: Now the most terrible forms of ruthless aggression and of oppressive injustice had suddenly become dominant in our world. Radical evil seemed—and was—in thorough control of history. Further, it was evident to all of us that in Europe as in Asia the spread of military violence, of oppression, and of radical injustice would cease only if there appeared some mode of resistance—yes, military resistance.

At once the ideal of peace, long dominant in our souls, found itself directly countered by the equally imposing ideal of justice. To my intellectual and moral consternation, in this historical situation these two ideals, the twin ultimates of liberal humanism, were in the starkest contradiction to one another. All of us ominously felt that soon we must choose between them.

At this point all this was only *felt*. It was not yet articulated, as later reflection would seek to clarify this very muddled situation. What we—or I—felt was a new bewilderment and confusion, a breakdown of things I had taken for granted, a contradiction of ultimate principles more than a lack of will. We found ourselves veering first this way and then that in anxious debate; correspondingly, there appeared a tendency in those months to imbibe much more than usual. Finally, there were signs of the onset of an incipient and debilitating cynicism. I recall after a long argument about what we should do, saying, with what I felt to be a very wise historical maturity: "Oh well, Europe has to be unified sometime anyway. Such processes of unification in history have always been ruthless and bloody—Hitler might as well do it as anyone else"—and hating myself afterward. Past evil viewed serenely in historical retrospect is one thing; present evil seen out the front window or just around the corner of your own street is quite another.

This deep moral confusion, this vivid contradiction between my two fundamental moral absolutes, peace and justice, and this dead end of helpless cynicism and even despair, represented a dimly discerned crisis in my moral humanism. That "humanist" way of being or of self-understanding was based on adherence to fixed principles—in my case peace and justice—and on the assurance that one could effectively follow them in the main issues of one's life. Together these two begot the confidence that thereby one could achieve both creative action and inner moral stability. As I had asked myself repeatedly during college, what else than this intellectual, idealistic, and committed humanism was needed to live a satisfactory life? Why was religion, why was God, at all relevant to this perfectly attainable enterprise of becoming fully human?

Later reflection on this uneasy situation has discerned within it three distinguishable, if never separable, dilemmas or questions that required an answer and that compounded together to form my inner discomfort. These were all felt, and flashes of what they were would light up frequently in my consciousness; they were *there* all right, even if they were not yet clearly spelled out.

My first dilemma was the awareness of a stark and practically (even if not theoretically) irreconcilable opposition between my two ultimate principles: if we were loyal to peace, and refused intervention, then we would inevitably be disloyal to justice and hence aid in the establishment of a radically unjust and oppressive world. There was no negotiation or compromise between these two principles; it was either intervention or, in effect, collaboration. In practical terms—and these alone counted—one must choose one or the other; one could not choose both or a little bit of both.

Second, if two absolute principles collide, what then? Cannot both be relativized a bit? Peace now, justice later, or the reverse? But if moral principles are made relative to any given situation—relevant for this issue, irrelevant for another—then is there any real moral guidance left? Is there anything to stop this slide into relativity, this absence in the end of any principles at all? Principles and ideals are the fixed stars of humanism; if they become relative, negotiable, on what basis besides self-interest does one negotiate? On the basis of what works? But if principles are gone, what can limit the claims of self-interest, what can define in a moral way "what works"? Why then is not the collective drive to security and well-being "moral" enough? Why, in that case, is not a successful Hitlerian empire fully justifiable? After all, it seems to work. To survive, moral humanism seems to require some absolute structure: principles that are inviolable and the moral character to choose them and adhere to them.[1] In most ordinary situations the collision and opposition of fundamental moral principles are infinitely obscured; but in this one they were in stark conflict. No wonder I felt I was sliding steadily toward a cynical indifference I neither recognized nor welcomed.

Third, as the second point hints, a humanist morality seems to require virtue and at least a sense of moral adequacy in the larger issues of life. To be sure, whether in secular liberals, in religious pietists, or in religious liberals, this consciousness of being capable of "good works" can build a smug self-consciousness of virtue—and become for others extremely objectionable. But that extreme concern about one's goodness is not what I mean; here I refer to a minimal sense of moral adequacy, of being in the right and being on the right side. Associated with this identity of moral action with inner moral adequacy is its consequence: the tendency to identify a moral commitment to good ideals with the virtue of compliance to those ideals. "We are for peace; therefore we are peace loving; we are for justice; therefore we are just," as the democratic allies in World War II

---

1. Later reflection, and later reading of ethical and theological texts, has suggested to me that Kant could well have understood our class's dilemma, though his language was to us hopelessly archaic. If you are going to be moral on a humanist basis, then some moral imperative which is absolute and categorical is required.

constantly asserted. Furthermore, since moral principles and virtue are seen by this consciousness to accompany one another, it must follow that those who are oppressed or attacked must be innocent and those who are exploited blameless. Victims represent not only the ideals of peace and justice but the virtue of adhering to those ideals. If a cause is just, those supporting the cause are likewise just. This is surely central to the liberal creed *and* the liberal self-confidence. Hence, as the final consequence, it follows that true idealists find it difficult to support an issue unless its adherents and their allies are themselves blameless. The agent, like the principles the agent represents, must have no balance of evil in a moral cause. Our allies, therefore, must be drawn from those whose "hands are clean." Otherwise there is no moral content in what we do, and we have joined the other side of the moral divide. Are not the victims of oppression ipso facto more virtuous than the perpetuators of oppression, the poor more virtuous than the rich, the unions who fight for justice more selfless than the owners, the attacked community that cries for peace more virtuous—yes, more idealistic—than the selfish aggressor? For the moral consciousness the clear (and proclaimed!) justice of a community's cause is identified with the virtue of the persons in that community. All of these were certainly my unreflective assumptions; I was a certified, if not very subtle, "liberal."

And it was these assumptions that kept causing us trouble, breeding moral impotence during that winter and spring. Was not Senator Walsh really right? The British empire was in fact oppressive, often brutal. It was organized and run for the ultimate benefit of Britain and seemed quite indifferent to its colonies' cries for freedom. Surely its hands were anything but clean. How, therefore, could we support it morally? We might do it for our own self-interest, but then how were either of us better than Hitler? Humanist idealism seemed to lead not only to the espousal of absolute principles that could be in stultifying conflict; it led just as inexorably to the requirement of innocence, of clean hands, of a sure confidence in the virtue of one's cause, if one were to participate.

Seemingly one could not be realistic about one's allies or one's self and act in the world. Moral idealism seemed inexorably to drive toward a blindness to the real ambiguity of the world, and of ourselves in the world; to an unreal division between the good and the bad that made one quite unable to deal with the real stuff of historical life. Just as a sense of the permanent ambiguity and relativity of even the highest moral principles stalled my moral consciousness, so the dawning of a self-awareness of ambiguity, even of guilt, in one's allies, in one's own nation, in one's self, and even in one's own cause had the same effect. But could one ever find a pure principle at work in history or uncover an innocent enterprise? Again, cynicism and the fog of despair seemed to be the inevitable term of a breakdown in humanist idealism.[2]

∞

Into this bewildered and dispirited situation a new voice entered, the voice of Reinhold Niebuhr. My father knew well my humanist stance and my feelings of the irrelevance, even the subjectivity, of religion. He knew I was wondering whether modern experience, reflectively pondered, could show anything remotely similar to the picture world of religion. He had read my senior thesis in philosophy, extolling the good sense, as well as the elegant language, of that charming philosophical skeptic and "naturalist," George Santayana. Thus it was probably no accident that he suggested gently, as was his wont, that I go to hear his friend Reinhold Niebuhr when the latter came to preach in the Harvard chapel in that spring of 1940. As before, I had no idea who Niebuhr was, but went out of curiosity and out of respect for my father.

The torrent of words, insights, and ideas that issued forth from that towering figure in the pulpit stunned me. This was not gentle and apologetic persuasion rounding out our "nice" ordinary experience with a moral and religious interpretation. This was from beginning to end a challenge to the assumptions of my sophisticated modernity. And that challenge came with a vividly new interpretation of my world. In fact a quite different viewpoint on everything was set before me, a viewpoint in which my confused and deeply troubled "ordinary experience" suddenly clarified itself, righted, and became for the moment intelligible. There was here no appeal to an extrinsic authority: on the contrary there was an exceedingly realistic analysis of just the social situation that was troubling me. But this was an analysis structured by a framework, a wider "ontological" framework, which was very new to me; it was in fact one of which I had never before been really conscious. To my astonishment Niebuhr identified his own utterly realistic appraisal of the domestic and international

2. These reflections about my own liberal sentiments were just that, *mine;* they represented the thoughts that were present in my reactions to the onset of "real" war in 1939–40. They do not claim to be a description of the liberal movement as a whole, or even of its major representatives. I then felt at home in the liberal, humanist world, and hence I feel the affinity of these reflections to that world—but this was my undergraduate "take" on that tradition.

situation (much more real than that of my philosophical mentors Bertrand Russell, John Dewey, or George Santayana) with what he called the "Biblical viewpoint." Further, he pointed out not only the "naive optimism" of the humanist and naturalistic philosophers I had treasured, but even more the experiential validity and the moral strength of this other, "Biblical," perspective. I felt overwhelmed, as if I had stepped into another space, one in which a new quality of light changed the social scene which was once obscure into what could now be comprehended. In short, he opened up the possibility of a realism about social affairs that did not lead to cynicism, and yet, on the contrary, led to a confidence in transcendence that supported a renewed and restrengthened moral commitment. I was by no means converted—but I was thoroughly disturbed and deeply intrigued.

I turned to a fellow philosophy student who sat there staring, and asked him: "Who the hell was that?" "Don't you know? That is Reinhold Niebuhr, professor at Union Seminary in New York [I only knew that my father had been a student there] and already famous for his books on society. He really stirs things up when he comes here." On my way out I asked a student assistant in the chapel if the preacher was speaking again in Cambridge. "Yes, this afternoon in Christ Church, and then once again this evening." I went to both, listened enthralled, and never recovered. Within two weeks I had bought and read hungrily three of his books: *Moral Man and Immoral Society, Reflections on the End of an Era,* and *Beyond Tragedy.* By the end of that time my understanding of almost everything had thoroughly changed—and for the first time I regarded myself as a Christian.

What was this message that so altered my world? I am sure I then had little awareness of its theological content, that is, the concepts and symbols that formed its structure. I felt or apprehended, but did not think out, its power and its relevance to my situation. But in that feeling or awareness there was an implicit conceptual structure of which I was then only dimly aware. This structure I shall here briefly set out; its more detailed articulation will be the purpose of this volume on the theology that formed the foundation of those sermons in 1940.

Most fundamental was the experience of an opening out, or an opening up. This represented a vertical expansion upward of reality, of my world, from the observable, tangible, evident, "immanent" world of nature and culture to which my thought had heretofore been confined. My world was, I suddenly realized, a confined one; however sophisticated and mature, it was the world of early twentieth-century culture and little else. The roof, so to speak, was suddenly lifted off this confined cultural space, allowing me to see that observable world as I had not been able to see it before and to breathe freely. Certainly the relevant word for this experience is *transcendence;* but I am sure that in this initial experience no such reflective concept as that appeared. What did appear?

What appeared first in quite new light was the actual historical world around me. I found that, as this ambiguous world was no longer for me all there was of reality, I could now look at culture and history realistically and thus honestly. I was at last able to recognize in them what I knew already—and had ignored—to be there, namely a universal *relativity,* a deep *ambiguity,* and an underlying, powerful *self-concern.* I could now see and admit that every earthly perspective—even our own, we the "peace-loving" democratic allies—was relative, a particular perspective shaped by our history, our wealth, our need for security, and yes, even our recent domination of almost the entire world.

The cause of our allies, therefore, was infinitely ambiguous: it represented a very partial perspective, and it was driven not just by the rhetoric of peace, order, and justice but also by the allies' fear for their status, their wealth, and their security. I could now admit that, despite the overarching importance of justice and peace, every community, whatever the nobility of its ideas, is pushed into action by the sharp gnawings of self-interest. Before, to admit all this rather than to deny it was to lose one's moral nerve, to slide into cynicism, to justify anything because "everyone else does it" and because for the moment it might work.

As Niebuhr said that day, the allies do fight for the noble cause of democracy and they do represent a more just rule—but they also fight for themselves, to preserve their domination and defend their security. The nobility of their ideals does not imply any absence in them of self-interest; the justice of their cause is something different from their claims to embody such virtue. With this it became possible for the first time for me to look squarely at the actual situation, a situation in which no side was completely clean, no cause untarnished with ambiguity or evil.

This realism about the relativity and self-interest of all the players did not, however, lead, as before it had always threatened to do, either to cynical indifference on the one hand or to the brutal affirmation that self-interest is the sole relevant principle in communal action on the other. To the humanist the domination of self-interest spells the end of moral idealism; if humans are the sole bearers of meaning, the admission that humans are universally selfish means that self-interest represents not only the highest principle of historical life, but more important, that it represents the only sensible ground for action. One is left only with the choice between a heedless self-concern and a prudent self-concern.

If, however, there *is* a reality that exists in and through itself, and that represents and upholds the good, a reality that in existence and in meaning transcends the ambiguous sea of corporate human life (as that life showed itself in the spring of 1940), then recognition of the presence of that ambiguity neither eliminates the reality of the ideal nor the legitimacy of responsible obligation. In this sense a dimension of transcendence over a surrounding and ambiguous culture preserves the continuity and authority of righteousness even in an unrighteous world—or, to use Niebuhr's language, God remains God even in a fallen world.

Let us note that it is the reality, or being, of God as transcendent to all historical relativity that is here important, not just God's goodness or the transcendence of God's goodness. A "god" who symbolizes only the projection of human ideals and nothing more—as in much liberal theology—disintegrates in a self-centered history as quickly as do the independence and permanence of those ideals. This sudden awareness of the possibility of a transcendent God, the self-sufficient ground of our ideals but infinitely more than they, secured for me a sense for the meaning of history, of obligation and of responsibility, and so of moral action in history even if history repeatedly failed to embody that meaning and those morals. Thus could one remain morally responsible even if oneself or the historical situation in which one had to act was seen to be saturated with the deepest ambiguity. I felt all this as I listened, though I had no appropriate conceptual grasp that would allow me to express it even to myself. In that spring, when France fell to Hitler, even though we were distraught by that, we were not in despair; I could breathe again, and, much later, I could live through the seething ambiguity of life in an internment camp without being cynical about others or myself. Ideals are relative, and they may contradict one another—but they do not therefore disappear.

Finally, there was the relativity as well as the apparent ineffectiveness of our ideals. Since peace and justice seemed irreconcilable in our situation, neither one could be absolute. Yet how could they be relative, the one possibility relevant now and the other irrelevant, if moral commitment and responsibility were to be affirmed? How could one stand up for, yes, suffer for, the "right" if the only "right" one could know was relative to all the real factors in a situation? This was the humanist impasse starkly felt but only dimly seen in that spring. If, however, the ultimate is a transcendent reality that unites being and value beyond our transitory being and our relative values, then obligation and responsibility can be redirected to transcendence—and the necessary negotiation between contending and relative ideals in order to fit the actual situation becomes possible. Our ideals of peace, justice, equality, and freedom are essential as guideposts in our moral and communal life. Nonetheless these ideals are pointers to, approximations of, the highest transcendent norm (love, as I later learned). They

13

cannot in and of themselves be absolute without the sort of contradiction we were then experiencing; however, if they be recognized as relative, they can now be applicable to the actual ambiguity of the real world.

All of this, both deep existential questions on the one hand and unexpected answers on the other, was felt, dimly understood and gratefully accepted. Only later did the conceptual structure of dilemma and of answer become clearer; that is to say, only later did the theological understanding appear that articulated in reflection that vivid experience of bewilderment and of renewed confidence and hope. As I read Niebuhr's early works in the week following his lectures, what he was saying—as well as what had been troubling me—became somewhat clearer. In fact, however, I did not really begin fully to understand Niebuhr's theology until more than a year later, when I had the chance to read more of his thought. Nonetheless, as was evident, a word had been heard, a word that was directly relevant to my actual situation—to my "existence." Theology as reflection on that encounter can in turn be an instrument of a further encounter of message and existence. I did not yet know the term, but looking back on this important experience, I could see all this as a "correlation" of question and answer—and so determinative of my own theological efforts from then on.

∞

My relation to Niebuhr's thought—I had not yet met him—remained crucial for me from then on. That summer I was already slated to leave for Beijing (to us at that time, "Peking"), where I had the very good fortune to be hired to begin in fall 1940 as an instructor in English as Yenching University. Immediately after hearing Niebuhr, I rearranged the elective course I was preparing to teach. That projected course was now centered on the critique of modern philosophical humanism rather than its celebration. And I refashioned that projected course all the following year in Beijing when I was really teaching my English courses. Because, however, the war against Japan intervened some fifteen months later in December 1941, and the Japanese in North China closed the university, I never taught that course. But just before December 7, 1941, my father sent me the first volume of *The Nature and Destiny of Man;* fortunately it arrived at the end of November 1941! I read and reread it as quickly as I could, beginning to understand at last the theology that lay back of my vivid experience of new understanding. When the war began and for six months we, the foreign faculty at Yenching, were put under house arrest, Lucius

Porter, a sixty-five-year-old philosophy professor at Yenching, and I (then twenty-two) offered to teach a class or seminar on this volume to all of our fellow faculty colleagues who were interested. By the end of two editions of that course in the following October, I knew that volume almost line by line. I was thoroughly and irretrievably a "Niebuhrian."

There followed in March of 1943 roughly two-and-a-half years in a Japanese civilian internment camp south of Beijing in Shantung Province. This experience itself was so vivid, demanding, and "down to earth" that it drove all thoughts of philosophy and theology quite out of my mind as I successively did the work on the housing committee, as a bricklayer, and then as cook and manager of a kitchen feeding eight hundred diners. But later reflection on that very rich if uncomfortable experience confirmed what I had learned in my senior year at Harvard, and, so to speak, solidified in terms of personal experience the understanding of communal life that Niebuhr had given me.[3] Thus when I returned to the United States in November 1945, I entered Union Seminary to study theology under Niebuhr, on whom my intellectual and spiritual existence had so long depended.

One final word. As this account of the transformation of my life and thought through the witness of Niebuhr indicates, it was much more his theology than his ethics that exerted this influence. As I have tried to show, he opened up a new *world* to me, a new understanding of the larger reality around us, of the history in which we lived, and so of the communal life of human beings in which we participate. It was an understanding of our being in the world *coram deo,* in the presence of God, that he gave me. The subject of ethics—what we should do and why we should do it—was of course continuously and forever important; this was where the whole problem began. Niebuhr was also very creative here—and most recent volumes on him have dealt with his ethics. But it was his uncovering of the deep ambiguity and relativity of the real historical world, even among the good in that world, and his disclosure of the reality and promise of the divine ground for that good, that touched and retouched me. These are the subjects of theology as he saw it—and as I have since understood it. Hence this volume seeks to articulate his important new theological understanding, what he aptly termed, in the title of a course he taught, The Theological Presuppositions of Christian Ethics.

3. This internment camp experience, and the theological reflections it inspired, are recorded in a volume entitled *Shantung Compound* (New York: Harper and Row, 1966). A further discussion on this experience, and its relevance to Niebuhr's theology, appears below in Chapter 6.

CHAPTER 2

The Structure of Niebuhr's Theology

The central characteristic of Niebuhr's thought from its earliest appearance is what I shall call the vertical dialectic: that is, the dialectic of transcendence and relatedness. It is as if he wished to push the roof off an
immanentist culture in which whatever *is* is confined to what comes before us in ordinary experience. The consequence is that in such a 'naturalist' culture whatever represents, or can represent, the ideal in life must be
resident in, expressed through, and also confined to actual cultural life. And
the further consequence is that if that life is very ambiguous, then one loses
the ideal entirely or else refuses to look squarely at the ambiguity. The
point, therefore, of this drastic upward expansion to transcendence is the
ability on the one hand to see and so to expose what is really there in social
existence, to achieve some permanent principle of judgment on the culture as a whole, and to let in elements of obligation, of grace, and of hope
from beyond that culture's ambiguous everyday life.

Thus *transcendence* is perhaps the key word in Niebuhr, and his use of
it has a unique and special character: First, transcendence and the transcendent have as their primary referent the divine, the God 'beyond' all we
know and experience in ordinary life around us. Second, transcendence
frequently refers to the principle or ground of reality, of meaning, judgment, and hope. And third (as 'self-transcendence') it may refer to the capacity of the human spirit infinitely to transcend itself (and relate itself to
God). However, solely considered in this last usage as a cultural and psychological category (as, for example, the transcendence of 'spirit' over 'nature'), 'transcendence' is not transcendent to Niebuhr. On the contrary, all
modes of human 'transcendence' reflect the finitude and the particular
perspectives of that human's cultural community. The heart of Niebuhr's

apologetic is that every culture, and each individual life, must find such a principle of genuine transcendence, and that 'Biblical faith' in a transcendent God supplies that need of culture's life.

Despite the fact that transcendence as Niebuhr sees it is not an aspect of the human psyche or of cultural history, this is a transcendence continually *related* to the world—related, that is, not only to individual persons, but even more to society, culture, and history. Transcendence is the originating and continuing ground of all human creativity, the principle of judgment and criticism on all human achievements, and the principle of the meaning and renewal of life. There is no genuine transcendence for Niebuhr unrelated to historical existence. For this reason Niebuhr was from beginning to end very critical of any philosophical or religious Absolute unrelated creatively and redemptively to the world's life; correspondingly he withheld his approval of any form of orthodox religion unconcerned with historical and social existence. Consequently, his criticism of religious liberalism was in effect a 'liberal' criticism, that is, a criticism that assumed, as the liberals did, the continuing relevance of God and of religion to the existence of all of life. The problem of liberalism for him was that, paradoxically, in its stress on immanence and in its indifference both to sin and to transcendence, liberalism failed in its own aim, namely, to judge, to reshape, and to redeem this existence. It could neither understand the deep travail of cultural life, nor could it provide grounds for the criticism and hence for the improvement and renewal of the world with which it was so deeply concerned.

Perhaps the best expression of this dialectic of transcendence and relatedness at the heart of Niebuhr's thought is the following:

> The most important characteristic of a religion of revelation is this twofold emphasis on the transcendence of God and upon His intimate relation to the world. In this divine transcendence the spirit of man finds a home in which it can understand its stature of freedom. But there it also finds the limits of its freedom, the judgment which is spoken against it and, ultimately, the mercy which makes such a judgment sufferable. (ND 1:126)

Niebuhr was convinced that all of culture—whether proletarian, Nazi, capitalist, or democratic, and whether one speaks of its norms and ideals, its goals, its rational principles and rational criteria, or its laws and customs—represented creative but relative achievements. What is more, each represented as well a warped or 'fallen' reality. Hence none is essentially or permanently virtuous; all are capable of becoming demonic and infinitely destructive. Thus, nothing in history, no culture or institution, for him can be absolute, nor supported or defended with absolute commitment; its rationality, its morals, its laws are relative to their time and place. None, therefore, is as absolute as it claims. Further, all, though relative, can and do claim to be absolute and universal, and so become, in Niebuhr's sense, 'demonic'. To see this 'reality' about historical life is for him not possible without transcendence. On the one hand to see the deep ambiguity of actual life without transcendence is to become cynical and irresponsible; not to see it at all is to be naive and sentimental. Hence human existence on its own is always in danger either of despair or of idolatry.

Transcendence means, therefore, transcendence over even what we consider the highest and best in our existence; Niebuhr's transcendence towers above the most rational and the most ideal of human capacities. Niebuhr sought, therefore, a principle of judgment on history beyond all historical relativities, a permanent principle of criticism—and so one paradoxically, necessarily, "beyond history." And he sought a principle of renewal and hope for history also beyond all immediate and so relative historical possibilities, a permanent principle of renewal. If even the ideal element of social life could disintegrate or become demonic, then a permanent principle of transcendence is necessary. When he described this transcendent principle as "beyond history," as he frequently did, it was often misinterpreted as unrelated to history, which was decidedly not what he meant.

Niebuhr's is a vertical transcendence. The divine transcendence is *beyond, above, over* people, society, and history. It is not a transcendence that essentially lies ahead, in the future that is to come—a transcendence that is, therefore, to be fulfilled in the future. The contrast is between the creaturely and the divine, the human being and the transcendent God, not between the past and present on the one hand and the future on the other. This understanding of transcendence as future is, interestingly enough, the essential meaning of transcendence both in Process thought on the one hand and in the Eschatological Theologies on the other. Niebuhr's is, moreover, a transcendence primarily conceived and understood as transcendence over history, culture, and society, over all the norms, ideals, laws, and mores, the modes of thought and of knowledge. In that sense it is an ethical and cultural, a political and religious transcendence, a separation or diastasis between human cultural life at all levels and the judgment, righteousness, and grace of God. It is a transcendence related to and so centered on culture; but it is hence for him by no means a projection of culture.

As a consequence, this is, secondarily, an *epistemological* transcendence. For Niebuhr even the highest rationality of culture is relative and one-sided; hence divine transcendence represents a meaning and a coherence beyond all our finite schemes of meaning and coherence, our canons of inquiry, and our criteria of validity—a thought quite as inconceivable to much of modernity, especially academic modernity, as it was to me when first I heard it. It is for him not through science or even through rational reflection that the relativity—and the "interests"—of our historical existence are transcended into the universal; for what is reflected back to us here are our own presuppositions and many of our own biases. As is evident, it is here in Niebuhr's analysis of culture and of history as relative and partial that are present the grounds for his affirmation of the need for *revelation,* by which Niebuhr means a disclosure that is not to us incoherent but one that comes from beyond, that challenges and so fulfills, the ordinary—and relative—canons of our own reason.

This is, in the end, also an *ontological* transcendence, a transcendence of God's being or mode of being over the contingent, temporal, and transient being of all creatures. For a number of reasons that I shall discuss, Niebuhr insisted that the Biblical 'myth' of creation, interpreted through the classical formula of ex nihilo, "out of nothing," represents the closest expression in language of God's paradoxical relation to the world. Here God transcends infinitely the world God made; paradoxically, however, God is at the same time in permanent and intimate relation to that world. Niebuhr was concerned with this 'ontological' doctrine only insofar as he saw it as the necessary backdrop for Biblical faith, the necessary presupposition in ontology for the modes of divine transcendence over history that I have described, namely a religious and ethical transcendence over the destiny and the norms and ideals of culture.

Despite the clear implication of the absoluteness of God contained in the myth of creation, Niebuhr would not have disputed either the hypothesis of evolutionary development or the 'related' God of immanent metaphysics—for example, that of Process thought. He assumed that permanent and universal relatedness of God to a changing world and argued for it. God is present continually to God's creation insofar as the creation exists at all and is orderly; and God is present in all of history in judgment, in the workings of providence, and in the grace of renewal. Further, God is present continually to our individual consciousness, in our sense of absolute dependence, and in our conscience, and to our consciousness of obligation and of guilt; and God is supremely present to us in the consciousness of judgment and of mercy. The dialectical ontological presence of God as absolute and yet related—one of Niebuhr's many "paradoxes"—forms the necessary presupposition for all of his theology.

Ontology was, however, never a direct concern of Niebuhr's theological reflection. In fact, he was constantly impatient with metaphysical efforts to smooth out the paradoxes of experience, and especially the paradoxes of faith—among them that of the absolute and the related God. These paradoxes were, he felt, fundamental for Biblical faith and for any understanding of the mystery of ordinary existence. To smooth these paradoxes out, to construct an ontology of the whole that is rationally coherent, was, he was sure, either to project a transcendent Absolute unrelated to the world or to conceive a divine immanence with no principle either of judgment or of genuine renewal in it. A too-coherent ontology—moreover, one coherent in terms of a logical or a physical necessity that bound the whole together—seemed to him to threaten the essential freedom of the human spirit, namely to choose itself, to create ever-new forms of personal and social life, and to rebel against God. Only language that granted to both creaturely and divine freedom each its fullest scope—namely the language of personal relations and of historical events, the language of myth—could possibly express the paradoxical certainties of Biblical faith. Surprisingly, therefore, Niebuhr's emphasis on the transcendence of God strengthened rather than diminished his polar emphasis on the spontaneity and freedom of the human creature. Again, as is evident, Niebuhr's conception of transcendence is better expressed through the paradoxical notion of a transcendent and yet related God than through that of a transcendent yet immanent ultimacy, as the concept is worked through, for example, in Paul Tillich.

∞

From all I have said, it is apparent that this is a *political* theology. That is to say, it is a theology concerned above all with the social existence of human beings and with the health and disease of that existence. It has, to be sure, individualistic, existential, and personal elements at its very center. Nevertheless the abiding focus, from beginning to end, is on society, history, and politics rather than on the inner, private, individual consciousness. As a consequence, despite many common elements, Niebuhr's is a quite different sort of theology than that of Kierkegaard, or of most of the European 'neo-orthodox', for example, Rudolf Bultmann or Emil Brunner, who concentrate their theological attention on the dilemmas of the existing individual, the individual's self-understanding, and the individual's relation to God. Niebuhr's theology is, therefore, in many ways exceptional. He is an existentialist for whom social rather than individual issues are primary. And he is a political theologian for whom the transcendent God is above us in the present, as in the past and the future, rather than, as with the eschatological political theologians, the God solely of the future. In contrast to what the eschatological theologians charge, here the vertically transcendent God does not "bless the present" nor create a private as opposed to a public theology. On the contrary, God judges the present as God has judged the past and will judge the future. Hence the impinging historical future is for Niebuhr a locus of continuing sin, of continuing judgment, and of promised grace rather than one of unalloyed salvation.

This continuing and dominant interest in social and historical matters means that social science and social philosophy, social psychology, anthropology, social ethics, and, above all, philosophies of human nature and of history represent the materials with which Niebuhr largely worked. They form the secular intellectual basis for his thought, and he knew them extraordinarily well. Unlike many liberal theologians of the first half of this century (the evolutionary theologians and Process theologians), Niebuhr appealed only rarely to developments in the physical and biological sciences or in contemporary metaphysical and epistemological reflection. His primary interest was in human, social, and historical studies, not studies of nature. Consequently, his concentration with regard to any metaphysical or epistemological philosophy is on its view of human beings, its understanding of reason, and its interpretation of human evil and human goodness.

As is evident from his writings about the history of philosophy and social theory, he knew a good deal about this history, learned a great deal from it—and appropriated important elements of it into his thought. To most readers, however, what is probably most noticeable are his sharp criticisms of the great figures of Western philosophical history. Pushing aside as fundamentally irrelevant their metaphysical speculations and epistemological inquiries—all that has made them famous—Niebuhr in each case went straight for their "doctrine of human nature," their views of desire and conscience, of reason and will, of evil and the meaning of history. He praised and criticized them solely with regard to these issues, that is, his own 'theological' questions. Niebuhr was convinced that at the heart of any philosophy, however explicitly it might be based on scientific inquiry or rational speculation, lay its views on these human issues, on the questions of the meaning of life. For him each philosophy's understanding of fate and the tragic, of human evil and human renewal, shaped all of its other speculations about reality and knowing. For him, in other words, each philosophy has as its "hidden" foundation a particular "faith" in life's meaning, and hence its explicit philosophical reflections in fact manifest a religious substance and a religious criterion. In that sense for him every philosophy is comparable to any example of theology.

The passion for social justice and for historical renewal is the driving force of Niebuhr's thought. In this, if not in his understanding of human nature and destiny, he is a devoted social gospeler, a reshaper of the liberal tradition he contested so sharply. For him the point of high religion and of sound theology, the criterion by which each is to be judged as valid, is its relevance to the renewal of social history. And, as we shall see, the real content of most classical theological symbols, their most important meaning, lies for him in their implications for the quest for justice. For example, as we have noted, what the transcendence of God *means* is the judgment of God on class, national, and racial pride and on the results of these in injustice. The hermeneutic that he applied to the biblical, the classical theological, and the philosophical sources alike was that of creative political action, what is now called "liberation." Although for me he was a more important theologian than an ethicist, nevertheless his theology was one of ethical intentionality. Theology is the foundation for creative action in the world, and little else.

∞

This is a theology of catastrophe, nemesis, and renewal in history, not one of progress. For Niebuhr history to its end will be characterized by tragedy, violence, and suffering as well as by creativity and radical change. This represents the point of sharpest difference with the liberal, progressivist culture that he criticized for its belief in steady moral progress. The point of faith for him, therefore, is to provide meaning, hope, and grounds for creative action and for new life precisely in such a real world of experienced ambiguity and tragedy. Correspondingly, the point of theology is to make this continuing character of historical life ("the continuity of sin," and "the continuity of sin in the life of the redeemed") intelligible in terms of the nature of human being and of God, to look at the real world and yet not become cynical. That is to say, to recognize that this ambiguity and tragedy, as well as creativity, represent the character of history, and, in the light of this understanding, to provide intelligible grounds for hope and for responsible action.

This sense of the ambiguity of history in time, plus the new emphasis on transcendence, created a radically different mood in American theology that is perhaps taken for granted now at the century's end but was astounding to Niebuhr's colleagues in the 1930s. One could say that he sought to reestablish the liberal concern for creative action in the world on a more realistic and so a more solid and, incidentally, classical Christian basis. If the grounds for action and for hope had previously been the confidence in an enduring and enlarging social progress, in "building the kingdom of God," and if that confidence and so those grounds had vanished in the turmoil of early twentieth-century history, then what motives for social action remained? If the kingdom really cannot be built in Detroit or New York, why persist in seeking to make these cities better? Or why endanger or even sacrifice oneself for such a hopeless endeavor? It is because Niebuhr feels the persistence of this liberal obligation for creative social action in the vastly new context of the twentieth century that he emphasizes the dialectic of realistic social analysis on the one hand and transcendent grounds for judgment and hope on the other. This dialectic precisely fit my situation in the spring of 1940. He wished to repair the broken nerve for social action, not to sever it.

Much of this new emphasis on critical and realistic social theory and radical social action is taken for granted by recent theology and ethics. When it appeared with Niebuhr it was startling, almost incredible to a still-optimistic culture. As anyone who reads these early books notices, the critique is uncomfortably specific: it is contemporary capitalistic and democratic culture, our own culture, that is under judgment; it is our wise men—secular, academic, and liberal Protestants—that he presents as naive; and it is the sanctimonious empires of the West, our allies, who are the objects of his prophetic witness. For him these cultures are not at all the manifestations of a civilization advancing in technology, in knowledge, and in morality alike—"developed," as we like to say. On the contrary, these "advanced" cultural forms are penetrated by greed and afflicted with imbalances of power, and so they are beset with continuing cruelty and deep injustice that inexorably spell out suffering for the victims of that culture and impending doom for its rulers—a doom signaled by the rise of fascism. Although there are in Niebuhr's thought significant changes on these issues over the years, this critical, judgmental stance toward culture remained as the initial meaning of theological transcendence throughout the development of his thinking.

On the theological level this new sense of the radical ambiguity of historical life led to the reappearance at the center of theological discussion of the categories of sin and of divine judgment—symbols that had largely disappeared in nineteenth- and early twentieth-century liberal theology. Yet in his new use of them, these "classical" symbols were with equal radicality reinterpreted by Niebuhr. That is, they are interpreted now as relevant to the understanding of society and history, not (as in orthodoxy) as applicable almost solely to individual life. Sin means here not so much individual

vice but the sins characteristic of the American community: racism, economic injustice, imperialism, and so on. Correspondingly, the concept of
sin receives at Niebuhr's hands a newly significant empirical content or
validation through his extremely sharp and original analysis of the troubled domestic and later international scene before him. In turn, redemption means the transformation, insofar as that is possible, of this
social matrix and of individual existence in and through that social transformation. Above all, sin connotes the 'fallenness', not of the unre-
spectable sinner in a respectable society, but the ambiguity and warped
character of ordinary life, of even the respectable, the powerful, and the
good. Niebuhr was sure that this understanding of sin as referent on the
one hand to social injustice and on the other to the ordinary existence of
all of us, righteous and unrighteous alike, was as true to the meaning of the
category in Biblical prophecy and in New Testament teaching as it was
fruitful for his understanding of actual social relations. It was for him one
pole of 'Biblical faith'.

A second consequence of this new vision of history as continually characterized by deep ambiguity and destructive catastrophe was an emphasis
on the inability of human powers to guarantee meaning to human life. As
his writings amply show, Niebuhr stresses as much as any modern writer
the great creativity of the human spirit: in rational power, in knowledge,
in techniques, in practical solutions to common problems, and in the
steady growth of moral and social ideals. All of this he shared with his liberal colleagues. But he also emphasized—and this was new—the relativity
and the ambiguity of all of these powers, their proneness to selfish and
one-sided use, and so the destructive possibilities latent in every human
achievement. Hence, none of the human powers on which the growing
humanism of the nineteenth and early twentieth centuries had depended
for progress could be counted on to retain permanently their creativity:
objective reason, scientific inquiry, education, democracy, and liberal religion. None of these was as objective or universal as they claimed, and
none was incorruptible. Hence these were the false gods of modernity's
optimism. This critique of the "heights of the human spirit" represents
one very significant meaning of transcendence: even humanity's highest is
under a judgment from beyond its partiality and self-concern.

We see here, moreover, the ground for a quite new interpretation of
idolatry. Here, idolatry is no longer the religious worship of an explicit idol
or even participation in a false religion. It is now understood in secular and
social terms as an ultimate faith in our own human powers and human
achievements, in what is partial and creaturely; it is a faith that character-

izes modern culture. In the broadest sense idolatry has become the self-concern, self-love, in effect the self-worship of the creature for itself and its community: making itself the center of the world, what Niebuhr calls 'pride'. Sin is thus not only understood in secular terms, as ordinary actions in the common world. Even more it is understood in social terms as the self-worship of the community. And the primary moral consequence of sin is not so much that individual depravity leads to damnation before God as it is that communal idolatry leads first to injustice and then to destructive conflict. One can see clearly the reinterpretation of classical categories into the terms of modern social and historical categories, even into a liberal understanding.

From this sharp critique of the redemptive potentialities of human powers, in effect a critique of modern secular faith, it follows that in Niebuhr's theology only a religious solution is credible as an answer to the question of human meaning. However creative human powers may be, and however many changes and achievements history therefore manifests, all are corruptible and will be corrupted—and catastrophe will follow. Correspondingly, history's major problems are spiritual, in fact religious, in character. An overweening or absolute trust in our own individual or communal power, in our intellect, in our righteousness, in our way of life, constitutes the pride that is unwarranted and destructive and is the essence of sin, as it is the deepest clue to the travail of history. Consequently, only if the self can locate its trust in something genuinely transcendent to the self and to human achievement, individual or social, can it become itself. Faith as the deepest trust in and commitment to God is the condition of the possibility of love and so of justice and peace.

Despite Niebuhr's passion for social ethics, the ethical is for Niebuhr subordinate to the religious; the second commandment to love our neighbor in effect becomes a function of the first commandment to worship God alone. As sin represents a break in the relation to God, so faith represents the reestablishment of that crucial relation—and it is sin that brings about the evil actions of history just as faith and grace determine its possibilities of moral renewal. The religious relation to God is hence no longer an expression of the human quest for the good and so of the goodness and idealism of human being, as it was in much of liberalism. On the contrary, the quest for God can only be infinitely frustrated until the actual religious relation to God is rectified—and that becomes possible only through God's initiative, through revelation and through grace. Theology has here returned via an emphasis on sin and grace to the centrality of the religious: of faith, of repentence, and of trust in God on the one hand and of revelation and grace on the other. Although, therefore, ethics is here subordinate to theology in Niebuhr, we should note that for him *politics* is not subordinate to ethics. This point will become clearer when we discuss the role of sin in the political.[1]

The important presence in Niebuhr of Pauline, Augustinian, and Reformation themes (at least as the latter interpreted Paul and Augustine) is undeniable. Niebuhr himself recognized this as did all who heard and read him. What is new and less recognized—and less characteristic of his continental colleagues—is Niebuhr's social and historical interpretation of these themes as the keys to understanding the travail of human political and social existence rather than the career of individuals. As in the thought of his colleague Paul Tillich, here, social hermeneutic—itself an inheritance of liberalism—opens up a new role for theology. The task of theology is no longer merely the elucidation of 'doctrines' from the sources of scripture and tradition, nor merely the effort to prove by reason the validity of Christian affirmations. It is now even more the interpretation of the mystery and travail of human existence, social history and personal history, by means of the symbols of Christian faith, to show that it is these symbols, and these alone, that make sense of the confusions of ordinary life. These theological changes, therefore, provide the ground not only of an innovative theological analysis of the entire scope of human existence, but of a new discipline as well, the theology of culture, or, better for Niebuhr, the theology of society.

As my description of the anatomy or structure of Niebuhr's theology indicates, this theology could legitimately be labeled, as it was, at least in America, "neo-orthodox." In this description, the word "orthodox" refers to the Pauline-Augustinian-Reformation strain of church theology, and not (as it does in Europe) to the orthodox dogmatics of the sixteenth- and seventeenth-century Lutheran and Reformed churches. If the former be the referent of the word "orthodox," then the post–World War I theology of Europe (also called *Krisis Theologie* or *Dialectical Theology*) can fairly be called "neo-orthodox"; if Protestant orthodoxy is meant, the label is then quite inaccurate. As a union of the classical Christian symbols (creation, sin, providence, revelation, incarnation, atonement, ecclesia, and eschatology) with many modern themes (the historical consciousness, historical criticism, modern physical science, etc.) this theology represents a new—

---

1. See also Niebuhr's discussion of the ambiguity of *all* political theories, and so of all ethical systems, at the conclusion of *Reflections on the End of an Era*, which I examine in the next chapter.

and so 'neo'—form of 'orthodoxy' as opposed to liberal theology. Whether the balance of this new synthesis tended more toward its orthodox component or more toward its modern and so liberal component is a question I shall discuss throughout this volume.

In any case, as is very clear, this union of disparate elements, traditional and modern, is even more characteristic of Niebuhr's thought. In each instance the classical symbol (Niebuhr regarded them simply as biblical)—creation, fall, sin, revelation, idolatry, pride, and so on—is used to provide the fundamental structure of his theology. It is the articulation of these orthodox symbols that directs and shapes the essential development of the theology. But the reinterpretation of these symbols is radical, and so 'neo.' It accepts, assumes, and incorporates into itself a very great deal that modern culture "knows" about nature, history, community, and the self, from cosmology and evolution, through historical consciousness, to modern interpretations of society and the self. It is, therefore, a genuine correlation (this is not Niebuhr's word) between a traditional theological symbol and modern self-understanding. Hence Niebuhr can as easily be termed a "neo-liberal" as he can be called neo-orthodox. Probably for a more careful analysis of this entire modern period, and especially of Niebuhr and Tillich, the label 'neo-liberal' will in the long term appear as the more adequate description of these theologies.

The only reason for reinvoking the original label "neo-orthodox" was that that name seems more faithful, I believe, to Niebuhr's and Tillich's own intentionality. Innovators in ideas are always very conscious, perhaps conscious only of the vast difference between themselves and their immediate predecessors. They are above all aware of being bearers of something new that seems to them the total opposite of what is at present established and also to them now being discredited. Thus were Renaissance and Enlightenment thinkers aware of their own stark opposition to the medieval period, the new Romantics of their opposition to their Rationalistic predecessors ("They kill in order to dissect," as Coleridge said). Correspondingly, the new theology of the post–World War I world was conscious only of its distance from, its opposition to, the preceding 'liberal' world.

So it was with Niebuhr: the sense of opposition to the then-dominant liberal culture, secular and religious, echoes and reechoes in his writings up to the 1950s. He hardly seems conscious in any way of all that he holds in common with them. Yet, fifty years later, the inheritance from liberalism, and from the post-Enlightenment culture that was 'modernity', seems to be fully as significant an element of his theology as were its appeals to the symbols of classical ('Biblical') theology. Because, however, of this character of their own consciousness as rebels against liberalism—even though this consciousness is one-sided—I prefer the label "neo-orthodox" to describe what was going on in the work of these theologians of the 1920s and 1930s when this theology developed.

Niebuhr's theology, then, was, like that of his contemporaries, genuinely a mixture of liberal and orthodox elements. It contained new syntheses not seen before; and perhaps its fragility, even its transience—for it did have a relatively short life—is a result of the precarious unity of these polar elements that constituted these syntheses. There are, I believe, three of these new syntheses.

(1) Reflectively and methodologically Niebuhr's theology represents the union of classical Christian symbols with modern scientific, historical, psychological, and social scientific understandings, a "correlation" of symbol and contemporary understanding not unlike that of Tillich. One methodological result was the appearance in theological language of a quite new category, namely 'myth', or what he called permanent or sophisticated myth. (2) Next is the synthesis that he recognized and applauded, namely that between the Renaissance (or, actually, the Enlightenment) and the Reformation. This synthesis combined on the one hand the post-Enlightenment recognition of the continual relativity and change of all historical institutions, mores, and concepts (including those of religion), the Enlightenment and post-Enlightenment affirmation of the creative originality of the human spirit, and as a consequence the modern confidence in the indeterminate possibilities of development in history. This modern sense of human being in history is in Niebuhr now synthesized with the Reformation sense of the continuity of sin, of judgment, and of the need for grace, and so the need for a transcendent fulfillment beyond history. One could add to this the union in Niebuhr's mind of the modern emphasis on the autonomy, the creativity, and the self-creativity of spirit with the Pauline-Augustinian tradition of theology. (3) Niebuhr offers a synthesis of the classical symbols of sin, judgment, atonement, justification, and new life with questions about and issues in social and historical existence, as now symbols interpretive of society, history, and our common historical future rather than primarily of individual life. We should note that this latter synthesis was with Niebuhr, as with Tillich, quite new.

CHAPTER 3

Early Political Writings

Reinhold Niebuhr's thought begins, as we might expect, deeply en-meshed in the social and political world around him. He is writing analyses of society, and at the same time he is reflecting on the character of history and the hopes for history. His questions are initially political and ethical ones: How is the achievement of justice possible? How, therefore, does society work? How and why do men and women behave as they do, and what sort of hopes are there as a consequence for justice in history? As we note, increasingly his reflections are driven beyond is-sues of social and political reform to questions about human nature and the character of history. We find him disagreeing more and more with the prevailing liberal views of his time (1925–35), as well as with his own earliest understanding; he is clearly at odds with both secular and religious "liberals," as the reaction of my father and of Harry Fosdick showed.

As is also evident, this increasing intellectual distance from his contem-poraries—with many of whom he cooperated politically—was partly the result of his interest in Marxism, which he had studied thoroughly and with much of which he then agreed. Apparently it was initially through the help of the Marxist critique of American capitalistic and democratic culture that he was able to get outside, to 'transcend', American culture vigorously enough to criticize it. But this was only a momentary assist. His own sharp eyes uncovered most of what he has to say in these early writings;[1] increasingly, he also became aware of what were to him the errors of the Marxist viewpoint.

∞

What was this prevailing view with which in these works he finds himself already disenchanted? It is generally called 'liberalism', and it characterized the dominant religious (Protestant) elite—the leaders and scholars of most Protestant churches and their middle-class congregations, and most if not all secular intellectuals and academics.[2] Probably its most fundamental assumption, appearing in both naturalistic and theistic form, was that reality (cosmos, history, society, and culture) represents a continuously progressive or "evolutionary" development. As the universe studied by astronomy and geology is now known to have developed over immense time from chaotic beginnings into its present coherent and orderly state, as the forms of life began with inchoate organisms and have developed into complex and so 'higher' species, so we now know that the realm of history itself began with barely organized and brutal forms of personal and social life and has gradually 'progressed' to its present levels of civilization. Barbarism, cruelty, and irrationality have steadily receded as ignorance, technological helplessness, and social confusion have diminished. Growth in scientific knowledge and in the use of tools, refinements of logical power and empirical inquiry, improvements of political ideals and of moral standards have all characterized this steady advance of civilization into higher levels of rationality and morality. The fruits of these advances in technical mastery, in lessened cruelty and conflict, in greater justice and equality are evident all around us. In both nature and history, therefore, there is a growing continuity between the natural and the ideal. Obscure at first, this continuity becomes more and more evident as the process unfolds, finally manifesting itself in a steady progress toward the ideal long latent within it. This assumption of evolutionary continuity in reality and of progress in history was fundamental for almost all reflective thought in America: scientific, political, sociological,

1. Perhaps the best example of these "sharp eyes" is in one of his very earliest and greatest books, his reflections on his experiences as a young minister in Detroit, described in *Leaves from the Notebook of a Tamed Cynic* (Chicago: Willett, Clark, & Co., 1929).

2. I shall discuss this general view from another angle in chapter 8 below, when I describe the "modern view of progress" as Niebuhr saw it.

historical, philosophical. Perhaps its greatest expositor was, ironically, Niebuhr's colleague in socialist politics, John Dewey. This vision of progress did not originate in America. On the contrary, it had characterized the dominant motifs in the eighteenth-century European Enlightenment and in new developmental forms in the nineteenth century.

There was also a religious form to this secular liberalism. In accord with the notion that history represented a progress of political and personal morals and of religious conceptuality and sensibility, religious liberalism tended to ascribe this progress to the work of the Divine Spirit rather than to the forces of nature or history alone. Religion provided, so to speak, the guiding and empowering inspiration for progress—just as, for evangelical Pietism, the Holy Spirit had provided the inspiration for personal sanctification. This progressive development represented for liberals the hermeneutical key to a true understanding of the biblical history: here we see a 'primitive' Hebrew view of God and of human obligation giving way slowly to a deeper religious and moral understanding. Through the covenant, the prophets, and the simple moral teachings of Jesus, these ideals—now at last prominent in modern civilization—have come to flower. Correspondingly, authoritarian religion, intolerant dogmatism, superstitious rites, and the parochial and biased spirit have given way to a more caring, tolerant concern for justice in the world—for "building the kingdom of God." As political absolutism has given way to democracy in politics, so arbitrary authority, dogma, and prejudice have been replaced by autonomy, cooperation, and tolerant understanding in religious communities.

Neither the secular nor the religious forms of this liberalism find evil—human evil—to be a lasting, overwhelming, or intractable problem. To be sure, evil characterized the historical past of barbarism, of Roman and medieval existence, and, unfortunately, of some contemporary unenlightened cultures. A "cultural lag" from the inherited institutions and habits of the past prevented the *social* reality of the period from being as civilized and advanced as its scientific and technical achievements might warrant. Thus much remained to be done, even in this progressive present. But hope is sustainable because the gradual elimination of evil is assured. The passage of historical time wipes out the preponderance of evil and gradually cleanses the character of history as historical life becomes more rational and more moral.

In this period, liberals tended to believe in the developing goodness and rationality of people, in the growing health of democratic and economic institutions, and in the certainty of a better and better tomorrow. Thus they downplayed—could not bear to see—the continued presence of evil in culture generally, the persistence of selfishness, irrationality, and brutality. Instead, they continued "to look at the good side." Hence the dilemma: moral idealists could hardly be realistic; if they became so, they became cynical.[3] Niebuhr castigated this view repeatedly; he identifies its refutation as the main theme of these early writings:

> Inasfar as this treatise has a polemical interest, it is directed against the moralists, both religious and secular, who imagine that the egoism of individuals is being progressively checked by the development of rationality or the growth of religiously inspired goodwill and that nothing but the continuance of this process is necessary to establish social harmony between all the human societies and collectives. (MM, xii)

As I shall demonstrate, Niebuhr finds many things wrong with this understanding of humans, of society, and of history. He hints, moreover, at many objections which are, perhaps, even more evident to us now than they were to him in the 1930s. First, the civilization—scientific, technological, industrial, individual, democratic—so rapturously celebrated in the liberal vision as universal, as the clear shape of a unified history's future, comes before our contemporary eyes as essentially partial and even local, as the ideal version of the present western European and American worlds. There are to be sure genuine ideals there, but they are clearly Eurocentered ideals, and the cultural forms manifested here are clearly the products of Western history and experience. That this very particular shape of things, even in its ideal form, can claim to represent the goal of all of history may certainly have been credible in 1910 and, in the United States, in 1925. After all, that civilization did in fact rule the entire globe! Nonetheless, clearly the assumptions, the norms, and the goals of a particular culture and of a particular epoch have in the theory of progress been made ultimate, the final goal of history. The present—our world—culminates the past and gives meaning to the vast strivings of that past; and the future will build on these potentialities latent in our own present.[4] It is in

3. For examples of this view in religious liberalism, see Albrecht Ritschl, *Justification and Reconciliation,* vol. 3 (1870); Auguste Sabatier, *The Religions of Authority and the Religions of the Spirit* (1900); Adolf von Harnack, *The Essence of Christianity* (1899–1900); and Walter Rauschenbusch, *A Theology for the Social Gospel* (1918) and *Christianizing the Social Order* (1912).

4. Intellectuals and academics in the 1920s laughed at Hegel for his "presumption" in seeing eighteenth-century German civilization as the epitome of historical progress—and his own philosophy as its centerpiece! Ironically, as progress was pictured in my youth during that same decade, it was assumed that history's persistent efforts had culminated not in early romantic Germany, but in scientific, technological, industrial, democratic, and Protestant(!) America.

the light of this very dubious privileging of the ideals of modernity as universal and absolute that we can understand Niebuhr's search for transcendence. He required a vantage point beyond this dominant and apparently ideal culture so that he could judge its particularity, its errors, and its injustices, assess its imminent destruction, and view some promise of hope beyond it.

∞

As we begin our analysis of *Moral Man and Immoral Society* (1932), we find Niebuhr clearly a 'political' theologian—if, that is, he can be called a theologian at all! His only concern seems to be social existence: how it can best be understood and how it can be made more just. His focus is on what we can call "the domestic political scene," the class conflicts of advanced capitalistic society. To him revolution and force may be necessary for any meaningful change to take place; he uses elements of Marxist theory as his lever of criticism of present society; and he has a limited but real confidence in the proletariat. Hence he has an undeniable "tilt toward the poor," and he is confident that an oppressive bourgeois society is shortly to destroy itself. History is for him dominated by class warfare, by the logic of such a historical process; and the resolution of this conflict is to be found in some mode of socialism. In all of this he is quite unlike the later Niebuhr and not unlike much recent 'liberationist' theology—and yet, as we shall see, there are also differences, and these differences signal important elements of his later theology.

There are four major theses in this important volume. The last one—the difference between individual and group virtue—is the most famous, but not, I think, the most significant.

The Ambiguity of Power

Political existence represents a contest of power, a conflict of wills driven by *interest,* the interest of each competing group, be it a class or a nation. Political life is thus not primarily a clash of theories to be carried on and directed by theoretical minds; nor is it one resolved by some mode of rational adjudication, persuasion, or agreement. The interests that dominate and drive groups are those of self-concern for the power, security, and status of the group; these interests are stubborn and resourceful. They will allow themselves neither to be persuaded nor deflected; they cannot be checked, limited, or overthrown except by the opposition of another and stronger group. At this point, Niebuhr labels this driving interest or self-interest "natural impulse," "the inertia of nature" (cf. MM xii, 35), and he compares it to "the jungle" (MM 81). In our present civilization this predatory interest and its issue, the drive to power, is obscured by the mechanics of a commercial and trading society, but it is nevertheless the will to power that is the dominant force in modern times as much as it was in ancient or medieval life.

It is this interest, the will to power, that is the major impediment to the achievement of justice. It is neither error in theory nor lack of education that perpetuates the economic structures that encourage oppression:

> The fact is that the interests of the powerful and dominant groups, who profit from the present system of society, are the real hindrance to the establishment of a rational and just society. . . . Policies are given their general direction by the pressure of the interests of the groups which control them; the expert is quite capable of giving any previously determined tendency both rational justification and detailed application. (MM 213–14)

Power not only impedes justice; a preponderance of power breeds further injustice. The group with dominant power always takes to itself most of society's privileges, defends them as its right, and refuses to relinquish any significant elements of them unless somehow forced to do so: "The individual or the group which organizes any society, however social its intentions or pretensions, arrogates an inordinate proportion of social privilege to itself" (MM 6–7). "Our interest at the moment is to record that any kind of significant social power develops social inequality" (MM 8). This expanding inequality in turn breeds a social discontent, and so in the end unequal power and unequal privilege destroy themselves in conflict (MM 11).

On the other hand, however ambiguous it may be, power cannot be completely eliminated in social history. Power is always necessary in order to bring unity and order to a community. In any community there are subordinate centers of interest eager to dominate other centers; without some central unifying power, any larger community is subject to the peril of anarchy—and in anarchy there is not only the actuality of conflict, but also in the end, since the strongest group will ultimately certainly dominate and oppress the others, there is the peril of a renewal of tyranny. Power is thus necessary to bring an uneasy peace to community life (MM 4). However, this necessary unifying role is always achieved by *one* group within the wider community, usually one class (what Toynbee calls a dominant minority).[5] This ruling minority creates and defends the whole, but it does not represent the whole (as it claims to do) as much as it represents the interests of its own ruling group. As a result, all unity, all order, all peace in society is inherently unjust because it is an order that represents and nurtures the dominant class (MM 6–7) and thus is in effect imposed (MM 19). Hence the paradox: "The power necessary to control the wicked is the danger, not the wicked" (cf. MM 16, 20–21). Because of the necessity and yet the ambiguity of power, society is continually, and inescapably, threatened with the dialectic of anarchy and tyranny and so continually plagued by injustice and potential conflict.

Finally, power is necessary if there is to be any increase in justice. No dominant group voluntarily surrenders its power and thus its privileges— a theme repeated over and over in Niebuhr's writings (e.g., MM xvii–xviii, 193, 253). As we shall see, rational and moral persuasion, while important, are not alone capable of dislodging a ruling group from its dominant position. Some mode of 'force' is necessary, be it that of legislation and law (not nonviolent because enforced by the unifying power of the state), that of economic and political pressure, or, as a last resort, that of protest and revolution. Niebuhr surely preferred the nonviolent forms of political power (cf. chapter 9 below), but he is clear that in the end the searchers after justice must be willing to use some mode of force to achieve their end (MM 171). And thus they too must face the further danger of misusing that force in their turn and in the end becoming themselves a dominant minority.

The Ambiguity of Reason

On the one hand, *reason* is for Niebuhr the principle by which men and women transcend their own partial interests to achieve a more universal viewpoint; thus it is the principle of creativity in human life (MM 25, 29, 31). At the same time, however, reason is the principle by which those partial and selfish interests are defended, justified, and expanded. Reason is, in other words, ambiguous. Liberals, Niebuhr says, wrongly negate power as

5. See Arnold Toynbee, *A Study of History,* vol. 4 (London: Oxford University Press, 1939–40), esp. C, 3, a, 1, 2, 3. Toynbee's theory of the "breakdown of civilizations" bears remarkable similarities to Niebuhr's—a dominant minority creates a new form of civilization, one very relevant to the problems of that time, but then it "idolizes itself" and its own early creative achievements; it "rests on its oars"; and finally it defends, long after it is relevant, that once creative response of an earlier time against all efforts to change these fundamental institutions.

inherently evil and wrongly celebrate reason as the objective resolver of our social problems. Intellectuals see only the universalizing, creative aspects of reason. This is what they do in their work, a work protected in many ways from the brutalities of the world; hence they regard the human intellect they feel they embody as capable of the same objectivity and disinterestedness in the political struggles of the world as it seems to them to possess in the library, the department office, or the laboratory. They fail to see that when a conflict of selves or of a group is involved (whether in a faculty, in commerce, or among nations), reason is the servant of interest long before it becomes its master, and that that mastery represents in fact a very rare moral achievement (MM xiv):

> Men will not cease to be dishonest, merely because their dishonesties have been revealed or because they have discovered their own deceptions. Wherever men hold unequal power in society, they will strive to maintain it. They will use whatever means are convenient to that end and will seek to justify them by the most plausible arguments they are able to devise. (MM 34)

In the first place, reason is used by dominant groups to justify their privilege and their power. There is, Niebuhr agrees, a class consciousness, and it acts on reason shaping the work of reason to further the interests of each group. As Niebuhr puts this in an oft-quoted sentence: "The will to power uses reason as kings use courtiers and chaplains, to add grace to their enterprise" (MM 44), and "Thus nature's harmless and justifiable strategies for preserving life, are transmuted in the human spirit into imperial purposes and policies" (MM 42).

Further, as the last implies, reason in fact extends and enlarges what Niebuhr then calls "the impulses of nature." It builds more effective instruments of aggressive action and simultaneously justifies that action. Most important, it is because of reason that humans are more anxious about the future than are the creatures of 'nature'. Humans can see that they are mortal; hence they are driven by this fear into aggressive and defensive actions, into a more persistent lust for power and security. Thus, in some memorable phrases, "mind sharpens nature's claws" (MM 44), and mind transmutes "the will to live into the will to power" (MM 18):

> The beast of prey ceases from its conquest when its maw is crammed; but man's lusts are fed by his imagination . . . and he will not be satisfied until the universal objectives which the imagination envisages are attained. (MM 44)

Here Niebuhr is developing some ideas that will themselves be thoroughly "transmuted" in his later theology. The original dualism of nature-impulse on the one hand and reason-mind on the other is in the process of being broken through: mind here affects and enlarges impulse, and it rationalizes, justifies, and enacts the resulting imperialism. 'Mind' in other words is now one important basis of the will to power; it is hardly innocent, nor is it as opposed to impulse as the older, dualistic categories Niebuhr is still using seem to imply.

The Ambiguity of Religion

Just as the other universal aspects of human existence, communal and individual, are fraught with ambiguity, so states Niebuhr is religion. To him religion is, like reason, the source of much that is creative in common life and yet also the source of much that is destructive: "Religion is at one and the same time, humility before the absolute and self-assertion in terms of the absolute" (MM 64). Profound religion in its relation to the absolute relativizes the ego and the group and hence encourages humility (cf. MM 52–63). At its best, moreover, religion emphasizes love as the highest ideal (MM 57) and breeds confidence where otherwise there might be despair (MM 62). But the concentration of religion on the absolute can also create real problems. On the one hand, concern for the absolute can lead to the identification of the absolute with the very relative values of our own communal life (MM 66); or, on the other hand, a religious absolute can obscure and minimize, if not simply negate, important "contrasts between good and evil on the human and historic level" (MM 67). It is this latter fault, said the early Niebuhr, that characterizes Augustine (as well as Barth), who saw "little value in the earthly city"—a critical judgment on Augustine's theology which Niebuhr will later thoroughly revise (MM 68–69).

In this new realism about religion (liberalism had held that these faults characterize only authoritarian and dogmatic religion), are the first signs of Niebuhr's very important later concept of idolatry, the tendency of the self and its community to identify itself with God, to worship itself, to "make itself God." This tendency Niebuhr will later term *pride* and will regard as the quintessence of sin. Here, moreover, there is the implicit recognition of the role of spirit in human evil, for a destructive religion represents a perversion of the spiritual relation to the absolute. But Niebuhr still names this destructive role of the absolute "the inertia of nature" (MM 198–99).

Except for this new realism about religion, Niebuhr's discussion of religion at this point is theologically very liberal: religion is a human creation, the work of the poetic imagination, painting the cosmos in human pictures in order to encourage moral attitudes (MM 52–53): "The truest visions of religion are illusions, which may be partially realised by being resolutely believed. For what religion believes to be true is not wholly true but ought to be true; and may become true if its truth is not doubted" (MM 81). One can feel in these sentences Niebuhr's Ritschlian background: religion sets morality in a cosmic framework. Even more interesting, one could say that Dewey might have written that sentence—except of course for Niebuhr's unquestioning assumption that religion, the humanly relative 'illusion', is a response to the presence and the call of a real and transcendent God. The ambiguity of religion, its destructive as well as its creative power, thus qualifies, if it does not quite refute, the optimistic hopes of humanism in the redemptive qualities of immanence. Thus it too drives Niebuhr's thought inexorably toward transcendence, if cynicism is to be avoided.

The Immorality of Groups

The thesis that while individual existence is or can be moral, group life cannot be, is generally taken to be the main theme of this volume. Although this is a point Niebuhr makes—certainly in the title, *Moral Man and Immoral Society*—there are, as I have tried to show, many more important themes at work here. What he seems to be saying—and this he will reiterate later—is that while individual virtue is difficult and rare enough, group virtue is well nigh impossible (MM 107). And certainly we cannot, as many liberals have done, conclude from the possibilities of individual selflessness the plausibility of a corresponding group selflessness.

There are three important reasons for this greater difficulty, this near impossibility, of group virtue:

1.   There is no single, unified, self-transcending consciousness in a group as there is in the individual. To be sure, a section of the community (usually a class, a dominant minority) unifies the wider group, shapes its common consciousness, and acts in the name of the group in all economic and political matters. But the consciousness of this ruling class is not identical with the consciousness of the whole, as in an individual. Rather it represents a particular group consciousness within the whole. Hence the interests that motivate the exercise of its power are by no means self-transcendent, selfless, or even the interests of the group as a whole; on the contrary, they represent the particular interests of a given class concerned with maximizing its own special power and privileges.

2. Groups are, therefore, not corporate individuals but communities composed of individuals. Thus there emerges the paradox or dialectic of morality in groups. The individual, who can be moral and who is called on by the group to be moral, in ordinary life becomes 'moral' by supporting, enacting, defending, and even sacrificing him- or herself for the welfare of the group. This individual morality and even sacrifice thus add fuel to the fire of group policies and interests, including any group's frequent 'immorality' toward other communities. For this reason 'moral' persons within the group can actually be immoral toward other groups, as 'moral' white people in a segregated and racist culture are 'immoral' and unjust to other groups and support that injustice. In such a case true morality is not to further the group's interests but, quite to the contrary, to challenge and even to oppose that communal immorality, that is, to refuse to sacrifice oneself for the group's purposes.[6]

Patriotism, says Niebuhr, is a paradoxical and ambiguous virtue. It combines the self-sacrifice of the individual with the self-interest of the group the individual serves; hence it produces, or can produce, the monstrous brew of fanaticism, group cruelty, violence, and conflict. To be 'morally' against the immorality of one's group is hence to become oneself immoral in the eyes of the wider community: a traitor to one's family, one's class, one's race, one's nation. But, as history shows, one is also a saint to other groups defending other, more universal sorts of 'interest', as the cases of Socrates and Jesus show (MM 91–93).

3. Finally, each group is invariably *hypocritical*. To ease the consciences of its individual members (MM 9)—or, later, its common conscience as a community—the group must claim to embody and to pursue the highest values rather than admitting the relatively dubious interests, the particular self-interests, that actually drive the group. The group, therefore, pretends not only that the values the community espouses are more universal than they truly are, but also that those values are the sole 'reasons' why it does whatever dubious things it does do. Thus each embattled nation fights for

---

6. It is precisely this capacity of the individual to sacrifice him- or herself for the group, what is frequently called altruism, that is identified by most of the biological and sociological communities as the essence of the moral. Members of these communities have not pondered the paradoxes of ethics enough to comprehend this Niebuhrian dialectic, namely that this individual morality can become quickly enough 'immorality' on the level of group life. Hence, paradoxically, the height of morality—e.g., in Socrates, in Jesus, in most martyrs—is precisely the refusal to be 'altruistic' in the social science sense and to refuse to give one's allegiance to the group.

peace and justice; each ruling class defends a universal order, unity, and peace; each dominant race defends law and property. Actually, in fact as Niebuhr said on a number of occasions, "no nation fights until its own deepest interests are involved." Because self-interest is insinuated into all corporate action and because humans remain moral, hypocrisy is the inevitable by-product of all social politics (MM 45): "It is the tribute morality pays to immorality; or rather the device by which the lesser self gains the consent of the larger self" (MM 95). Hence the morality of individuals can be channeled into service for the immorality of groups, and then, lest that individual conscience awaken, it can be kept quiet by the claim that the group's immorality really serves a universal moral purpose to which each individual should adhere. Clearly here we have an early form, on empirical grounds, one might say, of the very important later category of self-deception.

There are further themes in this volume that reflect Niebuhr's interest in Marxism and his adherence to socialist principles—as well as his relation to his 'descendants' in liberation theology. Only the poor, he says, can see the truth of the real social world; they suffer from its brutalities, its injustices, and its fatedness (MM 80, 166–67), and so they are vividly aware of the dominance of self-interest in all societies. The upper classes, and their 'chaplains'—the academic wise men—are protected and blinded by their privileges; they overlook the covert and overt violence that holds society in that form together, and hence they view social developments in an optimistic but hopelessly naive way. Niebuhr feels that economic power is the dominant form of social power (MM 164–68) and that the social goal of equality is a higher goal than the unrealistic and self-interested bourgeois goals of order and peace. And he is certain that out of the turmoil of an advanced capitalistic world, socialism of some sort will become dominant (MM 144, 164, 178–79). Finally, he finds many of the moral faults and the theoretical excesses of communism "understandable" in the light of the sufferings of the proletarian class it represents (MM 156–62).

In the midst of these at best mild reproofs of a view that Niebuhr will later strongly repudiate, there appear, however, elements of critical insight into Marxism that will grow as his own point of view develops. As he reiterates throughout this volume, any utopian vision for history's future is not only implausible but dangerous, and communist oligarchs, when they reach power and their idealism recedes, will probably be as oppressive as those whom they replace (MM 21). In fact he argues that communism is less a science than a religion, dependent on a 'myth' about history and on a deep commitment to the aims, the authority, and above all the eschatological hopes of that myth (MM 154–58). As in part a form of religion, communism especially should be self-critical unless it is to become dangerous. Communism shows as yet no sign of this self-criticism; on the contrary, it breeds the tendency to idolize its own class, the proletariat, as the universal representative of all humankind. Niebuhr's criticisms become even sharper as events in 1930s Russia develop.

This is a remarkable book. In the place of the 'naive' utopias of both liberal and Marxist theories, utopias that for that reason could not face the realities of their own developing world, it presents realistic, modest but still remarkably hopeful prospects for the future of society:

> The problem which society faces is clearly one of reducing force by increasing the factors which make for a moral and rational adjustment of life to life; of bringing such force as is still necessary under responsibility to the whole of society; of destroying the kind of power that cannot be made socially responsible . . . ; and of bringing forces of moral self-restraint to bear upon types of power which can never be brought completely under social control. (MM 20)

> His concern for some centuries to come is not the creation of an ideal society in which there will be universal and perfect peace and justice, but a society in which there will be enough justice, and in which coercion will be sufficiently non-violent to prevent this common enterprise from issuing into complete disintegration. (MM 22; see also 256)

And as I noted earlier, this volume—now read constantly in sociology and political science classes—evoked on its publication a very real storm of protest and disdain from socialists and from democratic and religious liberals alike.

∞

Most of the important themes of *Moral Man* continue in *Reflections on the End of an Era* (1934): society represents a struggle for power and security, that is, for interest; "reason is the servant of impulse before it is its master" (RE 17); all politics is laced with hypocrisy and rationalization; and religion is incurably ambiguous. The emphasis on class struggle continues. German fascism, for example, is seen as the 'delirious' defense of bourgeois rulers against communism (RE 165–66) (a serious error of interpretation and, ironically, one in thorough agreement with many capitalists who also saw fascism as a bulwark against communism). Niebuhr still thinks that the inevitable and ultimate outcome of the West's present class warfare will be the doom of capitalism and the appearance of a socialist world, the final victory of the proletariat. Ironically, barely half a decade later (1939–40), having successfully predicted the rise of fascism, Niebuhr's own subsequent reaction to that rise was just the opposite from what he had earlier foreseen: namely a newly invigorated defense of democracy. Finally, the blindness of liberal savants is repeated: separated from the brutalities of social existence and enamored with the coherence of their own rational abstractions, "with pathetic irony modern civilization proceeded to tear itself asunder in national and class warfare while its wise men dreamed of perpetual peace" (RE 14).

There are, however, several emphases that are new, and that together drive his thought increasingly in the direction of his later theology. One can feel, first of all, a quickened interest in anthropology (the theory of human nature) and in the philosophy of history. Both, as noted above, were present in *Moral Man,* but served more as the implicit background for Niebuhr's analyses of the domestic social struggle and of the possibility of domestic social justice. I believe that in *Reflections* they now appear as the explicit subjects of the volume. In fact, it seems to me that the latter issue, the nature of history and its developments, has become his major reflective concern, possibly because the social and historical events with which he was concerned had shifted from the domestic struggle against capitalism to the even more intense drama of the rise of Asian and European fascism and international communism.

The irony that a culture that thrives on its belief in historical progress marches in actual history toward its own doom is made very clear at the start of the volume. Let us recall that in 1933–34 Japan invaded Manchuria and Mussolini, Ethiopia; Hitler had just risen to power and posed an ever-increasing threat to the peace, and the life, of Europe. As a consequence, Niebuhr's central awareness is of the crucial events that appear to be leading inexorably to an international crisis of vast scope. He was then continually berated for being a "doom-sayer"; in fact, he was quite right in this gloomy intuition. And also understandably, the theoretical problem that dominates the book is the question of the direction and meaning of a history now in continuing and very deep crisis. The origins of the belief in progress are carefully cited (RE 3, 5); the way injustice leads to inevitable contradictions (RE 16, 18, 32, 87–88) and manifests 'judgment in history' (i.e., divine judgment) in and through the actual sequence of events is articulated (RE 51–52); and finally the now-obvious fact that no perfect society is possible is reiterated (RE 104, 246)—for "the world of politics remains the world of sin" (RE 247). This description of the way history seems to be working in the 1930s forms a clear preview of the theology of history that is to come in his later books. This developing philosophy of history is, I suggest, the dominant theme of this book; and this is new.

Correspondingly, the anthropology latent in *Moral Man* becomes much more an explicit subject of discussion. The categories with which Niebuhr conceives of human nature and its behavior, categories which organize and articulate "the facts of experience" as he sees them, remain largely unchanged, that is, liberal. On the one side are reason and spirit; on the other side are impulse and nature. It is the all-dominating force of interest that leads to the collective drive for power; and this driving interest, which makes the conflict, the violence, and the injustice of history inevitable, remains for him an irrational impulse, a function of 'nature'. Again politics is fueled by interest and not, as the liberals suppose, by theory: "The collective life of man moves by impulse rather than reason" (RE 34). Hence society remains more of a "jungle" than modern rationalists can believe; it is propelled by "the forces of nature" (RE 124, 178), or "the inertia of nature" (RE 196), forces arrayed against spirit, that is, against conscience and reason (RE 212). In effect, therefore, history is to be understood as under the domination of nature, a manifestation of "the order of nature" (RE 31).[7]

These apparently 'dualistic' categories—impulse and nature on the one hand, reason and conscience on the other—remain as the categories with which Niebuhr reflects on society. They show clearly the imprint of his liberal inheritance even while his empirical insights, the stuff of history as he increasingly sees it, are bursting these categories apart and so are calling for the radical shift of understanding that will soon come. The later Niebuhr would never have written that "the world of history is the world of nature" (RE 179) or "history-as-nature" (RE 236). Yet his sense of what this historical world is actually like (as opposed to the way it should be reflectively described) remains relatively unchanged from these early writings to his developed theology. For what he is seeking to say here by using the category 'nature'—namely that society is neither ideal nor rational but driven by interests—is precisely what he would later say with more intelligibility by using the category 'sin'. Hence what he frequently said about his critics and opponents—namely that the facts of history, the ordinary stuff of ordinary experience, fail to validate their categories of understanding—ironically applied precisely to the categories in his own early writings on human nature.

7. It is also ironic that much of the liberal thought that Niebuhr here disputes also saw history as "under the dominion of nature," except that there nature was viewed as obedient to an evolutionary process of development which then carried on "beyond nature" to direct history's progress to higher and higher advances in civilization.

One of the fascinating things about this volume is that the bursting apart of these categories is here developing almost before his (and the reader's) eyes. He sees that this dualism of nature and mind is beginning not to work, to require radical qualification. As he notes, it is reason that transmutes natural impulse into endless aggression, the relatively innocent will-to-survive into the deadly will-to-power (RE 6, 8, 17). And it is mind and conscience that provide the rationalization and the hypocrisy that hide and justify this egoism (RE 5). Two quotations show that these old wineskins are barely able to contain the new wine:

> Man is always most inhuman, not when he is unconsciously driven by natural impulse, but when he imagines his natural impulses and his relative values to be the instruments of some absolute good.
>
> The impulses of nature only achieve demonic proportions when they are falsely mixed with spirit and gain immunity from the moral censor by appropriating the moral prestige of the spiritual. (RE 171)
>
> The task must be performed by those who know that the world of history is the world of nature; but who also know that the greater degree of social cohesion of which human collectives are capable involves them in perils of anarchy and self-destruction of which the world of pure nature knows nothing. (RE 179)

Niebuhr is here at the threshold of new categories that will be supplied shortly thereafter by the Biblical symbols—creature, image of God, and sinner—and that will structure his later thought about human nature. Again, his frequent theme that ordinary experience cannot be understood without these later categories seems validated by his own intellectual development.

As we have noted, the structure of historical change, the philosophy of history in that sense, is—so it seems to me—now the central theme of *Reflections.* These are reflections on what is to him the clear end of our historical era, and so they concern what factors are at work in those contemporaneous cataclysmic historical developments. The irony of historical progressivism in the midst of a developing historical catastrophe (RE 3, 14, 16), the inexorable march of capitalism toward its own doom and, after immense travail, toward a new socialist world (RE 32, 81, 87, 88), these are given greater prominence here than in *Moral Man.* And as this indicates, the sense that history is determined by its economic relations and its class warfare seems to have grown (RE 10–12, 66–67, 90–91). There is an inexorable 'logic of history' (RE 143, 161); certain changes are 'bound to occur' (RE 18–19, 35, 37, 143). Thus there is necessity in the transition from capitalism to socialism (RE 181) and certainty in the victory of the worker (RE 161) so that 'the future belongs to the worker' (RE 146). Clearly these are Marxist themes, made more prominent by Niebuhr's increased interest in the question of the direction and meaning of history. The socialist understanding of historical change and of the social goals of historical development are to him still *the* way to see history. It is, I think, important to note that the significant change that is soon to occur in his understanding of history is as fundamental a change as is the shift in his understanding of human nature. Later, his statement, "Where there is history, there is freedom, where there is freedom, there is sin" (ND 2:80), manifests as radical a departure from his early Marxist determinism as his later insistence that it is spirit that transmutes a relatively innocent nature into the destructive evil of human affairs.

Nevertheless, despite this continuing and, in effect, fairly dogmatic use of Marxist categories in understanding history, the critique of Marxism deepens. Niebuhr was obviously shocked by the Soviet persecution of the Kulaks in the early 1930s. One of the first to make this point, he now states even more clearly his interpretation of communism as 'religion'—that is, as 'myth' (RE 193). Any view, he says, that gives to all of history a meaningful structure is neither science nor philosophy but myth. Meaning is only established by myth (RE 194–95), and myths are held by assent or faith and not by rational argument. Hence, as he will reiterate later, cultures are held together by their faith in the myths that give their common life meaning. If, therefore, communism be a religion, says Niebuhr in a classic phrase, we can understand the "consistent animus of communism for religion, particularly Christianity." For communism "combines the hatred of one religion for another with the repulsion of irreligion for religion" (RE 193).

Most interesting is Niebuhr's discussion of the spirit of vengeance. Making the point that it is vengeance that drives the long-suffering proletariat—and so the party—to the excesses of cruelty evident in Russian history in the early twentieth century, Niebuhr is clearly partly understanding and justifying this reaction as the natural result of a long history of severe oppression and exploitation. The victims of injustice "are activated as much by the spirit of vengeance as by the spirit of justice; this is inevitable but it is also dangerous" (RE 167). It is dangerous because, he notes, there is a residual egoism here, an egoism of class that, if not recognized, can become the basis of intense cruelty. When this egoism is blind to its own partiality and is combined with a sense of an absolute cause, it becomes a scourge of all other interests. The industrial proletariat have suffered evil, but they falsely identified their suffering with all suffering, and their victory with the victory of all humankind—hence other suffering groups with other interests are eradicated. This is the blindness of the spirit of vengeance, and the great danger for justice of the Marxist cause (cf. RE 187–89).

> Man is always most inhuman, not when he is unconsciously driven by impulse, but when he imagines his natural impulses and his relative values to be the instruments of some absolute good. (cf. RE 171).

> The communists are certain they are collectivizing the peasants for the latter's own good and their measures against peasant opposition therefore reveal the cruelty which always characterizes the will to power of righteous people who are certain that they are the instruments of a righteous cause. (RE 172)

One can see, moreover, with growing clarity that it is precisely the religious dimension of Marxism that inspired its most virulent forms of injustice and cruelty. The critique of religion has deepened with the result that a prophetic principle becomes necessary in all religion. Without some permanent and so religious principle of self-criticism, as well as criticism of the other, any religious myth—Marxism now included—can become quickly demonic, and this, Niebuhr notes, is the advantage of profound religion (RE 183–84). Later he understands the 'spirit of vengeance' and the demonic role of religion in Biblical terms; he then applies to both the new categories of idolatry (worship of a partial goal) and pride (the part making itself the whole). Later the issues of idolatry and pride become his major points of contention with Marxism. Instigated as always by contemporary historical events, this new, sharply critical perspective on Marxism seems to have become a second major factor impelling Niebuhr to new categories of understanding: his liberal dualism failed to understand human nature, and likewise the Marxist scheme of history failed to make intelligible the developments within socialism itself.

We have noted the appearance of the category of myth as the sole linguistic mode adequate for the elucidation of meaning in history. Niebuhr later develops and refines this conception into one of the main elements of his theology. In this, its first significant appearance, the category of myth is associated with three important issues: (1) Myth answers the question of the nature of history as a whole, that is, what history's final structure of development may be and what its direction or its goal, if any, may be (RE 194). (2) Myth answers our anxious questions about the problem of evil, that is to say, the reason for our suffering on the one hand, and the hope for our redemption from that suffering on the other (RE 196). (3) Myth, therefore, discloses the meaning of a community's life and so of each individual life within that community. For Niebuhr no community, and in fact, no individual, can live creatively without some affirmed sense of meaning, and since humans are communal, that necessitates a meaning for all of history, a historical myth.

We can see here developing very important elements of Niebuhr's understanding of the essential structure and role of religion, namely to provide the overarching principle of meaning in life. And it is this that makes religion in this sense an essential and permanent element in all human existence. Myth, therefore, can also take a secular form, as the liberal myths of progress and the Marxist myth of the dialectical movement of history toward its goal show: both give to modern communities a sense of the structure and goal of all of history. Both, therefore, provide meaning by answering questions of suffering on the one hand and of redemption on the other (RE 122–28, 194–96). All myths, moreover, transcend any simple rules of coherence; they cannot be made logically coherent. Hence they outrage the rational mind. Nevertheless, Niebuhr is certain that any philosophy, because it is dependent on a meaningful vision of the whole, is, in fact, a rationalized myth (RE 198).

Only Christianity is explicitly paradoxical (RE 207, 213–14) and thus 'absurd' to the philosophical mind. This discussion of myth sets the stage, moreover, for the apologetical character of Niebuhr's mature theology, namely the argument that myth is the only way these confusing facts can be made intelligible. But this paradoxical mode of interpretation of history is justified by the "facts of life and history" (RE 211, 217). Again, it is now only a step toward the more developed concept of 'Biblical myth' as the clue to historical understanding that appears in the sermons collected in *Beyond Tragedy* in 1936.

Perhaps the newest note in *Reflections*—one not in complete harmony with much in the volume—is his strong advocacy at the end of the book of a balance of power as the nearest a community can come to social justice and harmony. This new espousal of a balance of power is in sharp contrast to his former veneration of the proletarian cause and to his certainty of the truth of a socialist understanding of historical development. It bespeaks, therefore, a new sense of the relativity of all social perspectives (including Marxism), of the ambiguity of all social classes (including the proletariat), of the possibility within each of the latter to become demonic, and so to a new appreciation of the necessity of tolerance of opposing interests and opposing viewpoints. These are the virtues of liberalism, as Niebuhr gratefully remarks (RE 252–53, 258), and of the democracy that he had frequently felt to be quite ineffective in establishing real justice

(RE 54–56, 70–71, 156). Nonetheless, despite this tardy bow to these liberal principles, he still is no liberal: "Liberalism can tame life only if it is tame to begin with" (RE 261).

As always, his important change in political understanding came about not because of an intellectual change, a change in theoretical understanding, but because of the unexpected facts of contemporary history that his sharp eyes recognized and that confronted and confounded his own theories. He sees now that economic power is not so clearly the fundamental form of power he had thought; Marxism had merely exchanged economic power for political power, and oppression had only grown in intensity. The self apparently can use political as well as economic power to advance its interests. He sees that all political and social panaceas, all utopian and universalistic ideologies, however idealistic, represent particular interests and so relative perspectives; and this applies to the proletariat as well as to the bourgeoisie. All forms of power, therefore, whatever groups they represent and whatever their pretensions to universality and ultimacy, remain relative and self-interested; none represent an absolute position, and none can be trusted with absolute power. Since no particular class, nation, or ideology can rule safely without being checked, and since no positive blueprint is absolute, a balance of power among groups and perspectives is necessary so that none can become oppressive over the others (RE 231, 235, 243). "Without such a check [a democratic balance of power] every oligarchy becomes tyrannical" (RE 244). "Every balance of power and every equilibrium of social forces is a potential chaos which has been coaxed into a momentary cosmos" (RE 245).

Several important conclusions follow from this new insight.

1. If all economic and political theories are relative and potentially ambiguous, then the problem of social justice lies deeper than the political or economic argument between theories or the victory of one theory over the others, important as these debates may be. Any one of these can become the vehicle of tyranny. Hence the source of the problem of justice and of conflict lies deeper than any political or economic analysis can penetrate, and the source of the problem of injustice deeper than any particular social structure. This source resides in the inward life of the human self and its communities; and its discernment and articulation require therefore philosophical or theological analysis. With this understanding, Niebuhr is on his way to his later explicitly theological writings.

2. Correspondingly, politics moves in the opposite direction, that is, in a pragmatic direction suited to this new understanding of the relativity of all standpoints. Politics itself must become pragmatic rather than idealistic or utopian, directed by considerations of contemporary context and

factors rather than by strict ideological requirements. The task of political life is not to achieve the victory of one ideology or of one center of power over another, but to balance the forces within a community so that on the one hand a relative justice and peace are possible and that on the other hand the dangers of tyranny and of anarchy are avoided. The paradox of a political pragmatism buttressed by a profound theological analysis, for which he will become famous, has begun to appear.

3.   There is, Niebuhr concludes, no final answer to the problem of justice. Some political systems are better than others, and pragmatic choices must be made between them. Relative achievements of more justice, more equality, and more peace are, therefore, possible, if one's commitments are firm and one's policies tentative. History is always open to such relative progress, and it is this for which we should work. Catastrophe, however, is always possible, and every balance of power is a potential chaos. Thus we need an unflinching realism about our social world and especially about our own ambiguity within that world, an undiscouraged concern for more justice, and a permanent (and so transcendent) principle of criticism and of hope.

PART 2

Niebuhr's Mature Theology

CHAPTER 4

Meaning, Mystery, Myth, and Revelation

In this part of my study, I shall directly address Niebuhr's mature theology, represented by his major work, *The Nature and Destiny of Man,* and his subsequent theological expression of this theology, *Faith and History.* As I have shown above, Niebuhr's political reflections moved from the issue of justice in society "back," so to speak, to the sources of that issue: namely, the questions of human nature and of the direction of history, with which these major works are concerned. However, for Niebuhr these two fundamental questions themselves centered on the issue of meaning—much as Tillich's theology, which also began with the quest for justice, later centered itself on the question of being and of nonbeing. Hence I shall begin by seeking here to uncover how this important question of meaning functions in Niebuhr's theology. We have seen the issue of meaning slowly appearing in *Reflections* as the category most relevant to the understanding of history and of human action in history. Now, along with the question of the nature of human being, meaning moves to center stage.

For Niebuhr *meaning* is the main, though not the sole, gift of religion. In describing the character of various alternative religions, Niebuhr always begins with the notion of the meaning (or the lack of meaning) of individual and social existence. Whether or not a given religion provides a secure and creative meaning to our historical life is perhaps his major criterion of the adequacy of that religion. As is evident, meaning here is a category entirely referent to *history,* to the meaning of our life, individual and communal, in our allotted time. Niebuhr assumed that his concern with history and its meaning is the essence of "Biblical religion." Meaning here refers to a sense of worth, significance, or purpose in who we are and what we do; even more, meaning connotes the assurance not only of worth and purpose but also of the achievement of that purpose. The assurance of meaning thus gives confidence, courage, and self-affirmation to our common being in the world; it gives direction to our common projects and our acts; it is the principle of judgment on our relative successes and failures; it provides comfort and intelligibility in the face of discouragement and tragedy; and it gives hope for our future even in the possible grimness and suffering of the present. There are few persons, Niebuhr believed, who lacked entirely such a sense; if they do so lack, this then is what he meant by despair (FH 152).[1]

Meaning here is certainly individual—the significance of my own individual life. But for Niebuhr individual meaning is inextricably bound to social meaning; the meaning of each life is tied to the meaning of its significant group, be it tribe, family, city, class, or nation. Individual significance is not only judged by the criteria of the group; it is dependent on the group's success and failure in its vocation, that is, the group's meaning in the wider patterns of history. Thus since the meaning of the life of a group is itself inextricably bound up with the meaning of the history in which the group exists—that is, the patterns of historical change that shape and reshape, prosper or threaten, the life of groups—the religious question of meaning involves at once the wider religious question of the meaning of history as a whole. Hence the meaning of history is for Niebuhr *the* primary religious question, and for him, as for Tillich, the primary distinction between religions is that between historical and nonhistorical religions.[2]

Such a sense of meaning is, Niebuhr felt, absolutely necessary for an individual or a culture: "It is difficult if not impossible, to live without presupposing some system of order and coherence which gives significance to one's life and actions" (FH 153). Hence we can say that for Niebuhr there is a 'religious substance' (Tillich's phrase) to every culture, namely its vision of the whole of history and its role in that pattern of the whole. Such visions, as we shall see, are held by faith; they represent the implicit religion

---

1. This emphasis on the meaning of life in history, and its use as a criterion of other religions, is an example of how one perspective—in this case Niebuhr's interpretation of Biblical religion as 'historical'—formulates in its own terms the criterion of judgment of other religious perspectives. Another perspective, for example that of Buddhism, might not find the issue of the meaning of historical existence religiously significant at all! In this emphasis on history, Niebuhr is clearly a modern and Western thinker. Evidently he is also on this issue an example of 'liberal' theology in the sense that here the central focus of religious faith and piety has moved from the question of salvation in the next life to that of the meaning of this life.

2. Paul Tillich, *The Protestant Era* (Chicago: University of Chicago Press, 1948), chap. 2; see my further discussion of this point in chapter 8 below.

of even the most explicitly secular of cultures. This faith is expressed in and through every creative work of culture, and especially in its philosophies; it activates and directs all the members of that community. Prominent contemporary examples of such implicit religious visions of meaning that direct and empower their community are the faith in progress of modern liberalism and the confidence in the Material Dialectic of Marxism. Despite their explicit secularity, both liberal and Marxist cultures possess a religious vision of the whole of history and of its direction leading to a culmination, an end; and it is this vision, in each case, that gives meaning to the life of its community (FH 45, 153; ND 1:23).

Issues of meaning, then, represent the most fundamental issues for existence and for reflection on existence. We understand ourselves and our possibilities in the light of the meanings that we discern and affirm in our life. Niebuhr, I think, never doubted that such a sense of meaning was there in any individual life or culture that retained its creativity—nor did he seem to doubt at all that objectively history did in fact have a meaning, however obscure that meaning might be. Like ultimate concern in Tillich, a grasp of meaning was to Niebuhr universal; and its absence spelled despair, the cessation of the vitality that makes life possible. Thus Niebuhr does not try to prove one must have a principle of meaning. What he does seek repeatedly to prove is that alternative schemes of meaning are false and useless, subject on the one hand to refutation by events and so to despair, or on the other as lures to idolatry and so in the end self-destructive (FH 152–53).

This gives form to his most frequent apologetic for the Christian faith, for Biblical religion. The Christian scheme of meaning, he argued, makes more sense than the others on three important grounds: (1) it makes intelligible the contradictions and confusions of ordinary, and especially historical, experience; (2) it deals most creatively with the deep anxieties of being human; and (3) it guards against the twin perils of idolatry and despair. To him each of the secular alternatives to Biblical faith takes some finite and partial aspect of human life as both ultimate and saving. This inevitably leads on the one hand to reflective misunderstanding (see ND 1:1–100; or FH 1–100), and on the other it creates the condition for idolatry. None of the alternatives view human nature or historical change as centered beyond themselves, and hence they misunderstand.

> All three errors of most estimates of man, therefore, point to a single and common source of error: man is not measured in a dimension sufficiently high or deep to do full justice to either his stature or his capacity for good and evil or to understand the total environment in which such a stature can understand, express and find itself. (ND 1:124)

It is, in fact, impossible to interpret history at all without a principle of interpretation which history itself does not yield. (ND 1:141)

The meaning of life always appears against a background of deep, even infinite mystery. The infinity of factors and facts and the radical contingency of events in history mean that no complete or stable pattern of history, universal in its scope and timeless in its validity, is possible. A meaning in historical life is never demonstrable, either by science or by rational speculation. All are partial, perspectival, pictures at best of the meaning resident in the mystery of things, in short 'myths'. Hence all meaning is by faith and not by rational calculation: "The various principles of interpretation current in modern culture, such as the idea of progress or the Marxist concept of an historical dialectic, are all principles of historical interpretation introduced by faith" (ND 1:141). Meaning, therefore, is a partial disclosure within a surrounding mystery, a disclosure based on a fragment of experience and yet one taken by responding faith to represent a clue to the mystery of the whole (FH 141). Hence meaning expresses both the finitude of human being in the infinity of things and the infinite reach of the human spirit as it seeks to comprehend and relate to that whole. In turn, as both human faith and human idolatry reveal, mystery is not mere blankness and negation; it is rather fraught with a partial and fragmentary intelligibility to which all human life relates itself:

> Mystery does not annul meaning but enriches it. It prevents the realm of meaning from being reduced too simply to rational intelligibility and thereby given a false center of meaning in a relative or contingent historical force or end. (FH 103)

> In the same manner when philosophy approaches the ultimate issues of life and finds itself incapable of overcoming the ultimate ambiguities of human existence, it is forced to recognize the realm of mystery as both the fulfillment and the negation of the realm of meaning and to acknowledge the function of faith as both the fulfillment and the negation of reason. (FH 54)

I shall discuss this relation of history and history's meaning to faith further in chapter 8 below.

∞

Where, then, does this mystery, which surrounds, enriches, and also challenges meaning, lie? What are the clues to its universal presence in and over all of our necessary and yet finite schemes of meaning? Certainly we must, I believe, immediately answer, that mystery for Niebuhr is a pervasive and significant category primarily because he assumed that God was actively present throughout all of life. He sees a God who transcends all of our efforts to understand just as thoroughly as God transcends our creaturely being; yet this God is continually in essential and intimate relation to us. Mystery is in the first instance, therefore, a theological category. Still, there are points in our ordinary experience where ultimate mystery as mystery impinges, as does God, and discloses its strange, shaking, and upholding presence.

1.   There is a mystery in the origin and continuing being of things. However far cosmological science penetrates in seeking to understand the becoming—the coming into being—of the universe, it reaches an end of its quest. This is an end which, as Kant pointed out, nonetheless points thought beyond itself endlessly—as modern big bang cosmology itself witnesses. No completely rational comprehension of the mystery of ultimate origin is possible: "Actually belief in divine creation points to a realm of mystery which is at once both the beginning and the end of any system of meaning and which prevents it from being reduced to a too simple system of rational intelligibility" (FH 46).[3]

3. Further on in his own text (FH 48) Niebuhr cites a quotation from Whitehead to support the point he was making there and that I am pursuing here, namely that the symbol of creation represents the end or limit of clear intelligibility since, as he says above, it "points to a realm of mystery which is the beginning and the end of any system of meaning" (FH 46). The quotation from Whitehead (as quoted in FH 48–49) is as follows: "We must provide, declares Whitehead, a ground for the limitation which stands among the attributes of substantial activity. This attribute provides the limitation for which no reason can be given, for all reasons flow from it. God is the ultimate limitation, and His existence the ultimate irrationality." See A. N. Whitehead, *Science and the Modern World* (New York: Macmillan, 1926), 249. When, during my own labors to understand Whitehead, I spoke to Niebuhr about this quote, with which he was very familiar, I realized (as his own text implies) that he thought Whitehead agreed with him here, i.e., on the notion of creation. Both recognized a sharp limit to clear intelligibility, at the edge, so to speak, of universal process; both related that limit to God; and so both could reasonably name God, as Whitehead does here, "the ultimate irrationality." I do not think Niebuhr realized the immense differences on this point between his view and Whitehead's. In sum, this difference was that for Whitehead the natural process is all that there is, and outside of it there is only blank nothingness. This process has an arbitrary limitation; this limitation is as it is and so unfolds as it unfolds; it has no history and is not dependent on or related to history; no reason can be given, therefore, for just *that* limitation—it is the beginning of all reasons since all reasons are internal to the coherence of the process. This original limitation, the beginning of all process, is in Whitehead named 'God', or better, one aspect of God, the Primordial Nature of God. For Niebuhr, on the other hand,

Furthermore, this presiding mystery discloses itself within as well as outside of the scientific system of coherence: in the continuing appearance in nature of radical contingency and the new, in the consequent impossibility of entirely explaining any event or entity by its preceding causes, and hence in the appearance of spontaneity and randomness at even the lowest levels of natural life (ND 1:134; BT 8).

> Though the idea of creation is not in conflict with any scientific account of natural causation, which accurately describes the relation of an antecedent cause to a subsequent event, yet without the idea the antecedent cause tends falsely to become the sufficient cause of the subsequent event. This logic, when consistent, would exclude precisely the emergence of the novel in time, which it has been the achievement of modern culture to discern. (FH 48)

2.   There is, moreover, a permanent mysterious limit to human existence because of the infinite self-transcendence of the human spirit. The human mind is such that not only can it create innumerable schemes of coherence—as the history of culture and of science alike show—but it can also itself transcend each one of its own creations. That is, the mind can question, criticize, doubt everything that the mind produces; and it can, because of that infinite critical ability, refashion all its achieved forms of order into alternative forms. This is the basis for the dynamic character of changing cultural life and of novelty itself in human history; it is also a vivid sign of the relativity of all rational schemes of coherence. Because of this self-transcendence of mind, these latter human schemes are known to be relative, or are suspected to be such. Hence on the one hand they are ever unstable, and on the other their felt relativity tempts those who adhere to them to claim that they are not so, but are ultimate and universal. The ever-present possibility of doubt, and the erosion of secure meaning that this doubt threatens, creates deep anxiety and hence the ultimate danger of idolatry.

God is not an aspect of process, not even as its beginning; rather God transcends and creates the natural process. God is thus recognized as 'mystery' beyond the intelligibility characteristic of the process and available to finite minds. In this sense, namely that the divine transcends both process and its coherence, God is the 'ultimate limit' and the 'ultimate irrationality'. But the irrationality here is in the sense of a divine mystery transcendent to our understanding, but one still full of 'meaning', rather than in the sense of the blank unintelligibility of nonexistence quite outside our understanding. For further explication of Whitehead's notion here, see his *Process and Reality* (Cambridge: Cambridge University Press), esp. 521–25, also 135, 160–61.

However universal, objective, and timeless rationality may appear to be, reason is, nonetheless, itself creaturely, finite, and limited. It is always the reason of a particular self and of a particular community and culture; it represents, therefore, a located, partial perspective on the whole, not the whole itself. Reason is itself a part of the whole which it seeks to comprehend; and though it can rise in self-transcendence infinitely high, it never leaves or is free of this particular base. Mystery, therefore, transcends the reach of every effort of rationality; it is "a principle of comprehension beyond our comprehension."

> Insofar as man transcends the temporal process he can discern many things in life and history by tracing various coherences, sequences, causalities and occurrences through which the events of history are ordered. But insofar as man is himself in the temporal process which he seeks to comprehend, every sequence and realm of coherence points to a more final source of meaning than man is able to comprehend rationally. (FH 49)

All rational structures and meanings are, therefore, transcended by the mystery beyond them. Reason is thus both infinitely self-transcendent on the one hand and finite and creaturely on the other—hence it is partial and unstable, and reality as a whole remains to it a mystery. We note that for Niebuhr the divine transcendence is correlated with, not suppressive of, the infinite self-transcendence of the human spirit. Reason, therefore, cannot on its own terms and with its own criteria comprehend the whole in which it lives and which it seeks to understand. Niebuhr illustrates this thesis repeatedly: in the first chapters of *The Nature and Destiny of Man,* where he seeks to show the error and self-contradiction of each philosophy because it centers its reflection on one aspect of human nature alone, and in *Faith and History,* where he shows that alternative philosophies of history misunderstand history because they take only one set of facts as the clue to the whole of history. Each sees part of the truth but, by seeking to make that part the principle of the whole, falls into error.

Reason in fact articulates the particular scheme of meaning that supports, animates, and directs the cultural life to which it belongs. It gives coherence, order, meaning, and purpose to its vision of the world. Each philosophy is accordingly an expression in conceptual form of an underlying 'religious' scheme of meaning, a symbolic understanding of human being in its world, of the problems and possibilities of human existence and its grounds for hope. As a consequence Niebuhr feels—as his entire critique of philosophy shows—that all argument between philosophies is really a *theological* argument, that is, an argument between different schemes of meaning and so a debate between different 'faiths' or ultimate stances in life. He does not, therefore, argue so much philosophically with philosophies as theologically with them. That is, he explores the meaning that animates these philosophers, which makes his critiques unique and fascinating on the one hand and endlessly irritating on the other. Clearly here he differs from Tillich—though probably not as much as Tillich thought.[4]

There is, then, a mystery that grounds and limits every mode of coherence and meaning that humans can create. This mystery discloses itself in every facet of our existence; the meanings that lurk within it lure us to comprehension and commitment. Yet its infinite depths or heights defy and reject every claim to finality and ultimacy that we make for our partial understanding of ourselves, our world, our history, our destiny. The importance and creativity, and yet the relativity, of rational thought at every level could hardly be more forcefully stated.[5]

Niebuhr, let us note, leads us to this point by constant appeal to obvious 'facts'[6] of ordinary experience and by careful reflective argument from these facts: mystery transcends and impinges on all our meanings, and each necessary effort of ours to comprehend the whole remains itself partial, in some sense flawed, and in constant danger of becoming an idol. Having led us this far by argument, Niebuhr then draws these reflections to a conclusion with one of his stunning paradoxes—a paradox which, as he knew well, would be regarded as 'absurd' by those rationalists he was challenging. And perhaps the deepest paradox of all is the clear relation here expressed between divine transcendence on the one hand and human autonomy and self-transcendence on the other:

4. The reference is twofold: first to Tillich's insistence that arguments by theology with a given philosophy are philosophical and not theological arguments; but second to Tillich's equally frequent insistence that each philosophy expresses the religious substance of its culture, clearly a Niebuhrian thesis.

5. This is, it goes without saying, Niebuhr's largest difference from Whitehead. The latter maintained that every aspect of existence could be subsumed under one coherent set of rational categories; in this sense nothing within process lies outside the rational coherence a proper speculative system can give to it. As shown earlier (see n. 3 above), for Whitehead there lies outside the process only the blank irrationality of nothingness. This is significantly different from Niebuhr's notion of a divine transcendence beyond our understanding but one nonetheless redolent with meaning.

6. Interestingly, one of the 'obvious facts' appealed to in this cogent argument is the relativity of all things cultural: all philosophies, political theories, codes of morals, etc. Actually this "obvious fact" became obvious only with the dawning of the historical consciousness at the end of the eighteenth and the beginning of the nineteenth century (e.g., as explicated by Ernst Troeltsch and John Dewey).

The rational faculty by which he orders and interprets his experience . . . is itself a part of the finite world which man seeks to understand. The only principle for the comprehension of the whole (the whole which includes both himself and his world) is, therefore, beyond his comprehension. Man is thus in the position of being unable to comprehend himself in his full stature of freedom without a principle of comprehension which is beyond his comprehension. (ND 1:125)

Reason here has, with the help of Niebuhr, been led step by step to its very limits. But such is human existence that reason cannot fall back at these limits and surrender to skepticism; it must be supported as reason by a principle of meaning that transcends—and makes possible—its own principles of coherent and creative existence. A principle of meaning that envelops the whole is thus a necessity for existence. Considering the contingency and finiteness, the relativity, of all things human, even human reason, and the self-transcending questioning and wondering of human being, it follows that a principle of meaning that transcends our understanding is essential. Reason itself calls for the the transcendence of reason's limits—as the contingent being of humans calls for a transcendent ground of their existence, their confidence, and their hope. The Augustinian themes of a reason and an autonomy grounded in that which transcends reason, the Pauline theme of the justification of creaturely truth by a truth transcendent to our understanding, and the Kierkegaardian motif of reason surrendering itself to what is beyond reason in order to be rational are all certainly present here, as they are in Niebuhr's colleague, Paul Tillich.

Niebuhr was aware, as were Augustine, Kierkegaard, and Tillich, of the pervasiveness of human relativity and the consequent perils of radical skepticism and despair. As thoroughly as any liberal thinker, secular or religious, he had deeply imbibed the modern historical consciousness and its inexorable implication of relativity. However, while preceding modern intellectuals had avoided the chilling implications of relativity by means of a confidence in a progress of knowledge that was not relative, Niebuhr sought another answer. Granted, then, this same corroding relativity in a history that does not simply progress, a transcendent principle of meaning seemed to him inescapably necessary despite the scorn of an empirical scientific and rational culture for such a principle. The certainty of this need was not, he knew, enough for faith; a positive disclosure of meaning within the overarching mystery was necessary there. But it was enough for a new openness to the possibility of faith—and that was one first, large step in his powerful negative apologetics (see FH, chapter 10).

The need for meaning is, therefore, inescapable. It arises on the one hand from the finiteness and contingency of human existence, vulnerable before the vast forces of the wider natural and historical worlds, and on the other from the infinite reach of the human spirit, which seeks to encompass the whole in order to understand its place and its destiny. As we have seen, for Niebuhr, while mystery transcends all human meanings, mystery does not eradicate them; it is not blank nothingness, a stark rejection of that human demand for meaning to which Niebuhr has pointed.[7] Meaning is there, within the mystery of things; this Niebuhr never seems to doubt. The peril of meaninglessness is present to Niebuhr; but far more serious is the peril of idolatry. This danger is that the presence of ultimate meaning, deeply intuited by all human existence and expressed in every culture, tempts us to idolatry, to finding our own partial meanings not to be relative at all but to be identical with that transcendent meaning:

> Mystery does not annul meaning but enriches it. It prevents the realm of meaning from being reduced too simply to rational intelligibility and thereby given a false center of meaning in a relative and contingent historical force or end. (FH 103)

∞

This meaning within an overarching mystery is expressed in myth. Myth is for Niebuhr the primary form of religious speech. In its most general sense myth is the way in which the apprehended vision of the whole characteristic of a religion or a culture, and consequently the meaning for us within the whole, is expressed in language. As we have seen, the whole itself, as mystery, cannot be directly comprehended; it transcends any mode of coherence or intelligibility we may muster. Nevertheless the meaning latent within the whole can and must be expressed; this expression is essential, as we have seen, for the creative existence of any culture. Myths express this religious meaning in symbols and analogies that are central to the experience of the group and so are referent in the first instance to the finite life

---

7. For a further discussion of this point, see chapter 8 below. A very powerful statement of that blank answer to the human demand for meaning is in the writings of Albert Camus, especially in *The Myth of Sisyphus,* or, in a quite different version, Bertrand Russell, the modern naturalist (see *A Free Man's Worship*), except that Russell, like Dewey but unlike Niebuhr's contemporary, Camus, believed in the theory of progress.

around us and in us. In myth, however, these analogies from ordinary experience point beyond themselves to that which transcends that experience and yet is related to it. Myth represents an understanding of the transcendent and the infinite in the terms of the creaturely and the finite, "the other side in terms of this side," as Rudolf Bultmann put it.[8]

In the nineteenth century and the early part of the twentieth, most students of religion, and to my knowledge all biblical commentators, saw the term "myth" as properly referent only to premodern life, to early religions based on nature, and so to religions expressive of the power of nature and of a cyclical view of time. Although Niebuhr agreed with this general definition—that myth expresses the relation of the transcendent to the finite in terms of the finite—nonetheless here we see a quite different understanding of myth developing. What is new in Niebuhr's usage is that he applied this category from the history of religions to two quite new referents. First, as we have seen, he used the word "myth" to describe the two secular religions of progress and Marxism that were dominant in modern, not premodern, life; and second, he used the idea of myth to be expressive of the meaning of history and not just of the cycles of nature. These two modern myths were, he said, myths because they sought to understand the meaning of the whole of history in terms of a particular progress or dialectic visible in general experience, an understanding that resolved the problem of evil and that provided confidence and hope for the future, and so which gave meaning to the communities espousing them. And these were the essential functions of religion (see RE 122–36, 193–96). As I noted, this discussion of religion and of myth appears as early as 1934. Others had spoken of Communism as a religion (e.g., Nikolay Berdyayev, *Origins of Russian Communism*). Niebuhr, I believe, was the first to go further than this and speak of Communism as centered on a myth just as liberal culture was centered on the myth of progress. What is new here, besides the

---

8. Rudolf Bultmann, *Jesus Christ and Mythology* (New York: Scribners, 1958), pp. 18–19. Bultmann makes clear that while the Bible contains much mythology in this sense, this 'mythology' is precisely that part of the Biblical witness that is no longer relevant, helpful, or credible to modern men and women (19–20). The genuine Biblical message is of a God who transcends the cosmos and hence is not part of the cosmos at all—and mythology is an interpretation of religion in terms of the cosmos. Hence cosmological myth, whether we speak of archaic myths or even of those of Greek religion, has no relation to the Biblical proclamation of God. For this reason a program of "demythologizing" is essential properly to understand the Biblical message. Clearly this conception, both of myth and of the Biblical message, is very different from that of Niebuhr despite the 'existential' element in both of them. See also Rudolf Bultmann, *Essays* (New York: Macmillan, 1955), chaps. 1, 4, 12.

notion that modernity had its own myths, is that 'myth' is seen as expressive of historical and not only ahistorical meaning, as, therefore, the language appropriate to historical religions.[9]

The second, and even more radical innovation, followed from this point. This was to apply the category of myth to the Biblical and Christian symbols, which represent to Niebuhr the original and paradigmatic form of a religion centered on history. Again beginning with *Reflections* (1934), he describes the central Christian doctrines of creation, fall, incarnation, and eschatological end as 'myths', paradoxical in character, and essential, as are all myths, for any comprehension of the meaning of the whole (RE 122–36, 213–14, 217). In all of these cases myth remains discourse about the whole in terms of a part taken to be significant of the meaning of the whole. With regard to these Biblical symbols, however, the whole is centered on history, and myth concerns itself with the relations of the God who transcends history to the historical continuum. As we shall soon see, Niebuhr argues that Biblical myth, although paradoxical and even 'deceptive',[10] is the only creative means by which the whole as history may be comprehended without the twin dangers of idolatry on the one hand or ultimate despair on the other.

Although all myth expressing the whole in terms of a part of the whole is paradoxical, in Biblical myth the paradoxical element for Niebuhr grows in intensity.[11] This is because in Biblical myth the transcendence of God 'beyond' the world is increased, and hence any expression of the relatedness of God and the world becomes more paradoxical. Here eternity, conceptually the opposite of time, is nonetheless affirmed to be in relation to time; here the unconditioned, the noncontingent, the everlasting is juxtaposed in disclosure and in "acts" to the conditioned, the contingent, and the mortal world; in fact, the eternal is active in establishing that world, participating in it, and redeeming it. These are for Niebuhr paradoxes: that is, assertions of the juxtaposition of apparent opposites without the possibility of a comprehensible mediation between them. Theological speech, therefore, is for Niebuhr paradoxical and not dialectical, if the latter implies

---

9. See the references to myth as the vehicle of religion in *Reflections on the End of an Era,* above chapter 3. See also the sermons in *Beyond Tragedy,* 1936, and the essay "The Truth in Myths," in J. S. Bixley, R. L. Calhoun, and H. R. Niebuhr, eds., *The Nature of Religious Experience* (New York: Harper and Brothers, 1937).

10. See "As Deceivers yet True," chapter 1 in *Beyond Tragedy.*

11. Let us note that while Niebuhr calls this relation "dialectical" (BT 4), he did not mean by that word that it was possible for reason to mediate the pair of apparent opposites.

a final mediating principle that reason can supply.[12] For Niebuhr these paradoxes cannot be "smoothed out" by reason: neither side (e.g., neither eternity nor time) can be dropped out without sacrificing large ranges of fact in ordinary experience. To make ordinary experience rationally coherent, therefore, is to dissolve rather than to make intelligible the deep puzzles and confusions that make up the data of ordinary experience. Either the stubborn temporality, contingency, and dependence of the world of the creature is ignored, or the dimension of eternity, transcendence, and ultimacy within ordinary experience is denied—and in either case actual life is misunderstood.

For this reason, any who correctly or faithfully proclaim the Christian faith are, nonetheless, as Paul said, "deceivers yet true": "For what is true in the Christian religion can be expressed only in symbols which contain a certain degree of provisional and superficial deception" (BT 3). That is to

---

12. It is perhaps well at this point to state why I put "Biblical"—as in Biblical faith, Biblical myth, Biblical theology—in uppercase in this discussion of Niebuhr's theology. As I state frequently, Niebuhr assumed, and argued, that his theology was *Biblical*. That is to say, that it represented the authentic message of Scripture, or, put another way, that it was a valid and defensible reflection on the revelation witnessed to in the biblical documents. When, therefore, he spoke about Biblical faith, Biblical myth, Biblical theology, he referred to *this* theology, to *this* understanding and interpretation of Scripture, to *this* message for the churches and for us in our day. Biblical faith, therefore, represents a very definite and particular understanding of the meaning of the biblical corpus; Biblical in this sense is a proper name referent to what is taken to be the Bible's message for us.

This usage is, therefore, to be contrasted to the usual, and quite proper, usage for the word *biblical*. The lowercase word refers to the corpus of documents in the Scriptures and so connotes no particular or definite view or theological understanding of what those widely varied documents may say. Hence 'biblical myths' may well refer to the many remnants of myths from other preceding cultures scattered throughout the Old Testament. Further, to many, especially contemporary, biblical scholars, there is no such thing as "Biblical theology," that is, one agreed-upon religious message that the entire corpus offers to us. On the contrary, there are only the many possible 'theologies', which can be found in the many diverse parts of the entire corpus. The referent, therefore, of the word *biblical* is quite different from that of the word *Biblical*. The first refers to the diverse literature of ancient Israel and of early Christianity enshrined in the collection we call the Bible. The second refers in Niebuhr's usage to what he took to be the central, valid, and intensely relevant message of the Scriptures to us. It is, I think, very important to distinguish these two quite different usages and referents; we shall do so by using uppercase *B* for Niebuhr's Biblical theology, and lowercase *b* for the corpus of biblical documents. I will add that most of Niebuhr's 'neo-orthodox' contemporaries, biblical scholars and theologians alike, thoroughly agreed on this usage and spoke frequently in Niebuhr's sense of "Biblical faith" and "Biblical theology."

say, they paint the transcendent in terms of the experience of finite things and hence in part falsify the being and the activity of the transcendent to which they refer. These symbols are, therefore, and so must remain, paradoxical:

> A rational and logical expression of the relationship invariably leads either to a pantheism in which God and the world are identified, and the temporal in its totality is equated with the eternal; or in which they are separated so that a false supernaturalism emerges. (BT 4)

This strange, even "absurd," juxtaposition of apparent opposites cannot result from a rational inspection of ordinary experience, from philosophy, since as noted these paradoxes seem to defy the canons of rational intelligibility. They spring, therefore, from faith, and this in turn, as we shall see, is itself a response to a disclosure within experience of what transcends experience. Out of this disclosure arise these defiant paradoxes. However, once affirmed, these paradoxes are validated over and over by the "facts" or the "stuff of experience," both because other more rational alternatives falsify experience (FH 152, 164) and because to our surprise these same paradoxes make the strange and even irrational contours of experience intelligible (FH 165–67). And it is this "empirical" justification of what seems at first glance to be absurd that Niebuhr's theology seeks continuously to present to us.

All the central symbols of the Christian faith are, therefore, paradoxical and mythical, and only thus do they express the truth within the Christian message: creation, fall, incarnation, atonement, and ultimate redemption (BT 7–24). Our further discussion of Niebuhr's doctrines of human nature, of sin, of history, and of eschatology will fully illustrate this point (see the discussion in chapters 5, 6, and 7 below). For the moment, let us illustrate this in terms of Niebuhr's remarks on the symbol or myth of creation:

> The Biblical doctrine of the Creator, and the world as His creation, is itself not a doctrine of revelation, but it is basic for the doctrine of revelation. It expresses perfectly the basic Biblical idea of both the transcendence of God and His intimate relation to the world. The doctrine is expressed in a "mythical" or supra-rational idea. (ND 1:133)

In the doctrine or myth of creation the transcendent mystery of existence, God in God's mystery, relates itself to time and existence in establishing the world, a world that is real and yet not ultimately real, a world that is not God (*non de Deo*) and yet is 'good', a world that is not made out of preexisting matter (*non ex materia*) but posited by God out of nothing (*ex nihilo*). Hence this is a world whose temporal sequences and whose material and vital principles are not the source of disorder in the world but parts of a good creation. For this reason, this myth does more than set the framework for the other central theological symbols of Christian faith: the goodness of creation and the potential meaningfulness of historical life, sin, revelation, incarnation, and so on. It also provides the framework necessary if the mystery of human being, and the paradoxes of our strange existence are to be understood:[13]

> The Biblical doctrine of Creator and creation is thus the only ground upon which the full height of the human spirit can be measured, the unity of its life in body and soul be maintained, and the essential meaningfulness of its history in the finite world asserted, and a limit set to its freedom and self-transcendence. (ND 1:136)

The myth of creation thus encompasses the mystery that transcends all our modes of coherence; it apprehends meaning within "the realm of mystery which stands at both the beginning and the end of man's effort to comprehend the coherences and sequences of his world rationally" (FH 51). "Its role is to express the realm of mystery as both the fulfillment and negation of the realm of meaning and to acknowledge the function of faith as both the fulfillment and negation of reason" (FH 54). But as the above quote from *Nature and Destiny* shows, creation also articulates the significant realm of meaning in our existence that paradoxically appears within that mystery: the reality and goodness of our world, the unity of our existence, and the possibility of meaning within our historical existence.

The symbol or doctrine of creation is for Niebuhr a true myth. Its linguistic terms are those of a story set in time, and they imply an action of a divine agent; yet its content (the appearance and positing of an entire world out of nothing) points inescapably beyond that world of time and of action in time to its eternal source and ground in God. It puts together in a most strange mix the intelligible language, conceptuality, and models of

---

13. My own book *Maker of Heaven and Earth* (Garden City, N.Y.: Doubleday, 1959) is primarily an examination of the meanings inherent in the 'myth' of creation, meanings essential both to the other symbols of the Christian tradition and to an intelligible and creative understanding of human and historical existence. It is without question a 'Niebuhrian' book. That volume was preceded by a doctoral thesis with the same name (Columbia University, 1954) that also attempted to show that the 'paradoxical' doctrine of creation was in the end more intelligible than its rationalistic alternatives, namely the monism of F. H. Bradley and the pluralism of A. N. Whitehead. Here, therefore, both the negative and the positive modes of validation suggested by Niebuhr were illustrated.

science and history with the very different discourse about the God of Biblical theology. Thus its linguistic forms as well as its content are paradoxical, or, as Niebuhr said, a kind of 'deception'. And from this structure, essential to myth, stem some if not all of the subsequent problems of this doctrine, as for others, in theological history:

> The idea of creation relates the ground of existence to existence and is therefore mythical rather than rational. The fact that it is not a rational idea does not make it untrue or deceptive. But since it is not rational, it is a temptation to deception. Every mythical idea contains a primitive deception and a more ultimate one. The primitive error is to regard the early form in which the myth is stated as authoritative. . . . It is to this temptation that biblical literalism succumbs. (BT 9)

Thus Niebuhr distinguishes between permanent myth and primitive myth, the latter being for him a temptation, even a corruption, of the real meaning of the myth. Primitive myth is the literalistic interpretation of a Biblical symbol: Creation was an event in time six thousand years ago or so, an event that lasted over a period of six days; the true historical story of creation is followed by a true historical event of temptation and fall; and so on throughout the subsequent Biblical history. Niebuhr's entire theological effort was to remove this, to him, outworn shell of primitive literalism and to present to us as necessary for contemporary human self-understanding the permanent myths of Christian faith enshrined in these accounts, a clearly different enterprise from that of Bultmann.

On this issue of the primitive versus the real or permanent meaning of Christian myths, however, both Bultmann and Niebuhr, so it appears from the vantage point of the present, seemed surprisingly too liberal—or at least too progressivist—with regard to the coming dominance of intelligible, nonliteral religion. That is, they appear now (at least to me) to have felt that the literal or primitive interpretation of the faith was much less near to its historical center than in fact it was, and that, therefore, it had now become an aspect of a rapidly vanishing past. First, it is evident that both were in error about the role of literalism in the theological past. In fact, until the modern or liberal period, the entire tradition, including the "spiritual fathers" of both Niebuhr and Bultmann, accepted this literalistic deception or temptation as a significant aspect of the revealed content of these myths. From Augustine on, these myths contained authentic history as well as authentic symbolic content that pointed beyond history—and Barth agreed with both of them on this point. Second, it now seems evident that the problem of literalistic errors is as much a temptation for contemporary Christianity as it ever was for its earlier, primitive stages. To

Niebuhr and Bultmann, literalism was an irrelevant and archaic inheritance of little theological weight. In the present, a genuine and widespread fundamentalist or literalistic revival is an obvious part of contemporary Christianity, and it is possible that it is the liberal and mythical interpretation of revelation that may be archaic and vanishing!

∞

The intertwined meaning of our life and of our history, set as they are against a vast mystery, can neither be encompassed nor completed by our own powers. Our reason forms coherences and patterns of intelligibility. However brilliant, these remain incomplete and partial; they are never sufficient to give our life a secure intelligibility. Our actions too are fragmentary and wayward, and they create as many destructive consequences as they do fruitful ones. Hence on both the level of understanding and the level of the harmony of life with life, our common existence is threatened and insecure; we seem driven either into a false center of intelligibility and security, into idolatry, or into its opposite, a despairing resignation. Thus the human powers of rationality and of will 'call for' something beyond themselves. Revelation is not only received—as experience shows it is—it is also demanded or required by the common predicament of human being in time:

> The problem of the meaning of history is always the problem of the meaning of life itself, since man is an historic creature involved, and yet not involved, in the flux of nature and time, but always involved in a false solution to his predicament. Thus man always is in the position either of negating the meaning of history or completing it falsely, if he seeks to complete it from the standpoint of his own wisdom. Yet it can only be completed by a revelation, the acceptance of which is possible only through a contrite recognition of the human situation of sinfulness. Such repentance is possible in turn only if the judgment overhanging men is known to be prompted by love and to be crowned by forgiveness. (FH 140)

Clearly the key point here is contained in the themes we have just developed: the relativity of all reason and of all cultural achievements, and the consequent need of reason and will alike to point themselves to a true transcendent center, lest they complete their concern for meaning through some partial center, or, seeing the relativity of all centers, despair. Since all meaning, interlaced with mystery, is by faith (FH 113), the ultimate contest in life is between a faith in the transcendent that supports, judges, and renews our historical and social concerns and a faith in our own powers that in the end is idolatrous and leads to the oppression of others. The necessity for the intellectual transcendence of reason and of culture corresponds to the necessary transcendence of our own moral capacity for virtue if we would be whole. The one calls for revelation as the other calls for grace; an adequate and not idolatrous scheme of meaning appears only in response to the grace of revelation and through the reception of faith, just as the justified life of the sinner is possible only through the grace of forgiveness.

Niebuhr has taken the modern principle of the relativity of all things rational and cultural and argued from that to the necessity of faith in the transcendent, and he has combined this with the familiar Pauline and Reformation argument that the relativity of our virtue calls for a transcendent principle of grace as mercy. The application of the principle of justification by faith to the issues of meaning and truth represents, perhaps, an even deeper synthesis of the modern and the Reformation than the one he has explicitly recognized.[14] As we have seen, moreover, the recognition of the need for Biblical categories of interpretation—that is, for revelation in that sense—only became clear in his own intellectual development as the confusions inherent in his earlier modern categories of interpretation mounted. As Thomas Kuhn has suggested, it is the piling up of anomalies, inexplicable in terms of earlier theory, that prepares the way for the breakthrough of a new paradigm[15]—in this case a breakthrough of the Biblical symbols that resulted from revelation.

Niebuhr's interpretation, then, of human nature and of history, as of God and God's actions, is dependent on revelation. It is a 'Biblical interpretation' structured by the categories and symbols derived from Biblical revelation: creation, fall, incarnation, atonement, people, Word, and eschatology. In this way he sought to accomplish that which he knew was required, namely to "comprehend human existence in terms of principles that were beyond our comprehension" (see ND 1:125, 141). If this be so, we must ask, What is Niebuhr's understanding of revelation, of the symbols that issue from it, and of our relation to these symbols?

Unlike most of his continental 'neo-orthodox' contemporaries, Niebuhr recognized a general revelation of God in ordinary experience,

14. This was, of course, the synthesis mentioned by Niebuhr of the Renaissance emphasis on novelty and development in history with the Reformation principle of the continuation of sin in individual and corporate life (cf. ND 1: 300, 2: 204–12).

15. Thomas S. Kuhn, *The Structure of Scientific Revolutions* (Chicago: University of Chicago Press, 1962).

and he gave it—as did Tillich—a very positive role in his understanding of revelation. This universal and continuous (hence 'general') manifestation of God—not a "separate experience but an overtone implied in all experience" (ND 1:127)—is an "impingement or God upon our consciousness." It has, says Niebuhr, three aspects or elements: (1) a sense of "unqualified dependence" (Schleiermacher), the consciousness of a reality and a majesty upon which all contingent existence—and so we too—depends (ND 1:128), an ultimate source of being (ND 1:131);[16] (2) the sense of "being seen, commanded, judged and known from beyond ourselves" (ND 1:128), "of moral obligation laid on one from beyond oneself" (ND 1:131). In ordinary language, he says, this is conscience—but conscience here interpreted as disclosing a relation to the God who demands and requires of us. And (3) there is the longing for forgiveness (ND 1:131). One should add one further aspect of general revelation: (4) the universal truth (established by Niebuhr in the social analysis of his earlier books) that there is a moral order to history that manifests the judgment of God. "The most obvious meaning of history is that every nation, culture and civilization brings destruction on itself by exceeding the bounds of creatureliness which God has set upon all human enterprises" (ND 1:148; see also RE 139; ND 1:138–39).

As Niebuhr remarks, in this general and universal experience the first two points (sense of absolute dependence and a sense of obligation) are not at all sharply defined, and the third one (the longing for forgiveness) is "not defined at all." They all appear universally, but disguised, so to speak, in the infinitely varied forms of human culture and religion, and articulated in "various philosophies" (ND 1:129). These fundamental experiences of being grounded, of obligation, and of longing are the experiences in which we apprehend our own ontological being, our moral spirit, and our need for renewal. These are fundamental experiences of life and the formative elements of all religion; as a consequence, they are for Niebuhr experiences of the self in its relation to God. Interestingly—and quite at odds with the other twentieth-century theologians of revelation—Niebuhr calls these general and universal experiences of God *personal, individual,* and *private* (ND 1:127, 143). These are adjectives that Barth, Brunner, and Bultmann could have used specifically only in relation to special revelation, namely the encounter of the self in faith with the Word

16. This is certainly what Schleiermacher meant when he identified the consciousness of absolute dependence upon God with the deepest self-consciousness of the self. For an elegant exposition of this point, see Richard Reinhold Niebuhr, *Schleiermacher on Christ and Religion: A New Introduction* (New York: Scribners, 1964).

of God. For Niebuhr this continuous impingement of God in these experiences of the inner grounding of the self and its life, is "individual and personal," and he contrasts these individual experiences with "revelation in the context of social-historical experience," namely special revelation. Possibly by these categories 'individual' as opposed to 'social', Niebuhr also means 'inner' as opposed to 'outer and public'—that is, to revelation in and to a community, publicly expressed in witness, stories, myths, and rites, and enshrined in public norms, mores, and law. Certainly he means here by 'outer and public' a much sharper definition and articulation of revelation, a distinct particularizing of it into a definite tradition.

Special revelation for Niebuhr refers to "events" in history that become for a receiving community a self-disclosure, in fact the final and defining revelation, of the God who is already daily experienced and known in ordinary life:

> Faith in the transcendent God, as revealed in personal experience and in the character of the whole creation, is the ground upon which the Biblical historical revelation is built up. . . . It [this historical revelation] is rather the record of the events in history in which faith discerns the self-disclosure of God. What it discerns are actions of God which clarify the confrontation of man by God in the realm of the personal and individual moral life. (ND 1:136–37)

> The disclosure takes place in significant events in history. The revelatory power of these events must be apprehended by faith. So apprehended they prove to be more than ordinary events. They are "mighty acts" of God in which the whole drama of human life is made clear. (FH 105–6)

These events, discerned by faith to be disclosures of God, sharpen and define what has been dimly known: the mystery of the being that grounds us now becomes the Creator of a good creation; the obscure judge who claims and limits us is disclosed as the gracious Lord of the covenant and the God who is love; and the law that we fail to follow is transmuted by the Righteous One who redeems us through the mercy of grace.

> In these three types of revelation (i.e., the three phases of the general revelation of God) God becomes specifically defined as Creator, Judge and Redeemer. It is significant that each term represents a definition of divine transcendence in increasingly specific and sharply delineated terms; and yet in each the relation of God to the world is preserved. (ND 1:132)

For Niebuhr this series of crucial events begins with the covenant, with the choice of Israel despite that people's weakness and lack of special merit

(ND 1:137; and esp. FH 104). Here revelation appears not only as the source of a people's life and destiny, but even more as the critique or judgment of that people in the place of their idolatrous expansion:

> The idea of God choosing Israel as an act of grace, since Israel had no power or virtue to merit the choice, represents a radical break in the history of culture. It is, in a genuine sense, the beginning of revelation; for here a nation apprehends and is apprehended by the true God and not by a divine creature of its own contrivance. The proof of the genuineness of His majesty and of the truth of His deity is attested by the fact that He confronts the nation and the individual as the limit, and not the extension, of its own power and purpose. (FH 104)

This special revelation continues with the incarnation and atonement, which enlarge and sharpen these same themes of transcendence, judgment, and unmerited grace, and which, as we shall see, answer in final form the questions about human destiny that revelation, general and special alike, has posed.

In each case the significance of these events in history—perhaps "ordinary events," or as Kierkegaard put it, "incognito events" to those without faith—is only discerned by faith. Through the event, apprehended by faith, there occurs an encounter with God that alone can lead not only to a deeper relation and understanding of God, but also to a true self-understanding and a creative life: "Man does not know himself truly except as he knows himself confronted by God" (ND 1:131). Humans understand themselves and their history, and can live creatively within the latter, only when they are related to the transcendent God and when they apprehend themselves and their life in that transcendent dimension (see ND 1:124). Revelation clarifies the nature of God and of God's relation to the world, and also the nature, the problems, and the possibilities of the human self and its community.

This new understanding of God, of self, and of community, an understanding based on these significant (but from the outside, ordinary) events, spreads out to become the basis for an entire and quite novel vision of the whole: of the natural world, of the status, possibilities, and tragedy of human being, of the contours of history, and of the ultimate end of things. Hence arise the symbols, myths, or doctrines that characterize the Christian tradition: creation, fall and sin, providence, judgment and grace, and, finally, of last things. These particular categories, as Niebuhr said, are not "revealed doctrines," nor are any of them based on their own set of significant events apprehended by faith—as if the events of the creation of all things were media of revelation to some human group. Rather, these categories are implications to faith of revelation through those central historical events that faith apprehends as revelatory (namely, covenant and incarnation).

Creation, fall, and providence are in short the *presuppositions* of revelation and the *consequences* of revelation (judgment, grace, and eschatological fulfillment): "The Biblical doctrine of the Creator, and the world as His creation, is itself not a doctrine of revelation, but it is basic for the doctrine of revelation" (ND 1:133). The myth of creation, therefore, is present in proclamation not as a revealed doctrine but as the presupposition of the experience of judgment and of grace that is communicated through covenant and incarnation, as the myth of the eschatological end is a consequence of that experience with regard to our own ultimate destiny. For Niebuhr this is precisely the way these doctrines arose in the life of the religious community on the one hand, and the way they function in the Biblical account on the other, namely as the presuppositions of covenant and incarnation, of judgment, grace, and promise—presuppositions that set the world within which that gospel and promise make sense. Those symbols concerned with the nature and sin of human being, and the nature and destiny of history, are those I shall deal with in the following chapters.

In concluding this chapter I must say something of the nature of the faith necessary to the discernment and acceptance of revelation through significant events. Does this belief express merely the adherence to church or biblical doctrine, the setting aside of critical reason in order to accept traditional, dogmatic, or scriptural propositions declared true by some religious authority? Faith for Niebuhr is not in that sense doctrinal; it is not in that sense a synonym of 'belief'. Rather it is existential, closer, as many have remarked, to trust as in 'trust in someone'. The first element of faith is repentance, the recognition by the self not only of its fragmentary, finite, and creaturely character but even more of its tendency to claim more for itself, its views, and its acts than is warranted. At this level, Niebuhr is, like Tillich, an existentialist. We can know ourselves and God truly only when inwardly we repent and give ourselves to grace—and this inward act (not adherence to doctrine) is faith. God can be known by the self only when the self surrenders in repentance and trust to God. This occurs in encounters with God through the events proclaimed in the Word, in the message of the gospel; out of this existential relation to God arise "doctrines" for speaking and then for reflection—but these rational and coherent doctrines do not initiate the relationship.

> The Christian gospel as the final answer to the problem of both individual life and man's total history is not proved to be true by rational analysis.

Its acceptance is an achievement of faith being an apprehension of truth beyond the limits of reason. Such faith must be grounded in repentance; for it presupposes a contrite recognition of the elements of pretension and false completion in all forms of human virtue, knowledge and achievement. It is a gift of grace because neither the faith nor the repentance required for the knowledge of the true God, revealed in the cross and the resurrection, can be attained by taking thought. The self must lose itself to find itself in faith and repentance; but it does not find itself unless it be apprehended from beyond itself. (FH 151; see also FH, chapter 9).

∞

We have come in this chapter a long way; let me try to summarize our journey so far. There is, I have said, a paradoxical character to revelation and so to the myths that articulate that revelation. The final basis for this is that revelation and the responding myth express a relation between eternity and time, the unconditioned and the conditioned, the deepest mystery and the most apprehensible meaning. This relatedness of transcendence to our finite concreteness cannot be mediated, made rationally intelligible; this relation reaches beyond the limits of reason since reason itself, though here reason in relation to God, remains as creaturely and partial as is all else about us. The myth, responding to the revelation, expresses this transcendence-in-relation, a paradoxical referent if there ever was one.

This central paradox of transcendence-in-relation, moreover, manifests itself in four aspects of Biblical myth that are themselves paradoxical. (1) The form of the myth is transcendent to the limits of reason since the myth is myth; and since it is paradoxical, therefore it points beyond its own comprehensibility to mystery. Such a vehicle can neither be derived empirically from ordinary experience nor established by rational speculation. It requires, therefore, a recognition of the limits of reason in order that it be accepted as true. It represents a "challenge to humans as rational though finite creatures incapable of giving meaning to the total dimension of their individual and collective history" (FH 142). (2) In turn the message of the myth, dealing as it does with the relatedness of eternity to time, has a content expressible only in paradoxes, whose inherent opposites cannot be rationally mediated: eternity and time, God and human existence, and so on. Niebuhr cites what are to him the futile efforts of a rational Christian theology to make rational sense of its mythical and paradoxical symbols.

(3) The challenge of Biblical myth, moreover, goes even deeper than this confrontation with reason. The content of the revelation is also a chal-

lenge to the moral as well as the intellectual pretensions of men and women, to the continual effort of all of us to justify and to glorify the virtue of the self and its group:

> It is as difficult for a rational man to accept the possibility and necessity of such a disclosure as for the virtuous man to accept its content. Its specific content challenged the virtue of the virtuous; and its form and dimension challenged the self-sufficiency of human reason. (FH 145; see also 141–42)

Hence (4), finally, this revelation can be appropriated only by the paradox of an existential rebirth, namely an inner act of repentance on the one hand and trust on the other that surrenders the self and yet in that surrender finds the self again—an 'achievement' made possible only by grace.[17]

This theme of a faith that transcends reason only to become the creative ground of reason, and the theme of a self that surrenders itself only to become thereby a recreated and newly autonomous self—the theme of theonomy—is genuinely Augustinian as is the *credo ut intelligam* (faith seeking understanding) that also dominates Niebuhr's theology. When Niebuhr's Augustinian roots are spoken of, it is usually a reference to his theories of the state, of the necessity of justice and harmony for any community, but of the actuality in every community of self-interest and so conflict. This reference to Augustine's and Niebuhr's understanding of politics is certainly valid. However, a far deeper level is represented by this theonomous understanding of the self, of reason, and of history as grounded in God, yet as needing to be transformed, redirected, and reshaped by grace in order that they may become their true selves. Only the self dependent on God in love and faith can be the real self, in its understanding, its love, its justice, its trust, and its hope. The similarity at this point of Niebuhr with Tillich, whose category of theonomy is also Augustinian, is obvious. For all three, the self becomes its true and creative self only in relation to God; correspondingly, a true self, what Tillich calls a true symbol, is one that denies itself, points beyond itself, and thus remains creatively in union with its divine ground.

Despite this existential center of Niebuhr's theology, and its requirement of faith if there is to be understanding, there is here a principle of positive validation that should not be forgotten. Niebuhr would not have considered himself a natural theologian giving arguments based on expe-

---

17. Note how close Niebuhr comes at this point to embodying the important Tillician concept of *theonomy*, namely the identity of the presence of the Divine Spirit in the self with the fullest realization of the self's autonomy, power, and creativity.

rience alone for the existence of God; reason cannot as easily as that transcend its fragmentariness and partiality to establish such a union beyond experience. Niebuhr nonetheless is an apologetical theologian. By "apologetics" he meant a theology that argues with alternative viewpoints and seeks to show persuasively by argument the far greater validity of one's own position. Not only can the theologian show the inadequacy of alternative views of the human situation (negative validation)—as Niebuhr frequently and often skillfully does. Even more the theologian can show how the contradictory, confusing, and hence apparently irrational stuff of ordinary experience can be made much more intelligible by means of the Biblical categories. They clarify for our understanding the vast puzzles of experience that alternative categories fail to clarify—just as faith itself makes bearable and surmountable the tragedies of our life.

My further discussion of human nature, of human waywardness and sin, and of the confusions of historical existence will illustrate this. In each case Niebuhr argues that the Biblical understanding, in terms of those very paradoxical myths that reason rejects, interprets more intelligibly the apparently irrational stuff of ordinary experience than do any alternatives. Understanding is through faith and repentance, but understanding can then make itself intelligible to reason (to its own reason and to that of others) if it then interprets experience in the terms that have been disclosed to faith.

CHAPTER 5

The Doctrine of Human Nature

As I have noted, two theological themes had slowly become prominent in Niebuhr's early political writings, namely the question of the understanding of human nature and its behavior on the one hand and that of the interpretation of history on the other. These theoretical concerns appeared ever more clearly in his sharp analyses of contemporary Western social and political life where issues of social justice were at the center. And just as clearly, it was in dealing with these questions that Niebuhr underwent fundamental changes in his own theoretical understanding. In the late 1930s and throughout the 1940s these theological questions themselves form the major content of his two systematic works, *The Nature and Destiny of Man* (vol. 1 in 1941; vol. 2 in 1943) and *Faith and History* (1948).

These changes of focus should come as no surprise. The two issues of human nature and of history represented from the beginning the points where Niebuhr's developing thought had broken with his own liberal inheritance. At the same time, and far more fundamental, these issues also represented precisely the points where twentieth-century historical existence had challenged the liberal confidence in human rationality and morality and the liberal faith in historical progress, and had left as a consequence a vast spiritual vacuum. Out of this historical crisis and its accompanying intellectual confusion, Niebuhr's new Biblical understanding appeared as an answer, reflected clearly in the theology set forth in these volumes. We may note that much of the sudden—and possibly evanescent—wider cultural interest during midcentury in theology and its questions stemmed not only from the rare brilliance of its major representatives, Tillich and Niebuhr, but even more from an uneasy awareness of the importance of the questions these theologians (and not the philosophers) were addressing.

I should also note that it is in these volumes, especially volume 1 of *Nature and Destiny,* that Niebuhr's theological method—discussed in the preceding chapter—appears in actual usage; that is, as a method employed in thinking about something other than method. Here we see his continuing concentration on the empirical, experiential basis for all theory—in this case what Niebuhr called the "facts" or the "obvious facts" of social and historical existence. Correspondingly, we note his familiarity with and use of relevant philosophical, sociological, psychological, and historical reflections on these matters. All of these cultural materials based on common, shareable experience and cultural reflection thereon, form, so to speak, the content or materials of Niebuhr's analysis. A perusal of Niebuhr's description of human being, as creature or as *imago dei,* shows how thoroughly he has integrated into that discussion materials from the history of Western theory and literature on this subject. However, in each case—because the secular understanding of all of this is for him always flawed—these secular materials and their secular interpretation are in his own doctrines reshaped by the Biblical symbols that are given their form and their fundamental interpretations by the myths of Biblical faith.

In other words, we shall see here at each point a "correlation" between secular experience and secular wisdom on the one hand and Biblical symbols on the other, the former providing content or materials and the latter the forms for theological reflection. And, as it should do, the correlation goes both ways: while the Biblical forms transmute the secular materials into a Christian vision of things, in turn the secular materials, used by as modern an intelligence as Niebuhr's, transmute the traditional theological doctrines from their frequently literalistic and objectivist meanings into a modern symbolic and existential understanding, an understanding in touch with the scientific, the social scientific, and the philosophical reflections of its present world. This raises an intriguing question not addressed explicitly by Niebuhr himself, namely what of modernity did he challenge and what of modernity did he unconsciously appropriate in writing his theology? We shall be interested in pursuing this question as we analyze further his theology.

Niebuhr begins, as always, with a clear consciousness of the paradoxes, the dilemmas or puzzles, concerning the nature of human existence. These dilemmas and paradoxes are, he believes, apparent in ordinary experience, and they are reflected in philosophical reflections on human nature, a history of reflection, so he argues, littered with contradictions on the one hand and the ignoring of vast ranges of experience on the other. The confusions of this history, he argues, show that the reflective questions surrounding human nature are not resolvable in secular terms, that is, in terms of an understanding gained only by looking at ordinary, secular experience:

> Modern man . . . tries to interpret himself in terms of natural causality or in terms of his unique rationality; but he does not see that he has a freedom of spirit that transcends both nature and reason. (ND 1:96)

> They failed to understand the human spirit in its full dimension of freedom. Both the majesty and the tragedy of human life exceed the dimensions with which modern culture seeks to comprehend human existence. The human spirit cannot be held within the bounds of either natural necessity or rational prudence. (ND 1:122)

He regards these "facts of ordinary existence" ("The obvious facts of his history"; ND 1:95) as unquestioned and as forming the puzzling materials that all philosophies seek unsuccessfully to comprehend. These puzzling facts are clarified alone in terms of an interpretation that is centered on the transcendent dimension of human being, that relation with God which is present in experience but only disclosed to us in revelation and expressed in the Biblical categories. This is the heart of his apologetic: he does not prove this vertical dimension or the relatedness to God which it implies. Rather he seeks to persuade us that we cannot make either human nature or history intelligible without that dimension, that other viewpoints contradict either themselves or the facts, and that a Biblical understanding rightly interprets the common but otherwise incoherent facts of experience.

∞

Niebuhr suggests four interrelated sets of paradoxes in terms of which human nature may be understood. These are paradoxes because the "facts" to which they refer cannot be intelligibly comprehended in any coherent, and so rational, system. The reason is that each range of these facts points to an ultimate synthesis in a dimension quite transcendent to our common understanding, namely in the mystery of our relation to God. Hence to comprehend them 'prematurely' is to misunderstand them or to deny some of the facts; only the paradoxical myths of revelation make them intelligible. We note, however, that each side of each of the four paradoxes is factually warranted, an aspect of obvious experience; the puzzles are quite genuine; they arise from contradictory facts we experience continually in ourselves and in others. The four interrelated sets of paradoxes are as follows:

1. Humans are animal, a part of nature, and yet self-transcendent. They are subject to the necessities and perils of nature, and yet they are free and so both rational and responsible. In terms of Biblical categories humans

are both *creatures* and *made in the image of God* (note, not as earlier, "impulse" and "reason"). These two aspects of human being, while distinguishable, are not separable. Rather they intertwine, interact, and so form a unity.

2.   Humans are responsible, moral, and idealistic. They seek to know and to do good; yet they are also continuously and universally immoral and often cruel, even evil. Again, the two are interrelated.

3.   Humans seek and require meaning, and yet they despair. They demand significance, and yet they are obviously insignificant. They long for immortality, and yet they are clearly mortal.

4.   Finally, humans seem on the one hand bound in evil. Essentially, they seem the victims of an evil that always is already in them and so has overwhelmed and oppressed them. On the other hand, they are aware of being in some manner 'free' in this evil and thus responsible for it; they experience themselves as both necessitated and yet responsible, as both guilty and free. Although less obvious and much less remarked in secular, especially modern understanding, both sides of this fourth paradox, as in the others, are composed of "facts" that we all experience daily in ourselves and take for granted in others. No one escapes the feeling of being made a helpless captive and ruled by a sin that that individual did not choose; we all find ourselves to be innocent. On the other hand, no one escapes blaming others for whatever hurtful fault they exhibit, and hence asserting the freedom of those others to choose whatever hurt they give. Even more is this true of nations.

These four paradoxes form the content of our experience of ourselves and our fellows, illustrated in all literature and in all philosophical reflection. In fact, for Niebuhr these issues of human being, of its good and its evil and its prospects for meaning, represent the heart of every philosophy, the point from which its thinking really originates and the point at which, despite all its intelligible arguments, it is most vulnerable to criticism. In this sense, each philosophy has a religious base and is supported and informed by a 'faith' of some sort in human nature and its positive destiny. Nonetheless, for Niebuhr, on the basis of a reasonable survey of these common facts alone, no real comprehension is possible. One or another side of the paradox will be made the central principle, and the other ignored or distorted:

> Modern culture, particularly in its controversies between rationalists and romanticists, has illumined various aspects of the problem of vitality and form and of the relative contributions of nature and spirit to both form and vitality. But it has not been able to arrive at any satisfactory solution of

the problem because its interpretations of man were derived from metaphysical theories, idealistic and naturalistic, in which one aspect of reality
was made the principle of interpretation of the whole. (ND 1:27)

The Biblical categories—creature, image of God, and sin—to which
Niebuhr appeals in order to understand these puzzles and paradoxes of being human are the subject of the next two chapters. Let me give them at
present a brief summary and then explore them in more detail. (1) Humans are *creatures* formed in *the image of God* (*imago dei*) for relationship
with God and with one another; that is, for a life characterized by faith,
love, and hope. (2) Creature and image, while distinguishable, are not separable; rather they form a unity in each person, a unity that is creative at
once of the individuality of each person and of the human community on
which each individual essentially depends. (3) At the same time, this unity
of nature and spirit (creature and image) in us all is the source both of our
human creativity and the condition of our human sin. The change here
from the earlier duality of impulse and reason—however uneasy that duality was—to this understanding of human being as a unity of creatureliness and self-transcendence in continual relatedness to God is very great.
In a strange way Niebuhr was (as we saw) at once driven to these new categories by the increasingly clear implications of the "facts of experience,"
in conjunction as always with the tumultuous character of history in the
1930s. Yet he was also given these new categories by the new disclosures to
him during that decade of the meaning and relevance of Biblical revelation. Hence, as with all else in Niebuhr, this was a theonomous development.

∞

The category *creature* (in "man as creature") connotes for Niebuhr the whole
organic, biological, so-called animal nature of human being. Niebuhr sees
our creatureliness as without question the result of evolutionary development and so as part of the organic life we share with the animals and with
the rest of creation. He credits biological and hence evolutionary science
with instructing us with regard to these realities of our past. For him this
evolutionary past is part of the work of the providence of God. As a consequence, this is an aspect of our nature explored and disclosed to us by biological science, paleontology, anthropology, both physical and cultural,
and sociology. It includes our bodies set in space and time, our genetic

background, our instincts and desires, all our physical needs and insecurities, and our mortality. Moreover it includes as well our organic and biological need for one another, and so the communities that constitute history, beginning with family, clan, and tribe and continuing into modern societies. It is all of this that the romantic and later the naturalistic interpretations of humans have emphasized, and the present life sciences explore. Our creatureliness, as bodily and organic is, Niebuhr argues, the basis of human individuality and of human community. Our bodily particularity, organic inheritance, and natural self-centeredness (as opposed to 'inordinate' self-centeredness) represent the foundations of our individuality and selfhood; and our organic dependency on others, complemented by our most fundamental instincts and emotions of love and loyalty, establishes and preserves the essential communal character of all human life. As Niebuhr frequently said, history is the history of groups.

An important aspect of this creatureliness is for Niebuhr our mortality, which we share with all else in nature. As had most modern theologians since Schleiermacher, Niebuhr denies that we die because of Adam's sin (see chapter 10 below). With the rejection of that Genesis story as 'literal history', Niebuhr assigns mortality to the will of the Creator; and he seeks to show that, despite the strong Pauline tradition that death results from sin, the understanding of death as part of creatureliness is also authentically Biblical (see ND 1:173–77).

Even though our creatureliness receives heavy validation in our most general experience, as in the contemporary life sciences, Niebuhr regards this conception of the creatureliness of human being as authentically, in fact originally, Biblical. This view is, he argues, more realistic about the finitude and partiality of the human condition than any opposing views; alone it provides the framework within which that dependence and vulnerability can be borne creatively.

> The Biblical view is that the finiteness, dependence and the insufficiency of man's mortal life are facts which belong to God's plan of creation and must be accepted with reverence and humility. (ND 1:167; see esp. 167–77)

Not only, moreover, does the Biblical view recognize without denial the dependence, weakness, and potential suffering of our creatureliness, even more it insists that that creatureliness is good. It is good because God made it out of love: "The created world is a good world, for God created it" (ND 1:169). But, typically appealing also to experience and its possibilities, Niebuhr gives content to this Biblical affirmation in terms of the possibilities of life: the precarious and vulnerable character of existence can be accepted and borne serenely through trust in God, that is, in the faith that our very particular and fragmentary life contributes to the meaning of the whole. If supported by faith and a transcendent meaning given to life by God, our creaturely existence, however finite, temporal, and particular, and seemingly insignificant, can become a life of intense creativity and meaning. On these two grounds, Niebuhr asserts over and over that the Scriptures and so authentic Christian faith do not regard finitude, bodyliness, temporality, or even our mortality, to be evil or the source of evil.

> The fragmentary character of human life is not regarded as evil in Biblical faith because it is seen from the perspective of a center of life and meaning in which each fragment is related to the plan of the whole, to the will of God. The evil arises when the fragment seeks by its own wisdom to comprehend the whole and by its own power to realize it. (ND 1:168)

Human life, then, is for Biblical faith inescapably creaturely, set within the necessities and limits of nature, with our bodily and communal life alike driven by our instincts and emotions, dependent on immeasurable and immense forces and powers, and so vulnerable and fearsome in the extreme. However, established and supported by God, this same creaturely life provides the basic foundation for all that is creative and meaningful in our existence: the joys of existence—sensual, bodily, and aesthetic—our love for one another, our dependence on family and community, our ingenuity and faithfulness, our artistic and intellectual creativity, and the significant vocations that give point to our efforts. These 'goods' are not the whole, nor are any of them of ultimate significance; however, despite its fragmentary and insignificant character, our very finitude can be apprehended as contributing not only to our own brief joys and those of others, but also to a whole, to a plan and a purpose, transcendent to our understanding but available to each of us by faith. "The ideal possibility is that faith in the ultimate security of God's love would overcome all immediate insecurities of nature and history" (ND 1:183). It is faith that restores, or could in principle restore, the goodness and meaning of our life, individual and communal alike, despite the deep insecurities and anxieties of creatureliness.

∞

The second Biblical category for interpreting human being, namely the image of God, *imago dei,* refers to the dimension of spirit in human existence. For Niebuhr as for the tradition it is the *imago dei* that sets human life apart from the organic and animal levels of creation from which humans arose. As we have seen, humans share with the rest of natural life this bio-logical inheritance that constitutes the essential characteristic or structure of human existence expressed in the category 'creaturely'. As Niebuhr points out, the *imago dei,* what is uniquely human about us, has been vari-ously interpreted in the theological tradition, as in philosophy. Following the Greek practice, the theological tradition generally has identified the *imago* with reason or mind. Niebuhr, however, gives to this category his own interpretation, arguing his point from the Hebrew scriptures, the Pauline letters, and, perhaps especially, the writings of Augustine (see ND 1:151–58). At the most fundamental level, so he argues, the uniquely hu-man, the image of God, is the relatedness of each human to God (ND 1:152–53). God is the transcendent source of all existence, in relation to whom every creature has its being; in humans this relation includes the ap-prehended presence of God, as ground and as moral judge (as I showed in chapter 4 above). Thus essential to human being is a spiritual relation be-yond itself, beyond its world, and beyond all finitude to its transcendent di-vine source and ground.

In Niebuhr's thought each theological affirmation has its consequence in ordinary experience. Hence this relatedness to God is continually expe-rienced by us in the most fundamental characteristics of our humanity, namely our capacity for self-transcendence, for standing outside of our-selves, and hence surveying not only our world but ourselves in the world. All of human experience, and so every analysis of the human, in fact any empirical inquiry, presupposes this self-transcendence. This Augustine, de-spite his Platonism, saw. Of course reason is for Augustine an aspect of the human; but centrally for him the human manifested itself especially in memory and foresight, the transcendence over time that makes our con-sciousness of a self, of its world, and of time possible. Thus spirit "cannot contain itself" and "he [Augustine] concludes that the power of transcen-dence places him (man) so much outside of everything else that he can find a home only in God" (ND 1:156).

This self-transcendence, the vertical dimension in all human being, sets humans outside themselves in both space and time, as well as in space and time, with a 'before' and an 'after', a past and a future, a here and a there— and so arise the possibilities of the consciousness of self and world, mem-ory, the consciousness of history, and the awareness of options in the pre-sent, and of projects for the future (ND 1:161–62). In self-transcendence, spirit ascends, as the Platonic tradition saw, into the conceptual realm; it is the possibility of intellect and of reason, of knowledge and of planning, of both rational abstraction and of empirical inquiry, of critical as of con-structive, speculative reason. But even more important for Niebuhr, it is in self-transcendence that each self becomes a centered, free self. Conscious of its own givenness from its past, and yet conscious of choices in its future, the self here confronts the inescapable options, the moral calling, and the consequent travail of freedom—that is, of selfhood—which characterizes human existence. This is, therefore, the source of creativity—in techniques, in the arts, in projects, in thought; it is through spirit that new possibilities, better possibilities, appear in history, that novelty is introduced into historical time. In short, it is by its inescapable self-transcendence that each self is enabled—and forced—to choose itself and to plot its course in its world, or to lose itself and even to betray itself.

> Man is self-determining not only in the sense that he transcends natural process in such a way as to be able to choose between various alternatives presented to him by the processes of nature; even more he transcends in the sense that he transcends himself in such a way that he must choose his total end. (ND 1:163)

In self-transcendence humans are not only in time and in the world, but, being also beyond both and so able to survey the world and time, humans here know this of themselves. All creatures die, but humans alone know they are mortal. Because it reaches into infinity, spirit as self-transcendent knows its conditionedness, its finitude, and its mortality, and even the finitude of all its creations. Spirit is the principle of creativity in life, the source of creativity; but it is also, as is our creatureliness, the source of the anxious awareness of the creatureliness of all creatures, including our own creatureliness—and so spirit is the condition for the temptation to idolatry. This is the image of God, experienced in all human existence but not rightly understood either by the idealism that champions it as reason or the naturalism that presupposes it but tends to minimize it, if not deny it. It remains a puzzle until it is disclosed by revelation as the essential relatedness to God of all human existence, the latter's transcendent source and transcendent end.

Two central characteristics of Niebuhr's theology follow from this analysis of humans as creatures made in the image of God. First of all, the inescapable creaturely finitude of human existence and hence of all human creativity, in juxtaposition to the infinite transcendence of the human spirit over all it knows and achieves, means that no human scheme of coherence or center of meaning can suffice as a center for human existence. Each form of political order, each system of rational coherence, each center of meaning in temporal existence, remains partial. To make that partial principle of meaning ultimate (and self-transcending spirit requires ultimacy) is to become involved in idolatry, in "lifting some finite and contingent element of existence into the eminence of the divine" (ND 1:164), something we are tempted to do once we see how fragile and relative all of our achievements are. Hence,

> Implicit in the human situation of freedom and in man's capacity to transcend himself and his world is his inability to construct a world of meaning without finding a source and key to the structure of meaning which transcends the world beyond his own capacity to transcend it. (ND 1:164)

> Furthermore, a mind which transcends itself cannot legitimately make itself the ultimate principle of interpretation by which it explains the relation of mind to the world. (ND 1:165)

I have returned to the paradox discussed above in chapter 4: humans cannot comprehend themselves without a principle of comprehension that is beyond their comprehension. Again we see that for Niebuhr the transcendence of God is correlated with, not antithetical to, the infinite self-transcendence and inescapable autonomy of the human spirit.

By these reflections, moreover, we are ushered into the center of Niebuhr's understanding, not only of the infinite creativity of the human spirit but also of its essential ambiguity, its vulnerability to anxiety and emptiness, its weakness even in the midst of its prodigious strength. For it is the self-transcendence of the human creature that makes it aware of its perils in nature and society, and, even more, aware of the partial and relative character of its projects, its systems of coherence, its prospects of salvation. Self-transcendence, so to speak, is not only the principle of being in the human but also of nonbeing—if it does not find itself in God. Although the tragedy and evil that haunt human life arise from the "juncture of nature and spirit in man," it is more because of spirit than because of finitude that humans sin. We are, as we note, a long way from blaming sin on natural impulse.

> The fact that man can transcend himself in infinite regression and cannot find the end of life except in God is the mark of his creativity and uniqueness; closely related to this capacity is his inclination to transmute his partial and finite self and his partial and finite values into the infinite good. Therein lies his sin. (ND 1:122)

∞

Niebuhr has provided us with two Biblical categories for understanding human nature and behavior and shown how each is universally manifested in ordinary experience. But is this not just another 'dualism', one of creature and *imago* (nature and spirit) instead of his earlier 'impulse and reason'? Has he really escaped the dualism inherent in any rational interpretation of human being, be it speculative or scientific, idealistic or naturalistic? Can a human as inquiring subject (*imago*) investigate and reflect on humans as objects (creatures) without some sort of dualism, unless one or the other is denied?

The answer, I believe, is that Niebuhr has escaped this dualism by reason of his sharp sense of the unity of human being, that is, of the continual and pervasive *interweaving* of these distinguishable but not separable aspects of our being. As he began to see in his early political writings, these two aspects of human being do not leave each other alone. On the contrary, each continually affects the other, making the organic, creaturely level of our existence inescapably 'human' in character, and the highest spiritual capacities of our being inevitably 'creaturely'.

Creatureliness at each level is in humans touched and changed by spirit. This early insight ("Through reason the animal will to survive is transmuted into the human will to power" [MM 18; and RE 4, 6, 8, 17]; "Mind sharpens nature's claws" [MM 44]) has now expanded and deepened into a baffling but perceptive mutual interpenetration. There is no aspect of our creaturely, organic life that is not transmuted by spirit. Freedom transforms the given of natural instincts, for example, sexuality, into a wide variety of diverse cultural forms, into the highest levels of human personal relatedness and mutuality (eros and philia), into the capacity, uniquely human, of destructive perversity, and finally into the transcendent possibility of a love that is self-forgetful (agape). Correspondingly, the natural or organic communal relatedness of family, clan, and community are given by spirit the possibility of their infinitely various cultural forms in history, the continually destructive possibilities of social idolatry and oppression, whether in family or community, and the final possibilities of a justice transmuted by love: the kingdom of God. The natural orders of animal existence are thus continually broken and refashioned by spirit into an infinity of customs and mores both at the instant when human beings (hominids) first appeared and throughout their subsequent historical development. History is the transformation of nature—of creatureliness—by freedom, and yet history never ceases to remain nature at its base. Hence while there are general patterns of existence that can be called "natural"—sexuality, self-preservation, family, community, moral obligation, and so on—there can never be a specified, particular, and yet universal "natural law"; because of spirit, human existence at each level is dynamic and changing. The dynamic, refashioning power of spirit on nature in humans means that there are an infinity of diverse forms of human personal and communal existence, all of which are in one sense natural and based on a common creatureliness, and yet all of them are results of spirit's ability to create ever-new forms of common life. The disciplines of anthropology, history of religions, and history show this fact beyond question. "We cannot return to nature" (ND 1:99).

Correspondingly, there are no levels of spiritual self-transcendence and creativity that are not conditioned and so limited by the creatureliness, the relativity, and so the partiality of all human being. Every creative reach of reason—toward abstraction, toward a theory universally illustrated in the facts, or toward the overarching order of the whole—remains finite, conditioned by its time and place and by the self-awareness and interest of the mind that has created it. None is as universal or objective or coherent as it claims.

> The self is a narrow tower with a wide view. (ND 1:76)

> The self, even in the highest reaches of its self consciousness, is still a finite self. . . . It is always a self, anxious for its life and its universal perspectives qualified by its "here and now" relation to a particular body. (ND 1:170)

The image of God, however creative and noble, is always an *image* of deity, that is, an image that essentially and not accidently characterizes a creature. Both image and creatureliness are aspects of the essential structure of human being, and human being is a unity because each radically qualifies the other.

∞

The fundamental or essential structure of human being is that of creatureliness and self-transcendence (ND 1:231), a unified creation made in the image of God, or as Niebuhr calls it frequently, a being "at the juncture of nature and spirit" (ND 1:181). This essential structure is further clarified by Niebuhr through an important distinction—familiar in the entire history of thought about human being—between vitality and form. "All creatures express an exuberant vitality within the limits of certain unities, orders and forms . . . and thus there are two aspects of creation" (ND 1:26). The complex interweaving of these two "polarities" (to use Tillich's term) illustrates and fills out Niebuhr's understanding of creatureliness, image, and their unity.

Let us begin with Niebuhr's own description:

> Four terms must be considered in this situation: (1) the vitality of nature (its impulses and drives); (2) the forms and unities of nature, that is, the determinations of instinct, and the forms of natural cohesion and natural differentiation; (3) the freedom of spirit to transcend natural forms within limits and to direct and redirect the vitalities; (4) and finally the forming capacity of spirit, its ability to create a new realm of coherence and order. All these factors are involved in human creativity and by implication in human destructiveness. (ND 1:27)

Clearly we have here the way Niebuhr's early discussion of impulse and reason has been transmuted in his mature thought. And we note how unquestionably the implicit duality of that earlier formulation has broken down. All of human existence is creaturely, that is, based on vitalities and forms that we share with the natural world (and that biology and sociobiology rightly explore): sexuality; our needs for food, protection, and health; the drive to procreate and bear children; the necessities of family and community. In animal life these are set within an instinctive and so given order and harmony—an order we seem (in myths and dreams) to remember but which in actual life we find very elusive indeed. And the reason for this separation from instinctive order is the presence and continuing intervention of spirit; as Niebuhr said, "we know no impulse in pure form," and thus there is no set "natural law" for our life. The vitality (or freedom) of spirit continually breaks through these given forms, upsets them, opens up new possibilities, and then (the forming capacity of spirit) creates new forms of life—of sexuality, of family, of food gathering, of community, all the infinite variety of human customs, laws, taboos, clans and tribes, political and economic arrangements, and so on. It is into this never-ending variety of forms of life that anthropology and cultural studies inquire. Spirit thus introduces nature into history with its novelties, history as always the dynamic, ever changeable sequence of novel human individuals, events, and institutions. These remain creaturely; for all of these there is a natural base. At each level, however, even the most primitive,[1] there is evident the intervention of spirit: first, of spirit as vitality or freedom, creating diverse forms, and then, as a new result of this vitality, the fear of the possibility of still

---

1. Niebuhr remarks that the apparent lack of social, political, and religious 'freedom', and so the characteristic absence of novelty, in primitive human communities, is no sign of the absence of this essential characteristic of self-transcendence: "The lack of social freedom in a primitive community is a testimony of the inchoate freedom of primitive man" (ND 1:56).

newer forms of life, that is to say, the appearance of a new level of "spiritual rigidity" (customs, taboos, laws). Hence there follows the introduction of new or novel unities of vitality and form in all the varieties of human culture, and in reaction, the remarkable 'formal' and unyielding authority of all early religious and social mores.

Note that in the creation of this social diversity, spirit functions both communally and probably unselfconsciously: that is to say, not conscious, as it is in later stages of life, of its own creative, innovative work. Just as human existence is both creaturely and self-transcendent, so historical existence remains in nature and yet also more than nature, saturated from beginning to end with the freedom of spirit, as nature, to Niebuhr, is not. It is interesting that although Niebuhr unquestionably accepted the theory of evolution, nevertheless that theory had not influenced very much his constructive thought about either nature or human being, as it well might have done forty years or so later. For the presence of dynamic change of forms and so of genuine novelty is to us almost as evident in an evolving nature as it is in history; and, as sociobiology shows, the roots of spirit, even as Niebuhr describes spirit, can be traced not only into primitive human life but much farther back into the earliest organic life of creaturely nature. Spirit, as self-transcendent and as the possibility of culture (including religion), has arisen out of evolutionary development, out of our original creatureliness; and correspondingly signs of the presence of spirit can be found all the way back in natural existence.[2]

Niebuhr had always described himself as an Augustinian, that is, as emphasizing will and vitality against reason and form in his analysis of human being. As the above shows, however, this does not mean that he overlooks or even minimizes the role either of the forms of natural life or of the forming capacity of reason. Nonetheless, there is no question that in the

---

2. Sociobiology is quite correct in pointing to these biological, evolutionary roots of all aspects of 'spirit': moral obligations and religion, ideas and plans, symbols and imagination. The exploration of these earliest forms of the human by biology is a very rich and promising field. However, the fact that these aspects of the human, e.g., morals and religion, have such roots does not invalidate either of them; nor does a biological inquiry into their prior conditions explain either what morals or religion mean, nor the extent if any of their usefulness or validity. After all, biological science and genetics also have genetic and biological roots in previous life forms. And no geneticist, not even Richard Dawkins, would agree that a genetic explanation of the biological roots of biological science gives us a full explanation of either the meaning of its propositions or of their validity. As the positivists once noted, questions of causality are different from questions of justification. See Richard Dawkins, *The Selfish Gene* (Oxford: Oxford University Press, 1976), and R. Alexander, *The Biology of Moral Systems* (New York: Aldine de Gruyter, 1987).

end the principles of vitality and freedom—as aspects of nature, and of spirit or self-transcendence—dominate his discussion. Reason can, he has said, create new forms of individual, communal, and historical life, even new patterns of theoretical coherence and new schemes of meaning; spirit is, as rationalists say, the form-creating capacity of human being. Nonetheless, the character of spirit that Niebuhr stresses is its power of self-transcendence even over itself, that is, its capacity endlessly to transcend, to criticize, to refashion, or to dismantle the forms of life and of understanding that it has itself created. Hence even the new forms created by reason (cohering, speculative reason) are subject to the criticism of spirit; their finitude and partiality—their final creatureliness—can become evident to the critical powers of reason. Thus a principle of coherence and of meaning beyond any creation of the human mind, beyond our capacity to comprehend, to transcend, and to unravel, is necessary. Hence a new paradox: "The real situation is that man who is made in the image of God is unable, precisely because of those qualities in him which are designated as 'image of God', to be satisfied with a god who is made in man's image" (ND 1:166). Mystery always transcends any given meaning and coherence that we are able to create or to know, as God transcends the entire creaturely realm, and as revelation transcends the highest reaches of reason. As the vitality of spirit over nature and over nature's forms makes the romantic return to nature impossible ("Man does not have the freedom to destroy his freedom over natural process" [ND 1:99]), so correspondingly the vitality of spirit over reason makes the rationalist deification of reason impossible. Idealism "does not see to what degree man may, in his freedom, violate, prostitute and corrupt the canons of reason in his own interest" (ND 1:112). If one asks, therefore, What is self-transcendence? it is the vitality of spirit infinitely to transcend nature, history, and its own rationality— and so truly to find itself only in God.

∞

Appropriately, therefore, my discussion of the essential structure of human nature moves to its last subject—last, that is, before I broach the issue of sin. Niebuhr terms this last aspect of 'essential' human nature *justitia originalis,* the "original righteousness" of human existence. This terminology is certainly 'Biblical' because the Genesis account portrays the human situation in terms of a temporal story, the story of a good creation followed by the well-nigh fatal lapse from that goodness into something else. Hence reasonably enough, the tradition has articulated this created goodness of human being and its corruption into sin in terms of a temporal sequence; that is to say, an 'original' righteousness bestowed at creation and an actual unrighteousness characteristic of subsequent history. On this (literal) understanding an original righteousness was an actual constituent of created human being, a fact, so to speak, of actual history; and it was followed by 'an original sin', as a fact or event of actual history. In both cases, the word "original" has a predominantly *temporal* meaning, a first righteousness and a first sin.

As is already evident, Niebuhr accepts this myth as providing the profoundest interpretation of our situation. However, and this is the important point, he very carefully and creatively—for theological much more than for historical or scientific reasons—de-literalizes it:[3] "When the Fall is made an event in history rather than a symbol of an aspect of every historical moment in the life of man, the relation of evil to goodness in that moment is obscured" (ND 1:269).

As this quotation indicates, one of the consequences of this de-literalization of the story or myth of the Fall is the eradication of an actual temporal sequence between the good creation at the beginning and the subsequent fall from that estate. Since Niebuhr seeks to retain as far as possible the Biblical language, and since for good reason he prefers to use the mode of mythical discourse—expressing the relation of eternity and time in terms not of eternity but of temporal sequence, a story—he retains (perhaps without seeing its theological difficulties) this traditional usage: an original righteousness and a subsequent fall.

Niebuhr's insistence on mythical language instead of ontological language frequently made difficulties for him. As we have noted, mythical discourse contains a temporal form, but in Niebuhr's hands it does not refer to ordinary events in historical time, as does most historical, temporal language. On the contrary—and this is its essence—mythical discourse refers to the paradoxical relation of temporal events to the eternity that grounds, supports, and participates in them. Myth is temporal language

3. The scientific reasons are, of course, the entirely new understanding of time, of nature's processes prior to the appearance of human being, and of prehuman history and of human 'prehistory', which have appeared in the last two hundred years. This understanding of nature's history and through that of our human history became normative for all intellectuals, including most theologians, at least from Schleiermacher on. Niebuhr clearly accepts this evolutionary view of nature's and of humanity's past; he knows from biological and from anthropological science that there was no beginning of all things and no first human pair some six thousand years ago. But like most neo-orthodox theologians he hardly ever refers to the scientific sources of much of his own thinking. What he does refer to are the very good theological reasons for this de-literalization which his view of human being entails (see, e.g., ND 1:175; and esp. 260ff.).

that points beyond itself to the relation of time to eternity, of the created natural and historical process to God. The traditional usage of the Biblical narratives believed (so I have argued) that these narratives referred to actual, past events; Niebuhr has denied this reference, but insisted on retaining the language—an extremely tricky point.

Elsewhere, I have told the amusing story of an encounter between Niebuhr and his good friend and colleague, Paul Tillich, on precisely this point. In a conversation attended by students, Niebuhr had complained about Tillich's ontological language vis-à-vis the distinction between creation and fall, and he accused Tillich, in a friendly way, of ontologizing the historical, which in a sense Tillich did. And Niebuhr said Tillich should stick with the Biblical story as the only way to express the paradox of a good creation and a fallen actuality. Tillich smiled, sighed, and looked at his watch: "Tell me, Reinnie, when was it, this good creation, and how long did it last? Five minutes, an hour or two, a day? When was it? And if there is no time for your good creation, then can you speak simply of a 'story'? Do you not have to speak of a 'broken myth'—and are you not then in some mode of ontology, of a discussion of essential nature and its corruption?" Niebuhr knew perfectly well that he had been bested.[4]

As his further discussion makes clear, however, what Niebuhr is really talking about is not a first righteousness in the temporal sense, or a subsequent fall into sin. On the contrary, as Tillich knew well, Niebuhr is seeking to describe the essential, the created nature of human being and its corruption in actuality, a paradox or polarity that characterizes every moment of human time, or as he says, "a vertical rather than a horizontal relation" (ND 1:269). This transformation from literal story to discernment of essential nature and its actuality is clearer in his discussion of the fall than it is of original righteousness. As a consequence of this de-literalization, he explicitly identifies the original righteousness with the essential structure of human being (ND 1:269–76ff.). It is, therefore, clear that his talk of original righteousness refers to the essential structure of women and men, and it is this essential structure that has been the subject to which this entire chapter has been devoted. Hence his description of what is actually essential structure in terms of what he calls 'original righteousness' can be confusing, and this confusion has (for me at least) long obscured the important clarity of his whole discussion.

Niebuhr is adamant that the essential structure of human being, including the image of God, is not destroyed by sin. Humans remain human even in sin, and thus the essential structure remains (cf. ND 1:265–67). "Sin is a

4. Langdon Gilkey, *Gilkey on Tillich* (New York: Crossroad, 1990).

corruption of man's true essence but not its destruction" (ND 1:269; see also 265, 267, 286). Hence a distinction must be made "between the essential nature of man and the virtue of conformity to that nature" (ND 1:269, 270). It is, therefore, the corruption of the image and the nonconformity to our structure that characterizes sin, not the loss of that structure. As Augustine said, blindness is the corruption of the function of the eye, not the elimination of the eye, and disease the corruption of the structure of the body, not the loss of the latter (ND 1:277).[5] Hence even in sin, the creatureliness and the self-transcendence of human existence remain; the sense of obligation and so the uneasy conscience are there (ND 1:265, 267); and life is, as we have seen, dominated by the search for meaning and for reconciliation. Niebuhr often refers to our universal conviction that sin is "not normal" as "the memory of a lost blessedness" (ND 1:265); but more helpfully, he also terms the universal uneasy conscience of humans "the protest of man's essential nature against his present state" (ND 1:263).

The 'original righteousness' of human being is, therefore, the essential structure of our nature as humans. Hence that structure includes the entire nature as I have here so far developed it: "The essential nature of man contains two elements; and there are correspondingly two elements in the original perfection of man" (ND 1:270). These two elements, are, in some of the modes with which Niebuhr described them, the status of men and women as creatures and as made in the image of God, the "characteristics of human being as a creature embedded in the natural realm" (ND 1:270), and "the freedom of his spirit, his transcendence over natural process and finally his self-transcendence" (ND 1:270). All humans exist as both nature and spirit and as vulnerable and mortal yet related to eternity. Further, both our creatureliness and our self-transcendence are characterized by the polarity of vitality and form. And together, in remarkable unity, these two fundamental elements contribute to those other essential and polar aspects of our nature, our individuality on the one hand and our essential relatedness to community on the other.[6]

For Niebuhr the most important aspects of these elements of our structure are (1) that all elements are essentially good, gifts of a good creator,

5. See Augustine, *City of God*, 22.1.

6. Niebuhr carried on an extensive discussion of both individuality and community (especially the former) in ND 1, chaps. 2 and 3, showing the organic and the spiritual roots of this fundamental polarity. And I might add that he gives a corresponding analysis of 'power' and its relation to social existence. All are dependent on both our organic and our spiritual nature; all have infinite potentiality of good and of meaning—all are also subject to corruption. This represents, however, too complex and lengthy a discussion upon which to embark here.

and the potential bases, as he seeks to show, of all that is meaningful in our existence (see ND 1:150, 167, 169, 170). (2) Correspondingly, however, it is precisely this essentially good structure that provides also the possibility of sin, of the corruption of that structure, and so of the evil and tragedy that human action brings into the good creation:

> The evil in man is a consequence of his inevitable but not necessary unwillingness to acknowledge his dependence, to accept his finiteness and to admit his insecurity, an unwillingness which involves him in the vicious circle of accentuating the insecurity from which he seeks escape (ND 1:150; see also 276).

The key point of Niebuhr's understanding, the point to which this whole analysis has inevitably (though not necessarily) led, is that it is the relatedness to God of this self-transcendent creature that is crucial to the goodness or the health of the human being. And while both creatureliness and self-transcendence are available to ordinary understanding—and illustrated in every philosophical account of human existence—the relatedness of self-transcendence to God is not so easily discernible. It is, therefore, in ignoring this dimension that secular views fail and end in one-sidedness, in confusion and contradiction, and above all in obscuring the facts of ordinary experience.

Now it is the character of that relatedness to God, essential to the human as the center of its structure as human, with which Niebuhr's discussion of 'original righteousness' is concerned. The character of this relation is defined, for Niebuhr, by the crucial role that faith, hope, love—the so-called theological virtues—play in that essential structure. They constitute the conformity of the spirit to God, namely dependence of the spirit on God, in faith, hope, and love. That conformity corresponds in our existence as *spirit* (as *imago*) to our dependence as *creatures* on the creative power of God. Thus the theological virtues—faith, hope, and love—are not at all additions to the nature of human being as in the main body of medieval thought. On the contrary, they are requirements of human conformity to its own essence and so its own goodness, and they are requirements because their lack is, in the end, destructive of human existence.[7] If

7. See in Augustine, *City of God,* 11:24 and 22.1. Augustine articulates with great clarity the intrinsic dependence or relatedness of the structure of our religious and moral obligations to our 'ontological' structure; here the nature of our good, or *arete,* is dependent on the nature of our *being.* As we are in our being utterly dependent on God, so it is in our spiritual life, too: our faith and our love (*caritas*) should manifest our essential dependence on God. One notes the ontological grounding of ethics—in our created nature—in Augustine, in Niebuhr, and of course in Tillich.

humans conform to their essential structure in their relation to God, their existence becomes good; if, however, in freedom they contradict that essential structure, then self-destruction follows. For it is a capacity of self-transcendence and of the freedom it implies not only to choose options in life and to choose oneself, but even more to contradict the very deepest necessities of freedom itself, namely its relatedness to and dependence on God as the source and end of its being. "The freedom of man creates the possibility of actions which are contrary to and in defiance of the requirements of his essential nature" (ND 1:269).

The centrality of the relatedness to God, as has been evident all along, is the heart of Niebuhr's theological understanding, of what is to him "Biblical faith," and hence the heart of his apologetic enterprise. For on the one hand the absence of that relation in other views is the cause of the confusion and misunderstanding characteristic of all alternative views of human nature, and on the other the inclusion of that relation provides the only means of interpreting intelligibly the obvious facts of human existence (ND 1:96, 122, 151). But more important than the issue of theoretical understanding, a relation to God in our existence characterized by faith, hope, and love is for Niebuhr the only way that the creaturely freedom central to human existence can be lived out with the possibility of a creative and meaningful life, with loving relations to others, and without self-destruction:

> Faith in the providence of God is a necessity of freedom because, without it, the anxiety of freedom tempts man to seek a self-sufficiency and self-mastery incompatible with his dependence upon forces which he does not control. Hope is a particular form of that faith. It deals with the future as a realm where infinite possibilities are realized and which must be a realm of terror if it is not under the providence of God. . . . The knowledge of God is thus not a supernatural grace which is a 'further gift' beyond man's essential nature. It is the requirement of his nature as free spirit. (ND 1:231)

> Without faith in God's providence the freedom of man is intolerable. Hope is subordinate to and yet identical with faith. It is faith with regard to the future. (ND 1:289)

Correspondingly, love is the sole condition for the fulfillment of human being: love toward God, toward the self, and especially toward neighbor. As in the first and second commandments, love here is absolute: absolute love for God, absolute unity of the self, and absolute love—"a love in which regard for the self is completely eliminated" (ND 1:283)—in short, agape (ND 1:288–89).

How are we to understand this last? Is Niebuhr saying—as frequently he seems to say—that completely self-sacrificial love, the love which Christ embodied, is normative for us in the sense that a Christian should pattern her or his life on such self-sacrificial love and that anything else is un-Christian? What then of that organic and sensual love essential to love between men and women; the organic and spiritual love essential for family life, especially love for one's children; the care for oneself and one's own necessary not only for family but also for all community and for any vocation in the world; the requirements of justice to all, including one's own, as moral structures and moral obligations of communal life? And I should also mention Niebuhr's own recognition that force and possibly violence may be necessary if any justice is to be achieved. Is Niebuhr denying all this in his vision of the Christian life? Is he here proposing an essentially ascetic ethic of withdrawal or of self-sacrifice? Are all of these relations and obligations of ordinary life rendered obsolete by the one theological requirement of agape as the normative pattern of Christian existence—and in what sense, then, is such an existence either creaturely or 'creative'? These questions abound whenever Niebuhr speaks, as he does so frequently (especially in *An Interpretation of Christian Ethics*) of the absolute requirements of agape as providing the norm for authentic Christian existence. How are we to understand and not misunderstand what he is saying here?

It is my view, based on the entire discussion of this volume, that this absolutist or ascetic interpretation of Niebuhr is not correct. While agape is surely central to his understanding of the created goodness of human existence, agape is not for him morally constitutive of that existence; agape as self-sacrifice does not for him represent the sole moral content of the Christian life. On the contrary, the role of agape in Niebuhr (like that of the kingdom of God in his understanding of history) is to provide the transcendent or self-transcendent element to our moral existence, a self-transcendent element continually qualifying our sensual love, our mutual love, our love for family, and our responsibilities to our community (justice), that is, qualifying our conscience so that none of these can descend, so to speak, into self-destruction but are lured on toward our 'original righteousness'.

For Niebuhr sensual and mutual love are part of the essential goodness of human being, creative of individual and community alike. In both sensual and mutual love, and their combination, responsibility to the other and so justice represent the final moral norms, justice toward the other and also justice toward the self. This requirement of justice in every relationship constitutes one permanently valid element in the tradition of natural law, even if any given codification of that law represents a partial and temporal perspective on it (ND 1:270–71, 275, 280).[8] However, because of sin (the inescapable self-concern that insinuates itself into all of our natural relations), each of these—sensual love, mutual love, and even communal justice—is prone to become less than loving and less than just. Sensual love is corrupted by inordinate self-love, and the other is used as an object; mutual love quickly descends into calculation about how really "mutual" it is, a calculation dominated by a self-interest worried it is being used by the other; any concrete scheme of justice expresses an uneasy and unequal balance of power among persons and among groups in a community, a balance in which one side can easily dominate and in so doing defeat the desire to achieve real justice.

In each case, only if the self is at some level able to be heedless of itself, can it be toward the other as it always is toward itself; that is, in selflessness it can enact a genuine sensual love (eros), a genuinely mutual love (*philia*), or a genuine justice. If the self would act with true mutuality, it must be willing to risk itself—for in true mutuality there can be no anxious calculation. Agape—the willingness to risk or even to sacrifice the interests of the self, and in the end the self itself, for the other—is hence necessary if the natural law of justice, the harmony of self with other, and of the self with itself, is to be realized. This is such a crucial point to Niebuhr's understanding of the relation of agape to mutual love, to 'nature', that it is well to see what he himself says.

> Sacrificial love thus represents a tangent towards "eternity" in the field of historical ethics. It is nevertheless the support of all historical ethics; for the self cannot achieve relations of mutual and reciprocal affection with others if its actions are dominated by the fear that they may not be reciprocated. (ND 2:69)

> A self which seeks to measure the possible reciprocity which its love for the other may elicit is obviously not sufficiently free of preoccupation with self to lose itself in the life of the other. (ND 2:82)

8. One can see here how Niebuhr, like Augustine and Tillich, is not only 'ontological' in his interpretation of the requirements of the human, i.e., in his ethics, but how he can also be legitimately described as a theologian of 'natural law'. For the ultimate requirements or virtues of humanity (faith, hope, and love) are requirements set by the 'nature' of human being and hence represent in the original Greek sense the 'natural law'. One might surmise that it was his 'memory' of that deeply ontological understanding of human being characteristic of Patristic thought (a memory perhaps he was not inclined to admit) that made Niebuhr, despite his many sharp criticisms of the role of natural law in orthodox Roman Catholic canon law, nonetheless always sympathetic to natural law theories in ethics.

> The preservation of cultures and civilizations is frequently possible only as individuals disregard their own success and failure and refuse to inquire too scrupulously into the possibility or probabilities of maintaining their own life in a given course of action. (ND 2:88)

> But such strategies of mutual love and of systems of justice cannot maintain themselves without inspiration from a deeper dimension of history. A strategy of brotherhood which has no other resource but historical experience degenerates from mutuality to a prudent regard for the interests of the self. (ND 2:96)

As a requirement, therefore, agape functions in two ways: as a continual principle of criticism of any established balance of power, or any mode of sensual relationship, of any arrangement of mutuality, and any scheme of justice; and it also functions as a lure. What agape seeks to do is to prune our relations of the dominance of self-concern that can corrupt them, and then to persuade them into a fuller realization of their innate possibilities. After all, for Niebuhr all of creation is good, including vitality and form in all of their diversity. Hence relations with and to our bodies, relations (sensual and mutual) of the closest sort to another person, relations to our families and to others in the wider community are a part of that good creation and are central ingredients to all human meaning. Justice is the norm for those relations of self to other selves and to itself; but conversely justice needs agape to become itself.

In Niebuhr's thought, love (agape) must temper and qualify, criticize and lure mutuality and justice for a number of reasons. The diversity of nature and especially of human community means that a strict equality is never really just; exceptions must be made in light of individual differences; an inequality of positions is often necessary; and hence no law is able to achieve final justice. This diversity of need increases in personal relations, where the uniqueness of each self can only be reached by a relation grounded by love:

> The freedom and uniqueness of the other also raise moral requirements above any scheme of justice. The other has special needs and requirements which cannot be satisfied by general rules of equity . . . the obligation of life to life is more fully met in love than is possible in any scheme of equity and justice. They are negated because love makes an end of the nicely calculated less and more of the structure of justice. (ND 1:295)

Hence love both negates (in the first instance) and in the end fulfills justice. Again the essential structure of human being, its natural character, is completed by the transcendent relation represented by love of self to other and of self to itself. Mutuality and concern for the other, which always involve concern also for the self, must be touched and qualified by that which transcends all self-concern, namely agape.

Thus as the natural finitude, vulnerability, and mortality on the one hand, and the self-transcendence of human being on the other are alone made bearable by faith ("without faith in God's Providence, our freedom is intolerable" [ND 1:289]), so the harmony of the self with itself and with the other requires the continuing presence of a self-transcendent love, a heedlessness of self that qualifies all of these relations. And this heedlessness is possible only in faith: "Without freedom from anxiety man is so enmeshed in the vicious circle of egocentricity, so concerned about himself, that he cannot release himself for the adventure of love" (ND 1:272). The relatedness to God, expressed in the fundamental requirements of freedom—faith, hope, and love—is hence the center of the structure of human being. Without these requirements of freedom the entire good creation goes astray and sin results; with them there is the new possibility of approaching the goodness for which we were created. And as this discussion has now revealed, if we are to understand at all clearly this conception of the nature of human being, we must proceed to the further and final aspect of human existence as we see it in experience, namely the sources and lineaments of human sin.

CHAPTER 6

Sin: Anxiety, Pride, and Self-Deception

With the doctrine of sin, or as Niebuhr put it, "man as sinner," we reach the pivotal center of Niebuhr's thought, the concept for which Niebuhr was rightly famous and on which all else he said in theology—and especially about history, his other major concern—depended. As we have seen in his earlier writings, there were two 'faiths' characteristic of modernity that Niebuhr believed to be false faiths and that he ceaselessly challenged: (1) the goodness and rationality of human being, "the easy conscience of modern man," and (2) the confidence in moral and religious progress, as manifested by a belief in the gradual but certain eradication of evil as history unfolds. He was sure that the "obvious facts" of contemporary history showed the falsity of both of these bases of modern meaning, and that in both cases the Biblical view much more accurately interpreted these facts. Chapters 6 and 7 are devoted to his challenge to the first false faith in the name of the Biblical understanding of sin; chapters 8–10 focus on his reinterpretation of progress in history into what he termed "the Biblical view of history."

Niebuhr denies over and over that human wrongdoing or human evil (i.e., sin) is the result either of our material bodily state or of our finitude, as many other explanations of our universal waywardness have maintained. Insofar as we are evil, we are not so because of our instincts or desires, or because we are particular individuals in history. As we have seen, the bodily creation in all its particularity and individuality, its complement of desires and instincts, its dependence, its vulnerability, and its death, is nonetheless 'good', replete with possibilities under God of a creative and serene life.

> It [the Christian view of man] insists on man's weakness, dependence and finiteness, on his involvement in the necessities and contingencies of

the natural world, without, however, regarding this finiteness as, of itself, a source of evil in man. (ND 1:150)

> The fragmentary character of human life is not regarded as evil in Biblical faith because it is seen from the perspective of a center of life and of meaning in which each fragment is related to the plan of the whole, to the will of God. (ND 1:168)

Besides, bodily life and finitude are "essential" characteristics of our nature. If they were the source of evil, there would be no responsibility on our part for the wrongs that we do, nor, so long as we remain creatures, would there be any hope of redemption from evil.

On the contrary, for Niebuhr sin is the anxious attempt to hide our finitude and to make ourselves the center of all life, to take the place of God. This usurpation is an act of spirit, and hence an act of freedom for which we are, and know that we are, responsible.

> Man is insecure and involved in natural contingency; he seeks to overcome his insecurity by a will-to-power which overreaches the limits of human creatureliness. . . . Man is ignorant and involved in the limitations of a finite mind; but he pretends he is not limited. He assumes he can gradually transcend finite limitation until his mind becomes identical with universal mind. All of his intellectual and cultural pursuits, therefore, become infected with the sin of pride. Man's pride and will-to-power disturb the harmony of creation. The Bible defines sin in both religious and moral terms. The religious dimension of sin is man's rebellion against God. . . . The moral and social dimension of sin is injustice. The ego which falsely makes itself the center of existence in its pride and will-to-power inevitably subordinates other life to its will and thus does injustice to other life. (ND 1:178–79)

Sin and injustice, therefore, are not necessary; there is always the ideal possibility that in trust (faith, hope, and love) humans can bear this finitude and vulnerability and the anxiety that results from them, and so use these gifts creatively. Hence, estrangement from God, "unbelief," is presupposed as that which transmutes our finitude into a problem. Then anxiety about our life and its meaning becomes the inevitable temptation to sin.

∞

To understand what Niebuhr is saying, we must look again at the nature of human being, its essential structure, as providing the structural possibility, the ontological precondition, for this strange free and yet unfree, individual and yet universal, character of all of us, namely our actuality as sinners. We exist at the juncture of nature and spirit; we are at once creatures and *imago dei,* finite and self-transcendent; and these two are in intense unity (see ND 1:180–81). Anxiety arises out of this union of vulnerable and insecure creatureliness with the awareness of our temporality and mortality that spirit makes possible. Since creatureliness and spirit are both aspects of our essential structure, so anxiety is also an essential aspect of our human condition. Anxiety is on the one hand the source of human creativity, of the drive to make life more secure, more harmonious, and more meaningful (ND 1:183). But, shorn of the serenity given by faith, anxiety becomes unbearable, and the will to power that breeds pretensions over others inevitably results.

> In short, man being both free and bound, both limited and limitless, is anxious. Anxiety is the inevitable concomitant of the paradox of freedom and of finiteness in which man is involved. Anxiety is the internal precondition of sin, . . . the internal description of the state of temptation. It must not be identified with sin because there is always the ideal possibility that faith would purge anxiety of the tendency towards sinful self-assertion. (ND 1:182–83)

We are vulnerable, insecure, and mortal creatures, in constant peril. As self-transcendent, we feel and in fact see this situation and are anxious. And since our self-transcendence and the imagination that springs from it are unlimited, there are no possible limits to our anxiety about our security in either space or time. If we control our own valley, we can picture a new enemy on each neighboring hill—and every succeeding hill. If we have sufficient food for the present winter, we can imagine now our hunger in the next year—and every subsequent year. Our anxiety—hence our will to power and our greed and hence again our imperialism against every potential neighbor—is unlimited. Once we have become the center of our own world, conflict with and injustice toward every other inevitably arises. Here for Niebuhr in the union of finitude and spirit shorn of transcendent trust lies the source of the inordinate egotism that he terms *pride of power,* which in turn is the source of the social, economic, and political conflicts that plague history. These he once termed "impulse" or "the necessities of nature"; now he sees them as the work of spirit, an estranged spirit, in union with our essential creatureliness (cf. ND 1:186–89).

We are finite, and hence we are relative and partial; as creatures we represent this particular perspective and these special interests. Yet as self-transcendent we are made for the truth and for righteousness; conse-

quently we are aware that our truth and our own goodness are not ultimate. This finite-infinity of spirit makes trust in a transcendent truth and
righteousness necessary; but it also makes doubt and skepticism possible—
for we can always see the fallibility of what we are and of the truth we
know. Anxiety about our truth thus once more drives us to claim ultimacy
for the partial truth we know and for the partial good our lives and our
mores represent. Again, as anxiety instigates imperialism, greed, and violence in economic and political life, so now anxiety about the truth and
about the good impels us to ideology and self-righteousness, to what
Niebuhr terms *pride of intellect* and *moral pride*. And as pride of power results in conquest and oppression, so pride of intellect and pride of righteousness result in intellectual and moral revulsion at the other, scorn for
the other, and an even more intense cruelty to the other (ND 1:194–99).
The worst of all is *spiritual* or *religious pride:* here pride of intellect and of
moral righteousness unite with certainty of one's own religious eminence,
of kinship with the divine—or being the emissary of the divine—that
characterizes religious history and makes it, in combination with the other
forms, the most terrible form of pride (ND 1:200–203).

One notices the clear delineation of two levels of anxiety and likewise
two different levels, so to speak, of the sin of pride. These correspond, of
course, to the two aspects of human nature, as creature and as spirit or
image. Each of us is aware of creaturely anxiety about survival, security,
economic well-being—in fact it is this awareness that impels us all to participate in most of a culture's activities, that is, it inspires us to work to live
and to enhance and defend our lives and the lives of others who depend on
us. We are probably less aware of anxieties about our truth and our goodness; but the effects of these anxieties in dogmatism and intolerance on the
one hand and self-righteous disapproval and condemnation of the other
are just as evident and just as harmful.

As Niebuhr consistently points out, these two levels of pride are never
separated in actual life. A given political group that (to others) is clearly
dominated by its own self-interest—as are the individuals within it—always parades in reality as the virtuous (and selfless) bearer of the truth and
the good; and each group defends its own interest accompanied by the
claim that those interests represent universal values. (In present history, these
values are generally secular and normally include peace, justice, democracy,
etc.; in past history they usually were religious, and were associated with our
Christian nation, the glory of God, the glory of Christianity, etc.) Hence
politics is always saturated with ideological and moral pretensions.

The distinction between individual and collective sin, frequently apparent in Niebuhr's earlier works, has now very much diminished. Niebuhr's

eye, as always, is on the collective sins of humans against one another that have caused so much of the suffering, oppression, and injustice of history: sins of nations, of classes, of races, of gender. Now he has sought to locate the source of that universal trait of history's injustice and violence deeply within the human person, and so within individual persons, in their anxiety as mortal beings who know they are mortal. He certainly still implies that collective sin is even more inevitable and intractable than that of individual persons (ND 1:210). But even so, the fact that for Niebuhr our greatest freedom as individuals comes in the act of recognizing our own sin (ND 1:258–60) shows that now in his view sin is quite universal, an aspect of each individual life as well as of each community.

In addition, very few individuals are capable of 'making themselves the center' of their social world—though this is perfectly possible in the smaller communities of family and town. Thus most of us resolve our individual anxieties on a communal level, through the power, the truth, the value, and the glory of our group. Collective egoism is, therefore, a compound of the 'displaced' egoism of individuals, an extension of that egoism into the field of history, where its results are so destructive. However, as Niebuhr pointed out much earlier, this individual self-concern thus present in collective sin remains hidden, incognito, covered by the genuine moral sacrifice of the individual for the welfare of the group. In patriotism (which stands for all such selfless and so "moral" participation in group behavior) the sacrifice of each individual for the group creates a moral situation that covers the implicit collective egoism present in the group's action. Hence in actual practice the morality of individuals now serves and increases the immorality of groups. Paradoxically, the selfless sacrifice of the individual makes the collective egoism even more invulnerable to criticism (ND 1:212). And finally, the ultimate 'prophetic' requirement to challenge the immorality of one's own group again paradoxically requires that each such individual conscience appear to the group as 'immoral', as having no value, as a moral outcast. Here the requirements of a genuinely moral politics approach the unworldly, transcendent norm of the figure of Jesus on the cross or of Socrates accepting the hemlock.

As we have seen, there are anxieties on both the creaturely and the spiritual levels of human existence, anxieties about security, about truth, about goodness, and about ultimate meaning in life and history. Niebuhr is clear that these anxieties are the sources of human creativity: in civilization, in science, in culture and the arts, in morals, and in religion. But the same anxieties are also the ground, granted estrangement, of sin and injustice. Hence "spirit" in all its facets can be demonic as well as creative—a new note in theology, whether orthodox or liberal. This is also—as Neibuhr did not say—a new note for Niebuhr:

> Sinful pride and idolatrous pretension are thus the inevitable concomitant of the cohesion of larger political groups. This is why it is impossible to regard the lower morality of groups, in comparison with individuals, as the consequence of the inertia of nature against the higher demands of individual reason. (ND 1:210)

One can see here his disagreement at this stage with his own earlier liberal inheritance.

If the fault is spiritual and not natural, then a spiritual resolution is required at the very deepest level: not mere education, more inquiry, more intelligence, excellent as each of these may be. Rather we need the religious recognition of our own involvement in pride, humble repentance about our claims for security, for truth, and for virtue, and finally the acceptance of forgiveness and the beginning of trust. There is, hence, in Niebuhr a final transcendence of humanism, even the best humanism, into the necessity of the vertical dimension inherent in being human. To our surprise, moreover, we find ourselves here in the midst not only of religion but even more of the piety of justification by faith: of repentance on the one hand and trust in grace on the other. Lest, as this analysis shows and as the Reformers reiterated, we fall again into pride at our piety or into despair at our failures. Merely battling for the righteous against the unrighteous, while possibly necessary on one level of action, is not sufficient. For we too are also the unrighteous; without recognition of that, the cycle can never be broken. Here Niebuhr has made the piety of justification by faith relevant to politics and history, as he and Tillich had already done with the issue of truth.

Two more comments before we move on. (1) The important theological words in this analysis are words expressive of the vertical dimension: lack of trust, unbelief, making one's self the center of the world, rebellion against God—these are, let us note, *analogies*. This is to say that each of the above is a word that is referent originally to a human situation in ordinary experience, usually in relation to another person. Like the crucial theological concept *encounter*, such words (lack of trust, unbelief) are now being used in quite a different context, that of the vertical relation to God. Furthermore, these words do not point to conscious acts as they do in ordinary usage. For example, one could well ask, When did I make myself the world's center or show lack of trust? As Niebuhr shows, these acts are, however, not thereby completely unconscious; we are dimly aware of our responsibility and so our freedom here. Nonetheless, the words refer to a level of awareness below or behind the conscious thoughts, decisions, and actions of ordinary experience; they are only dimly seen. Although, moreover, this deeper level is not thereby one of determining necessity but in some sense of freedom and responsibility, still it is noticeably different from our experience of our ordinary decisions and personal relations. Much like the level of the "unconscious" of psychotherapy, or that of class consciousness in Marxism, both of which affect our surface lives and yet are not directly 'seen', these words point us to a different stratum, that of the vertical dimension, and hence these words apply differently, analogically, and not 'literally'. As Niebuhr makes clear, here neither clear, conscious choices and decisions nor a simple deterministic model are applicable (ND 1:181, 204); in fact the expressions Niebuhr uses seem to participate in both of these language games of ordinary experience. Hence we are dealing with analogies. Niebuhr is not at all clear on this point. Failure to clarify this usage is, perhaps, one of the reasons that the personal language of belief and trust on the one hand and of decision and rebellion against God on the other seems to make our situation of sin more consciously perverse than he meant it to be.

Finally, (2) if Niebuhr's analysis is accurate, then *normal* life, individual and communal alike, is judged as askew, as in fact "unnatural," as "fallen." Seeking security, advancing one's own interests, proclaiming one's own truth, and so on, are accepted in normal life as 'good'—and only their illegal or rude perversion is wrong. Ordinarily, we almost feel that unless something is declared illegal, it is not only acceptable to the state but acceptable to all moral judgments. Hence the conventionally respectable in any society are considered moral and only those who are in one way or another deviant are immoral. In Niebuhr, however, all this is turned around: the normal self-seeking of human being in terms of inordinate self-concern is precisely the 'normalcy' that is named sin and described as the cause of historical suffering, oppression, and conflicts.[1] Thus Neibuhr agrees with the traditional theological dictum that all humans are sinners

---

1. Any theological student, at least any student of Niebuhr's, recalls with some amusement the shock that both media and public felt when President Carter, a dedicated and informed Christian, said without any hesitation in an interview, "Of course, I am a sinner; I have sinful thoughts; and I am with some difficulty able to control them." Niebuhr would have said the same. The media collectively gasped: "Was Jimmy secretly playing around? Did Rosalynn know? What would Jimmy's fellow church members, especially the other Sunday school teachers, think?" Actually the latter probably also gasped—but Jimmy was "right on" with regard to classic Pauline and Reformation sensibility.

and consequently that history, all of history, is fallen and in this sense 'unnatural'. He regards this view as not only Biblical but also as an obvious fact about common experience—as the turmoil of the twentieth century seems to show. In social affairs it is the 'normal' behavior of ethnic, national, class, gender, and racial groups—'moral' people being ordinarily 'moral'—that causes the universal suffering of men and women, not just the few 'wicked' or 'immoral' people who live off that behavior. Correspondingly, real virtue—really seeking the welfare of others, really being indifferent to the fate of the self, really challenging the pride of one's group—this is rare, not at all normal or to be expected. In fact as a norm for our behavior such self-sacrifice must be 'revealed'. This is a radical interpretation of human communal life, more radical than that of *Moral Man and Immoral Society*. Niebuhr really means it when he says—as all Christians also frequently repeat—"There is none righteous, no, not one" (Rom 3:10, and see 3:10–18).

∞

A theme long present in Niebuhr's analysis of social and political behavior has been the universal presence of rationalization, the finding of moral (or religious) reasons for acts that are really motivated by self-interest. This theme now reappears under the labels "self-deception," "dishonesty," and "deceit."

> Man loves himself inordinately. Since his determinate existence does not deserve the devotion lavished upon it, it is obviously necessary to practice some deception in order to justify such excessive devotion. . . . Its primary purpose is to deceive not others but itself. The self must at any rate deceive itself first. Its deception of others is partly an effort to convince itself against itself. . . . The dishonesty (i.e., hypocrisy) of man is thus an interesting refutation of the doctrine of man's total depravity. (ND 1:203)

Humans cannot face the reality of themselves or their group, that is, as inordinately self-concerned; this would require the uncomfortable acknowledgment that their own moral behavior is immoral or wrong. The natural and well-nigh universal course is, therefore, denial of one sort or another of any responsibility or blame, mostly through rationalization or self-deception. Only those who are oppressed by that behavior—for example, someone from an oppressed racial, religious, or sexual-preference group—see through this moral rhetoric to the self-interested bias in the ordinary moral conventions of a community. The others, those on top, do not see it because they have convinced themselves, deceived themselves, that their behavior and the social mores they defend are not only moral but right and that their actions constitute a defense of the good and the true. And they must perpetuate this self-deceit in order, first, to defend the social structures that privilege them, and, second, to avoid the shattering realization that their own existence illustrates the very self-interested and immoral behavior they deplore in others.

The result of this self-deception is that all of our important deliberate actions seem to us to be good, to be according to the moral law, or, in modern usage, according to our moral ideals or values. Hence the hypocrisy of all politics: each policy, favorable to a particular class, race, or nation, parades itself as devoted to higher values. Yet, Niebuhr cautions, this is not simply perverse: "The dishonesty which is the inevitable concomitant of sin must be regarded neither as purely ignorance, nor yet as involving a conscious lie in each individual instance" (ND 1:204). We have (unconsciously yet consciously) deceived ourselves that what we do is really good, and because of that deception, we are enabled to continue our drive to power, our pride in our virtue and our truth—and the oppression of others, often of course for "their own good." Hypocrisy accompanies sin because there remains, despite our estrangement, enough of our authentic nature to force us continually to placate that essential self: "Hypocrisy is the bow sin makes to virtue." As Niebuhr remarks, however, this deception never really works, "because the self is the only ego fully privy to the dishonesties by which it has hidden its own interests behind a facade of general interest" (ND 1:206). Thus the self now faces a new insecurity, namely that the deception—and its confidence in its own virtue—will be discovered, and "the self in its nakedness behind these veils . . . will be recognized as the author of the veiling deceptions" (ND 1:207).

Just as the theological categories of creaturely self-transcendence, of anxiety and insecurity, of unbelief and of consequent pride and will to power had illumined Niebuhr's earlier insights into the 'impulses of nature' that drive us into social conflict, so now the categories of self-deception and the new anxiety of self-disclosure expose the universal patterns of rationalization, of dogmatism, and of ultimate fanaticism which he had seen in society. The false rhetoric of politics, the claims to embody and defend universal values, is neither arbitrary nor merely irrelevant 'public relations'. It is very significant and necessary in order to allow the self and its community to pursue self-interests without the hindrance of conscience and in order to quiet new and deeper anxieties of spirit that we are in fact more guilty than we admit and less virtuous than we proclaim. "No modern nation can ever quite make up its mind whether to insist that its struggle is a fight for survival or a selfless effort to maintain transcendent and universal values" (ND 1:211).

Values are values, and no community can get along without them. They make common and so also individual life not only bearable but good—creative, joyous, and fulfilling. Mutual kindness and trust, caring for one another, tolerance, generosity, freedom, as well as cooperation, personal autonomy, and personal responsibility—these are values utterly essential to creative community and individual human life within community. They are for most of us socially enshrined best within the more general 'political' values of democracy: assent of the governed, freedom of speech and person, equality in the public sphere, individual rights before the law, and so on. Niebuhr thoroughly believed in these values—or found how much he believed in them (as did many of us) when they were seriously threatened. And he was prepared to defend them. They were, therefore, for him not just rhetoric; nor did they represent the perverted moral justifications of ruling-class dominance. However, their clear and intrinsic value—which he affirmed—did not mean that they could not be misused. Every human virtue, like all human achievement, can be misused to create self-righteousness (moral pride) and intolerance, disdain of and cruelty toward the other. The very nobility of a community's ideals represents a temptation to such pride, and, as one of its direct consequences, can be used as the justification for vanquishing and dominating the other. Niebuhr saw this clearly, and his wariness about our common democratic social values thus reinforces rather than contradicts his own devotion to those values.

∞

We come now to perhaps the most intriguing (and most frequently misunderstood) paradox in Niebuhr's initial discussion of sin: the equality of sin and the inequality of guilt. This paradoxical formula epitomizes Niebuhr's understanding of sin and its relation to society and politics, as it does also his interpretation of Biblical faith. Perhaps more than any other of his important paradoxes, it also illustrates the strong influence of modernity (and with it, of liberalism) on his reinterpretation of the Biblical viewpoint and of Christian tradition—a point I will address in more detail later.

I have shown how central the traditional Christian doctrine of the equality—or universality—of sin is to Niebuhr's understanding of society: no group (or individual), however apparently righteous or idealistic, is free of anxiety and the self-concern that can breed inordinate pride and lead to the centering of the world around the self or the group. The men of power certainly show this; but so equally do the wise, the good, and even the spiritual. And each form or level of pride results in its own way in injustice toward the neighbor, "There is none righteous, no, not one."[2] Sin is universal in all of us; with regard to our broken relation to God we share a strange equality—a kind of reverse side to our equality of value in the sight of God.

Niebuhr sees very clearly that this emphasis on the equality of sin "imperils and seems to weaken all moral judgments which deal with the nicely calculated less and more of justice and goodness as revealed in the relativities of history" (ND 1:220). And he asserts that this equality, overemphasized by Protestant orthodoxy, has cut the nerve of Christian social judgment and action in society: if every group is equally characterized by sin, what is the basis for any sort of social action for justice? It was precisely this insight—namely that all imperial powers are equal in their self-concern, all are guilty—that enervated many college undergraduates in the spring of 1940, when Germany overran France and threatened England. More than one Pelagian liberal, convinced that social action must be undertaken by the "idealistic forces" against the "materialistic and selfish interests,"[3] saw Niebuhr, despite himself, as returning to that quiescent stance of Protestant orthodoxy.

This paradoxical formula, equality of sin and inequality of guilt, is Niebuhr's answer to his own query and to this complaint. If we understand this formula aright, he says, we will see that even though we are all sinners, there are crucial distinctions to be made in the amount of 'guilt' that each group (and individual) bears, and hence we must, in the name of justice, choose between historical forces, and side with those who have the least guilt. And typically he argues that not only was this paradox 'Biblical', but also the two apparent contraries (equality of sin and inequality of guilt), when properly juxtaposed, clarify each other and illumine the puzzles of our common social experience.

How, then, are these two categories, sin and guilt, distinguished? How can we have equality of the one and inequality of the other?

2. Rom 3:10; see also Ps 14:1–3, Ps 51, Ps 53:1–3; Is 59:7.

3. It is interesting that this dualism between idealistic forces of good and materialistic forces of self-interest characterizes not only much of the liberal religion of Niebuhr's time but also the work of such secular naturalists as John Dewey. See "Science and the Future of Society," in *Intelligence in the Modern World,* ed. Joseph Ratner (New York: Modern Library, 1939), chap. 4; and John Dewey, *A Common Faith* (New Haven, Conn.: Yale University Press, 1934).

Guilt is distinguished from sin in that it represents the objective and historical consequences of sin, for which the sinner must be held responsible. . . . Guilt is the objective consequence of sin, the actual corruption of the plan of creation and providence in the historical world. (ND 1:222)

In other words, sin refers to the vertical relation to God, which in all of us has become characterized by a break in that relation which Niebuhr has defined as pride, lack of trust, and "centering the world around the self." Guilt, on the other hand, refers to the consequences of this break, namely the injustice we inflict on others. Niebuhr applies the category of sin to the vertical, religious relation to God, and guilt to the horizontal, social, and moral consequences of sin in historic injustice. This is not only consistent with his analysis; it also resolves the moral dilemma that the equality or universality of sin seems to raise.

Niebuhr argues that there is another theme in the prophetic (Biblical) consciousness besides that of the universality of sin, namely the "antiaristocratic" emphasis. The prophets, Niebuhr says, are not at all unbiased in the social situation: "Specially severe judgments fall upon the rich and the powerful, the mighty and the noble, the wise and the righteous . . . which oppress the poor and crush the needy" (Am 4:1, 6:4, 8:4). The severer judgment on the mighty, the preference for the poor, continues in Isaiah and is culminated in the Magnificat, in Paul, and especially in the teachings of Jesus. Thus the prophetic consciousness sees the mighty, the wise, and the noble as bearing more guilt than do the weak and even the unrighteous, a radical reversal of our ordinary social and moral judgments (see ND 1:222–27). How, then, are we to understand this paradoxical prophetic consciousness: All are equally sinners, but are some more guilty than others?

The answer is that eminence of any sort—of political, economic, or social power, of knowledge, of morality, or of spirituality—tempts those who possess it to magnify inordinately their glory and so to claim from those who are weak more than is deserved. Eminence of any sort establishes the capacity to rule, to effect what others cannot effect, to shape the common life as others cannot do. Thus the sin of those persons of importance has more effect than does that of ordinary mortals.[4] Those who have

---

4. Recall: "Man's pride and will-to-power disturb the harmony of creation. The Bible defines sin in both religious and moral terms. The religious dimension of sin is man's rebellion against God, his effort to usurp the place of God. The moral and social dimension of sin is injustice. The ego which falsely makes itself the center of existence in its pride and will-to-power inevitably subordinates other life to its will and thus does injustice to other life" (ND 1:179).

more power are those whose acts result in the greater number of unjust consequences; they cause, much more than do the weak, the suffering of others. They are, therefore, more guilty:[5]

> Wherever the fortunes of nature, the accidents of history or even the virtues of the possessors of power, endow an individual or a group with power, social prestige, intellectual eminence or moral approval above their fellows, there an ego is allowed to expand. It expands both vertically and horizontally. Its vertical expansion, its pride, involve it in sin against God. Its horizontal expansion involves it in an unjust effort to gain security and prestige at the expense of its fellows. (ND 1:226)

This fundamental inequality of guilt, in which the mighty offend against the weak, and through which justice is betrayed and torn asunder, is for Niebuhr first seen and made clear as part of the Biblical or prophetic consciousness, and so of revelation. Much of Christian tradition has overlooked it and refrained from critical judgment on the powerful; and it is surely one of Niebuhr's main goals to reestablish this 'bias toward the poor' as a part of Biblical and Christian faith.

Niebuhr adds, moreover, that this important insight into the greater guilt of the rulers and the mighty is not denied but furthered by the other Biblical motif, namely, the equality or universality of sin. Each dominant or ruling class within society not only controls and manages the society's economic and political arrangements; perhaps more important, they establish, shape, and defend its social, moral, and even religious norms and ideals—and bend these latter to favor the interests, habits, and mores of their class. Thus the moral judgments of a society are slanted in favor of its dominant groups: for example, the old nobility, the bourgeois middle class, the white race, males, not to mention the Pharisees and Sadducees (ND 1:225). Hence the 'poor of the land', the proletariat, the dispossessed and enfeebled in each society, are unable to represent or to live up to the standards shaped and defended by those who are better off. It requires, therefore, Niebuhr says, the conviction that *all* are sinners in order to pierce this false veil and see the pride, self-concern, and cruelty of the 'moral' upper classes:

5. "Capitalists are not greater sinners than poor laborers by any natural depravity. But it is a fact that those who hold great economic and political power are more guilty of pride against God and of injustice against the weak than those who lack power and prestige. Gentiles are not naturally more sinful than Jews. But Gentiles, holding the dominant power in several nations, sin against Semitic minority groups more than the latter sin against them. White men sin against Negroes in Africa and America more than Negroes sin against white men" (ND 1:225–26).

It is at this point that the Biblical insight into the sinfulness of all human nature actually supports rather than contradicts the prophetic strictures against the wise, the mighty, the noble and the good. For without understanding the sinfulness of the human heart in general it is not possible to penetrate through the illusions and pretensions of the successful classes of every age. (ND 1:227)

One other twist. The equality of sin also pierces through another illusion about the 'righteous' and injustice. The weak, the dominated, and the exploited are, as we have seen, in many ways far less guilty than their oppressors. However, they are by that token not necessarily at all less sinful, or potentially less sinful. The rightness and justice of their cause—established by the inequality of guilt—does not indicate, says Niebuhr frequently, a special hold on virtue. When, after a radical change of power, the oppressed become the rulers, their pride, self-concern, and tendency to absolutize *their* cause will mean that they in turn will be unjust toward those dominated by them.

How quickly the poor, the weak, the deprived of yesterday, may, on gaining a social victory over their detractors, exhibit the same arrogance and the same will to power which they abhorred in their opponents and which they were inclined to regard as a congenital sin of their enemies. . . . This is the self-righteousness of the weak as opposed to the self-righteousness of the powerful. (ND 1:226)

Therefore,

It is only by an ultimate analysis from beyond all human standards that the particular guilt of the great and the good men of history is revealed. (ND 1:227)

Thus are the two sides of the paradox brought together as a means of illuminating the obscurities, and yet the validities, of historical experience. We are all equally sinners, and it is only by understanding this equality that we can see through the illusions of our partial social judgments and the truth of our inequality of guilt.

∞

This theological analysis of the collective sins of humankind has been heavy going. I would like, therefore, to pause briefly to illustrate what has been said by outlining a true narrative that seems to me, in retrospect, to have enacted its main points. As Niebuhr always said, experience—concrete experience—provides the best medium for understanding the meaning of theological symbols. I spent most of World War II—two and a half years—in a Japanese civilian internment camp on mainland China, having gone to Beijing to teach English as a young college graduate in 1940. The Japanese army had invaded eastern China in 1936, and they occupied it—including Beijing—until 1945 at the end of the war. Hence during the time I was teaching at Yenching University, we were surrounded by the large Japanese armed forces then in North China. The attack on Pearl Harbor and the commencement of hostilities between Japan and the United States in December 1941 startled us in Beijing as it did everyone else. Quickly at that beginning, the Japanese rounded all of us up and kept us under close surveillance. In March 1943 all "enemy nationals" in North China—British, American, Belgian, Dutch, and later Italian—were imprisoned in an internment camp in Shantung Province, three hundred miles south of Beijing, located in a then-abandoned Presbyterian mission compound near Weihsien. The camp was managed and run by the Japanese Consular Police, a force staffed by soldiers and officers for the moment on noncombatant duty. Enclosed by a high wall complete with barbed wire and machine guns, this was a small compound, an area of roughly 100 by 200 yards; into this space were crammed two thousand people housed in the classrooms, the hospital, and the student rooms of the old mission school.[6]

Of course we had to do all our own work; to the vast unease of that population, made up mostly of colonials, no servants were present. Thus we organized ourselves into work groups; we baked, cooked, stoked, pumped water, carted the meager supplies the Japanese delivered to the gates, and sought as well to educate, to entertain, and to discipline ourselves. Existence was intensely difficult, especially for those many (some four hundred) who were over sixty years old, and for the mothers of the four hundred children under twelve. Life was cold, dirty, muddy, inconvenient, and lacking adequate food, sanitation, and space. We did not suffer in any drastic sense (I was then twenty-four); but, for any who were over forty, it was life definitely lived on the margin, infinitely precarious and insecure, replete with hardships in the present and anxieties about the very uncertain future. Soon, however, to my astonishment, all of this vastly uncomfortable, inconvenient, and precarious life, with its forced simplicity, hard work, boredom, and hunger, became 'normal' to us; we accepted it

6. A much more complete account of this experience is found in my book *Shantung Compound* (New York: Harper & Row, 1966).

and quite creatively built a bearable life on it—but underneath our daily consciousness ran the dark undercurrent of continuous insecurity and so of nagging anxiety about the future.

Generally everyone showed enormous cheerfulness, courage, and especially ingenuity. In our bakery, our kitchens, our repair shops, our hauling teams, we gradually created what we proudly felt to be a remarkably viable civilization. Nonetheless, at times crises arose, particularly when the securities we had so laboriously achieved were threatened; and so, to my continual amazement (though I had read and reread Niebuhr), people (and I certainly include myself) acted very much more selfishly than I would have expected. This included not only the gunrunners, the streetwalkers, or the shady characters in the camp, but also the "nice" people, the 'moral' people, often Christian, who would be horrified to do the wrong thing. During the camp I was aware of only the political and moral level of these events, that is, of the destructive political and social consequences of such actions of us all; the theological meaning of this experience did not then, I must admit, enter my head. After the camp, recalling this whole experience, I saw, as in an archeological dig, its deeper layers that were relevant to the theological analysis we have here traced. In the end it seemed to me to be an amazingly apt illustration of what Niebuhr called "the facts of experience," facts that seemed to validate in very large part the Biblical interpretation he had articulated.

My first hint of the presence of what we can call moral or spiritual problems came right at the start of camp life, when I found myself the junior member of the camp Housing Committee. Our initial responsibility was to make the quarters of the internees more fair and so more bearable. The Japanese had parceled out the housing very quickly at the beginning, and so there were great inequalities in the living spaces people possessed. We also had to make room for new arrivals, which forced us continually into the unpleasant role of even further crowding some of the internees. Basically everyone was hopelessly crowded, though clearly some more than others.

Single men and women were piled into classrooms with only two feet between beds—not hard at all for twenty-year-olds but very difficult for middle-aged or older women and men. In one small classroom we found sixteen men; in a classroom the same size across the hall, there were fourteen. The solution, so rational it glowed, was easy: move one from the first room into the second. I proposed this to the second room and received an unexpected response: "Send him in here, buddy [or "mate"], and we'll boot him out again. We aren't crowding up one more inch!"

"But this is absolutely fair, and clearly just: fifteen persons in two rooms each of the same size as the other."

"We couldn't care less; that is their problem and not ours."

So much for Descartes' clear and distinct ideas! I went back to the housing office considerably sobered.

The second case was if anything even more surprising. Besides the class buildings, the compound contained rows of small rooms for students at the mission middle school. These rooms were nine feet by twelve and were intended for two students. Hence for a couple they were, for camp life, exceedingly generous. But for a couple with two children, they were hopelessly overcrowded. At the beginning of camp, the Japanese had given only one of these rooms to families with two small (under twelve) children—a miserable situation for mother and father, especially in winter when the entire family, and all it owned, had to exist, play, eat, and sleep in that small space. Families of four, and there were about twenty-five of them, with children over twelve, were given two rooms next to each other. The result was the one case of luxurious living in the camp: two teenagers in one room and frequently located next to a family of four in one room.

In any case, shortly after the camp began, a delegation of mothers of small children came to our office to demand that we do something: "You are making us bear the entire burden of the war!" And they were nearly right. So we combed over the camp again looking for space in which to move teenagers into dorms so that the other families could expand a bit. We found the space in some empty schoolrooms and arranged for an adult teacher to move into each new dorm to supervise it. One of these was Eric Liddell, the Olympic winner in 1924; he was later a missionary in Tientsin and so was in the camp. He was, of course, the hero of the film *Chariots of Fire*. Then we approached the twenty or so families of four with small children, who had two rooms, to discuss this move, which, unhappily for them, would vastly reduce their space.

I was by now hardly surprised that none of the families agreed to this move, nor that two of them adamantly refused to talk to us about it. One of them, a British business executive, threatened, as he slammed the door, to sue me for harassment. "This is my castle, and I will not give you an inch of it!" I recall asking him through the door what court we should meet in: Japanese, Chinese, British, or American? Fascinated, my partner and I called on each of these families and urged them to comply. Most of them had good reasons why they should not, could not, give up family space. "I am a preacher whose sermons are very important to the missionary community; I need space in which to write my sermons"—this from a Lutheran pastor. "We have prayed carefully over this, and received the answer: maintain a good Christian home for your two boys"—this from a prominent, Princeton-educated, Presbyterian missionary. When we asked this worthy pair, "How about the good Christian home of the over-crowded family next door?" the reply was, "Aren't the Japanese wicked?" In a meeting of all the families together, each side (some forty families) only saw the rationality of their own arguments.

Finally, after much soul-searching, we took the fathers of the most re-calcitrant families to our Japanese boss. We prepared the way carefully, and made the latter promise not to punish them in any way. He kept his promise and merely told them to obey the camp committee—and meekly as well as immediately, they submitted. It was, apparently, easier to bow to an order backed by enemy power then to an argument backed by only col-legial reason and, hopefully, morals. Finally, therefore, the families adjusted themselves, the dorms were formed, and those with small children had more space.

The final case that I shall discuss was much the most dramatic. It was also the most troubling. It showed with startling clarity not only the self-concern and self-deception of all of us, even the 'moral' among us, but even more the direct connection between injustice to our neighbor and social violence—how self-concern breeds injustice followed by conflict.

There had been a repatriation of Americans from Japanese-held Asia—and a corresponding one of Japanese from the United States—in the sum-mer of 1943. One boat from Asia and one from America met at Goa, In-dia, and exchanged their cargoes. Two hundred Americans left our camp in August 1943. They were, of course, a carefully selected group: men who had been imprisoned by the Japanese, older people, single women, and men whose wives had earlier gone home at State Department request. Young men of twenty-four were at the bottom of everyone's list, includ-ing my own. The camp, I must say, lost greatly by this evacuation; it seemed to those of us left behind that most of the creative, cooperative, and cheer-ful of the four hundred Americans were now gone.

We did, however, gain as well as lose by this exchange, for the American Red Cross took advantage of this event to send to American internees in Asia generous parcels of food. Hence, to our amazement and delight, nine months later, in July 1944, the Japanese delivered, with a covering letter, one parcel to each of the two hundred Americans left in the camp. These were extraordinary parcels: forty pounds of carefully chosen supplies, they included tinned meats, butter, cheese, dried milk, sugar, jam, dried fruit—and cigarettes! (Looking back from the year 2000, that seems strange in-deed.) As we found out, such a parcel could keep its owner from hunger for six months. What a vast amount of wealth! These parcels were gener-ously shared by the Americans with the other internees and the extra food helped keep off radical hunger well through the fall of 1944.

By December, however, the benefit provided by the parcels was gone, supplies continued to drop, and we all wondered how we would make it through the cold North China winter. (The war would be over in another seven months, but we did not then know that.) Then early in January, this time quite without warning, the front gates opened, and donkey cart after donkey cart piled high with the same sort of parcels rolled in. No one knew to whom these new parcels were addressed; all we knew was that again they were from the American Red Cross and that there were fifteen hundred of them; one hundred more than the fourteen hundred persons in the camp. They were unloaded and stacked in the center of the camp, where they were guarded by the Japanese soldiers and became the object of the fascinated gaze of every internee. As we stood, a dazed crowd around the huge piles, speculation about the packages began: "How wonderful," said the British, "fifteen hundred parcels and fourteen hundred of us—why, that is one apiece this time with a half parcel extra leftover for each of the Yanks!" "How wonderful," said some of the surrounding Americans, "this time it's seven and a half parcels for each of us." Needless to say, harsh words quickly followed these comments as the crowd became increasingly uneasy. I remember thinking how ironic it was that the arrival of so much material good for us all should threaten to create serious and ugly dissension.

Soon a notice from the commandant went up: the parcels were to be distributed the next morning, one for each internee and one and a half for each American. My friend Stu and I decided that this was a remarkably sensible decision on the part of the Japanese authorities, one capable, we hoped, of keeping the already vocal "100 percent Americans" among us satisfied. The next morning everyone lined up for the distribution. It is hard to describe adequately the joy, the relief, the abundance of good spirits that characterized that crowd, or the gratitude for the continuing "generosity" of America for providing so bountifully for everyone in the camp.

Suddenly, however, a Japanese guard strode up to the front of the two long lines and put up another notice. People who read it came away looking angry; Stu and I went up to it with sinking feelings. It said that, due to protest from the American community, the parcels would not be distributed now and that a query about what to do had been sent to Tokyo. Immediately fights began to break out in the compound, frequently between men who long since had become very good friends. Suddenly from a relatively cooperative and international community we had degenerated into a brawling set of outraged nationals. For the first time guards had to patrol our walks to prevent violence and conflict. The destructive sequence of insecurity and anxiety leading to a driving self-concern and resulting in injustice, conflict, and the ultimate destruction of community was crystal clear. Had we been left alone and armed, we might well have destroyed ourselves over those parcels.

That night a number of us—all single or without children and so not so sorely tempted as some of the other Americans—got together to see what we might do to help restore our shattered community. We were sure that these protesters—eight or more youngish Americans—did not represent the majority of the two hundred of us and that if we could show this by a survey, we could help restore our mutual trust. We were aware that the community could survive only through mutual cooperation and that some level of mutual trust was necessary for that cooperation. So the next day we each went among the Americans on our list asking each how he or she felt about the parcel distribution.

The first I met was Benny, a rather tough character from Chicago. Benny looked me straight in the eye and said, "Look, these are *my* sandwiches, not theirs. I intend to get every last one of them that is coming to me. Don't talk to me about sharing them!" At least, I thought, Benny is very honest. Next I ran into a young American lawyer from Tientsin. "Look Gilkey, you understand I'm not interested in the parcels. I'm interested only in the legal principle involved: this is American property, given us by the generosity of the American Red Cross. The Japs have no right to distribute them to others; it should all come to us. But understand, I'm only interested in these important principles of property. Where would we be without them?"

Last of all came an older missionary. "I'm not interested at all in the parcels, Gilkey; you understand that. My only concern is that this distribution be a moral distribution, and freely made by each of us and so made for the right moral reason. A distribution ordered by the Japanese authorities is coercive; it has no moral content since no one voluntarily wills to do it. There is neither virtue nor merit there. I say, give the parcels to us, and let us freely and voluntarily give them to others. The whole thing will then be moral."

"How many parcels, Reverend, do you think you would give away of your seven and a half?"

"Oh certainly at least three!"

The fact that a more even distribution among the internees might be more just and so more moral—not to mention that it would certainly feed many more hungry people or that his pious plea for voluntary choice cloaked a selfish concern for four and a half parcels, instead of one and half by 'coerced' distribution, never crossed this pious man's mind. He assured me, vigorously, that he, like the lawyer, was only interested in moral principles.

When we got together that evening to pool our results of the day, we were all very discouraged. It was evident that a majority of the two hundred Americans opted, mostly for the very noblest of reasons, for keeping the parcels. Since we were ourselves not really tempted in the matter—though sorely so in others—we found this hard to believe. But that these actions based on legal and moral principles could lead to violence and conflict, of that we were certain. Meanwhile the camp seethed uneasily for a week while the soldiers patrolled our streets. Finally another notice was put up: word had arrived from Tokyo that each internee would receive one parcel and that the remaining one hundred parcels would be sent to another camp! Not least among the ironies of this event was the fact that a divine justice—which abstracted from the treasure of each American one-half parcel—was mediated against our common wishes by our enemy and not by ourselves.

Looking back, I can see that everything we have here discussed was in this experience: our contingency and vulnerability, our awareness of that vulnerability and so our anxiety, our consequent driving self-concern that led to obviously 'unjust' demands and potentially destructive actions—and our need to deceive ourselves that all this was 'good', a matter of principle, an act of the highest virtue. Among those I talked to, only Benny was honest. I have experienced no clearer example of the way injustice arises from anxious self-concern, the way injustice cloaks itself as noble virtue, and the way that injustice leads, or can lead, to violence and conflict. These were strange, unexpected, and paradoxical 'facts of experience' that were, for me at least, made surprisingly intelligible by the Biblical interpretation Niebuhr was able to give them.

One final ironic note. When I returned from China, I began to give speeches about the camp experience to schools, Rotary Clubs, women's luncheon clubs, and so on. This was certainly to help raise money for graduate school—I had, needless to say, earned no salary during the war, nor did I receive the GI Bill. But I also wished to use this experience to illustrate what to me was an important message. Not yet that this was an example of "original sin"; the insight that this was the case only came to me later, after much more reflection. Rather the message was that a community could die from a lack of moral strength as quickly as it could expire from material want; that hatred, conflict, and self-destruction followed from injustice and a dearth of sharing as night follows day. As Augustine had said, justice is as necessary for a community's survival as are material supplies and self-defense. Over and over I told to these audiences the above story—and some other experiences—of how very normal people, even Americans (!), might act 'immorally' under the intense pressure of anxiety, and the grim results that followed for a secure community from selfish be- havior. Each time the audience was shocked and horrified to think that Americans could act that way toward their neighbors in want. And each time I drew the contemporary parallel: America was now rich and our for- mer allies were poor, and that therefore the United Nations Relief Associ- ation and then, a year later, the Marshall Plan, were not only the expedient thing to do but the *right* thing, both being utterly necessary for any hope of a creative and peaceful world community. It was a persuasive case. And over and over the audience would withdraw, would deny the parallel— and some would begin to mutter that once again 'foreigners' were trying to get hold of what belonged to us. Each time my mind was carried from the tree-lined streets of suburban America—and its well-stuffed cupboards— back to the grime and misery of Weihsien. I felt right at home. Whatever Niebuhr was trying to tell us about ourselves was still there, then and now.

Sin: In Bondage yet Free, Inevitable but Not Necessary

We have worked our way through the major categories of Niebuhr's analysis of sin: creature and image, insecurity and anxiety, creativity and pride, rebellion and injustice—and self-deception. Niebuhr has tried to show, with some success, that these 'Biblical' categories from the classical tradition of theology,[1] "absurd" and irrelevant as they are for most modern eyes, really fit the confusing facts of our ordinary individual and social experience better than any other modes of interpretation (e.g., ND 1:225–26, 249). Now I proceed to the center of that classical tradition, where the most stunning paradoxes of all are to be found: the apparent contradiction that each of us is in bondage, yet free; that our common sin is universal, yet

---

1. I have marked the word 'Biblical' because Niebuhr regarded what he considered 'Biblical' symbols not only as basic or fundamental to Scripture but also as representing the center of the 'classical' tradition in theology. By these symbols (creation, fall, revelation, incarnation, atonement, church, eschatology) he—and a whole generation that followed his—meant those symbols that provided, as we shall see, the structure for his theology, and for that of his 'neo-orthodox' contemporaries. And in truth these were the symbols that provided the structure for most of the theological tradition, especially the Pauline-Augustinian and Reformation line. It was, I believe, because they were held to be at once 'Biblical' and 'classical' in this sense (not in the sense of Hellenic or Hellenistic) that they were so deeply honored during this period. It is also the reason, as we have noted, that this school of Biblical theology was termed "neo-orthodox." Hence arose the surprising fact that the second generation 'Biblical' neo-orthodox found themselves much more interested in, and much more impressed by, the historical tradition of theology than were either the liberals that preceded them or even the Biblical theologians that taught them. This was also, perhaps, one of the surprising bridges so often crossed in my generation between Biblical theology and the Anglican and the Roman communions.

not a necessity; that therefore sin is inevitable, yet we are responsible. Niebuhr insists that these paradoxes—this conjunction of determinism on the one side and freedom on the other—not only express, if interpreted correctly, the Biblical view of sin; even more they fit the confusing yet undeniable facts of our experience (e.g., ND 1:249, 262–63). Let us try to see how Niebuhr argues these two claims.

He begins with what he admits is an "absurdity":

> Sin is natural for man in the sense it is universal but not in the sense it is necessary. . . . Sin is to be regarded as neither a necessity of man's nature nor yet as a pure caprice of his will. It proceeds from a defect of the will, for which reason it is not completely deliberate; but since it is the will in which it is found and the will presupposes freedom, the defect cannot be attributed to a taint in man's nature. (ND 1:242)

What this paradox means, as Augustine had formulated it, is that humans are in truth free—they can decide to do this or that: "I can clasp my knees when I wish" (Augustine, *Confessions,* 8.8). But they are not free to change their will, to love as they may wish, or as they intend to do, or as they should do (ND 1:243–44). As Augustine had said, "I can move my arm, but I cannot change my love." Sin exists at a level seemingly out of easy reach of our simple exercise of freedom, at the level, for Augustine, of our fundamental love, which is the level that determines all else we do. Moreover, Niebuhr, again following Augustine, contends we do not sin deliberately; in fact we do it against our conscious intentions. Yet it is not a necessity, for we do it "willingly," "voluntarily," through our freedom. And in remorse or the experience of conscience we know inwardly that we are responsible for what we have done. All this we experience: an enslavement to ourselves we cannot seem to shake even when we seek to lose our egotism; and yet one for which we experience a sense of responsibility. Most strange of all, this enslavement or bondage that captures and enthralls our free will is itself an aspect of our freedom, an inevitability for which we know we are responsible.

These Augustinian paradoxes have been denied as contradictory and absurd by the tradition called "Pelagian" and, in agreement with that tradition, by most of modern reflection on ethics. According to these views, we can only be held responsible for that which we have consciously chosen in freedom to do. Hence anything we term 'sin', for which we recognize we are held responsible, must be the result of a genuinely free choice. Sin is, therefore—I phrase this position as precisely as I can—the 'conscious choice of a known evil, a deliberate transgression of a recognized law.' Thus since the experience of responsibility seems to require that in each act the will will be free to do either the good or the evil, any "bias toward sin," which is also a part of universal experience, comes not from the will itself but from outside the will: from the bodily senses, from impulse, from nature (ND 1:245–46), or as many contemporary biologists insist, from our genes, our 'selfish genes'.[2] In short, that bias, so interpreted, is necessitating, something that impels our will from outside the will and so something for which we are not responsible. As Niebuhr notes, liberal theology (and the early Niebuhr) followed Pelagius at this point and regarded sin as always a conscious and deliberate choice and the tendency toward sin the result of our animal inheritance, our primitive desires, the "impulses of nature."

Augustine, following Paul's lead, rejected this understanding of sin as composed of conscious acts against the law, as deliberate acts of malice, as did the Augustinian tradition that followed them: "The good we could and would, we do not do" (Rom 7:14–24); "I can move my hand, but I cannot change my will" (Augustine)—that is, the will that wills to do this or that is not able to will itself to love God, even if it wants to.[3] The will thus experiences itself as unable on the one hand to be its true self, dominated by what seems to be an alien force, in some sense bound. Nonetheless, on the other hand, it also experiences that it is the will itself that binds itself, not 'nature', body, or necessity, for in remorse we recognize our voluntary involvement in this and so our responsibility. Niebuhr now agrees

2. See esp. Richard Dawkins, *The Selfish Gene* (Oxford: Oxford University Press, 1976), and R. Alexander, *The Biology of Moral Systems* (Amsterdam: de Gruyter, 1987).

3. *Confessions,* bks. 7 and 8; see also *City of God* 7.6, 9. Augustine interprets this bondage in terms of a bondage of love. Love is, he says, "the gravity of the soul," i.e., a force that propels the soul in the direction of the soul's love. Soul for Augustine is, of course, immaterial, that is, Greek. It is the principle of life, of intelligence, and of will, the seat of choice and so of freedom. But as is here clear, the soul is—and the will is—determined by its love, not by its mind. If the soul's love is for God, the soul rises to a knowledge of the truth and the possibility of loving according to its nature. If, however, its love is for the world, of worldly things, and of fame, then the soul is propelled downward, away from God, from itself, and from its true nature. As a consequence, it cannot rise again by its own power until the direction of its love is transformed by grace, i.e., from *cupiditas* to *caritas.* The soul has once chosen this false love, but once chosen, it is unable to change its "gravity." Clearly this fascinating analogy with gravity was based on Aristotle's *Physics,* where gravity was the force that propelled each body to its "proper" place, up or down. These Augustinian conceptions of love, which see our sin as the warping of our love into a false love of the world and view our attainment of *caritas* as our love for God given to us by a grace that transforms our love, quite dominated the medieval world (*City of God* 11.28 and *The*

thoroughly with this tradition: sin is neither a necessity of nature for which we are not responsible, nor is it a deliberate defiance of the good. On the contrary, it is done "under the misapprehension that it is good"; that is, as Niebuhr has shown, because we have deceived ourselves that what our self-interest pushes us to do is really the good, our moral wills should will to do.

This analysis, so far conducted, let us note, 'empirically', appealing at each step to ordinary experience, has brought us within hailing distance of the classical doctrine of original sin. That ancient doctrine sought to explain the experience of bondage, to tell us why we find ourselves apparently forced by our will against our will to do what is wrong. And it also seemed to explain why the world suffers so grievously from evil, violence, conflict, and destruction; it is because of 'original' sin that we suffer internally and externally, and it is because of 'original' sin that we die.

Interestingly, Niebuhr has not mentioned that doctrine (and barely the Genesis account) prior to this, his final chapter on sin (ND 1:242–43). Clearly, he has not deduced his analysis of our experience of sin from this doctrine, which was widely scorned in the liberal theology that preceded him. What he has sought to show, as he always does, is that the empirical content of our actual experience—our anxiety, pride, self-deceit, and now our experience of bondage—can only be understood in Biblical terms, and so in terms of those symbols drawn from that Biblical account. It is plain, therefore, that the main bases for his theological arguments are these undeniable aspects of experience, aspects now guided, shaped, and so illuminated by what he regards as the Biblical viewpoint. Considering the many similar reflections on these same themes in his own early 'pre-Biblical' works, it is clear that an appeal to experience constitutes as much a major element of his method as does the appeal to the new Biblical categories that have for him—and for many who heard and read him—clarified or brought into reflective order what he had found in experience. As in his entire mature theology, the *content* or *materials* of his theological

---

Trinity 8.5, 6, and 10.7, 11). As I remarked in another context, Augustine here is not so far from the position of the Reformation as history's conflicts seem to show. A love for God that allows the soul to be thoroughly itself, i.e., loving toward others and itself (*caritas*) is set by Augustine in the categories of Hellenistic culture but otherwise is not so different from the Lutheran "trust" in God or commitment to God as "faith," which is the response to the grace of *agape,* and from which follow all the works of love that make a human truly human. Here faith or trust has replaced love as the determining center of the soul's life—but in many ways the essential contours of these conceptions are similar.

understanding—in this case sin, the bondage of sin, and yet the responsi-bility for sin—come from experience and from reflection on experience, while the *categories* or *forms* that shape, illumine, and make sense of that ex-perience arise from what is for him Biblical revelation.

On the basis both of experience and Biblical authority Niebuhr, as had Augustine, disputes Pelagius: sin is not always (in fact almost never) a con-scious and deliberate choice of known evil; on the contrary, it is done be-lieving it is the good. It is, therefore, both unconscious and conscious (ND 1:250), the first because we believe our own self-deception, and the latter because we know secretly not only of our own dominant self-concern in this matter but also that we have eagerly deceived ourselves. We are dimly aware that we are not as good as we claim to be. Hence we seem to be in bondage to a force, outside our will and yet inside it too, that drives us al-most against our will to do what we do not intend—or know that we should not intend. And we know, through our experience of remorse, that this force itself is in fact our responsibility and so is intertwined with our freedom.

If, then, this is our experience, the question arises: What is this force ly-ing back of our conscious will? Why is our will, although apparently quite free to choose whatever it wishes to choose, still not free to be itself, to be less hostile, less egotistic, more loving? Why is our freedom not free to be itself? We know well enough that self-forgetfulness and love represent the conditions of authentic humanity and authentic community. We also know that egoism, hostility, and conflict are the conditions of destruction, of persons, of families, and of societies alike. And we can see the effects of hostility all around us. Why can we not be our real selves?

Let us note several aspects of these questions. First, this search for the 'bias toward sin' has been a modern as well as an ancient quest. Perhaps the longest reflective tradition has, like the Pelagians, assigned that bias to the workings of factors outside the human will: the influence of the body and its desires (the 'animal nature' of men and women), of certain cultures, of family, even of 'blood', and so on. Interestingly, Hellenic philosophy, Enlightenment rationalism, and postevolutionary liberalism (*and* the early Niebuhr) joined in ascribing this bias to the 'lower' forces of instinct and desire as opposed to the 'liberating' forces of mind and moral will. Closer to Niebuhr's later view is the tradition of Greek tragedy, in which Ate, at the command of the gods, blinds the tragic hero and hence precipitates, through his subsequent free acts, his downfall. Closest of all are, strangely, the modern sociological and psychological traditions in which forces working within the mind and the will transform both into attitudes, ideas, and actions that are unexpected and not wanted—and hence cause the victim's inevitable destruction. In classical Marxism and Freudianism, class consciousness and neurosis, respectively, work 'under' and 'behind' the conscious surface of life, corrupting our norms, deceiving our judgments, diverting our intentions, and ultimately producing intentional actions that lead to destruction. The contemporary debate as to whether it is 'nurture' (family, community, society) or 'nature' (genes or biological inheritance) that is the 'cause' of evil (why not of the good?) in the human situation, constitutes in the present this old theme.

For Niebuhr these modern explanations of our waywardness represent an interesting and universal recognition of the experiences of the bondage of our freedom, the unconscious deception of our minds, and the unintended corruption of our wills. But to him all fail to see the freedom latent within that corrupting force itself: it is not an external or alien power over against our will, but an inner power resident in our will itself, a result or effect of our freedom and hence a bias for which we are, however obscurely, responsible. We are neither as free in our ordinary acts as most modern moral reflections suppose, nor are our 'slips' and our 'sins' as innocent as most modern 'scientific' explanations of evil argue. An inevitable self-interest diverts even the good and intentional acts of our freedom, and responsibility and so freedom qualify even the bias toward sin that we repudiate.

> The actual sin follows more inevitably from the bias towards sin than is usually assumed. On the other hand the bias towards sin is something more than a mere lag of nature or physical impulse or historical circumstance. There is, in other words, less freedom in the actual sin and more responsibility for the bias towards sin (original sin) than moralistic interpretations can understand. (ND 1:250)

Niebuhr is adamant that the experience of remorse that signals our continuing responsibility is neither neurotic nor an illusion. The self is responsible—and, therefore, in some sense free—at even the profoundest level; any hint, therefore, of necessity, of an external causation that renders our action not at all 'our fault', is for him unempirical, a sheer denial of the obvious facts of experience: "The fact of responsibility is attested by the feeling of remorse or repentance which follows the sinful action" (ND 1:255).

To regard remorse or repentance, the experience of conscience, as an illusion or a neurosis is for Niebuhr absurd; no man, he would say, maintains this posture for long in actual life. It is assumed in every court of law—even by psychiatrists who testify there—that persons are in some measure responsible for what they do and that an absence of 'conscience' bespeaks a gravely abnormal, if not psychotic, state. To deny, therefore, our responsibility and so our residual freedom, is a purely 'theoretical' endeavor, and it is one in which the attachment to an objective method is allowed to overcome the clear data of actual personal and social experience. It is to throw out arbitrarily certain experiences (e.g., those of blame, of remorse, and of guilt) in favor of other experiences (e.g., experiences of sensory falsification or verification) because the latter fit a presupposed empiricist viewpoint or dogma. As we have repeatedly seen, for Niebuhr inner or 'personal' experiences, individual or social, represent as valid clues to reality as do so-called outer or objective experiences of the external side of social relations, or even sensory experiences of causal relations between entities. In the end, all represent 'our' experiences. And each of us, in our actual life, considers both sorts to be valid clues to what is real. All are, in one mode or another, 'inner'; and yet all are in one mode or another shareable, and all are taken to be clues to what is real. All, therefore, must be considered in any valid interpretation of the whole of life. On the validity of inner experience, Niebuhr agreed with both idealists and existentialists and with many of his contemporaries, for example, Whitehead and Tillich.

It also seems evident that experiences of both outer social evil and inner personal participation in sharing in that evil increased in scope and intensity in the first half of the twentieth century. Clearly the educated classes of the eighteenth and nineteenth centuries had no similar experiences of comparable weight. As Albrecht Ritschl said in the 1870s about original sin: "The concept [of original sin] is quite useless as a guiding principle in judging our conduct, just because the intensity of our consciousness of moral opposition to the good is much less, and exaggerations of that kind could only serve to make us untrue to ourselves."[4] And even the experiential theologians of the later nineteenth century and the empirical theologians of the early twentieth, found no "experimental" validity—only dogmatic authority—in the tradition of Pauline, Augustinian, and Reformation theology that had grounded itself on just those inner experiences of bondage, of responsibility, and so of repentance. But if works of literature, drama, and theology, not to mention art, are any indication, in the first half of the twentieth century the general experience of a pervasive, and intractable evil, followed by destruction of self and society, became

4. Albrecht Ritschl, *The Christian Doctrine of Justification and Reconciliation,* vol. 3 (1870–74; English translation, Clifton, N.J.: Reference Book Publishers, 1966), chap. 5, sec. 41.

very much more widespread. Almost certainly this trend was initiated by the turmoil of that period's social events, by the conflict, cruelty, and destruction of those decades, and the evident disorientation of persons in twentieth-century society. During the twentieth century we have, apparently, returned in part to the sorts of sensibility about human evil that characterized the end of the Hellenistic era, the early medieval period, and the Reformation and early modern period, when these theologians (Paul, Augustine, et al.) were accepted as formulating accurate descriptions of our real problems and providing desperately needed answers to those problems.

Granting, then, that these experiences, and the theologies that emanate from them, point to something real and pervasive in the human situation, we can understand the sense of validity that had for so long accompanied the 'doctrine' of original sin, and the continuing importance of that doctrine in our tradition.[5] This strange doctrine has been there not only because of the apparent authority of the Biblical story, of its Pauline interpretation, and of the dogma that grew out of that story. Even more it has persisted because it seemed to explain a widely experienced puzzle in ordinary life: Why are my life and our life (in family, in institutions, and in community) in such a mess, so out of control, so dominated by a self-concern in which we know we participate and a consequent suffering that burdens us all? Above all, why are each of us, who are free, quite unable to rectify that situation, to be serene as we want to be, to be rational, above all to be loving? We know these things are necessary if our common life is to be normal, even bearable—Why are we so continually unable to achieve them? As Kierkegaard said, only when you have reached this sort of question, this stage of self-understanding, can you comprehend what this doctrine is about; and as Luther said, "A theologian is a theologian only by living and dying and being damned." These are, unfortunately, twentieth-century questions, uncomfortably familiar to us all, as they were often in the past—and that is my point.

The doctrine of original sin sought—on the authority of Scripture—to answer this urgent question: Why are each of us, and the world with us, in such a mess? And the answer was: we are in a mess because all of us are dominated by an inherited 'taint', something we are born with but that is not part of the nature that God gave us. That good-created nature explains why we long to be good; but it does not explain why we so consistently fall

5. One can certainly say the same of the categories of *maya* in the Hindu tradition and of *desire* in the Buddhist tradition.

short of that longing. And that continual missing of the mark is something we have all inherited from our first ancestors, Adam and Eve. This taint is, according to medieval doctrine, "concupiscence," an inordinate desire we cannot control. This inheritance comes to us as a result of the Fall, that fatal act of the first generation with whose baleful consequences all subsequent generations are born. Then, having been born with this taint, with concupiscence, we each become in turn its agents, doing freely what our wounded will determines. Because of it we too sin, and because of our sin, we die.

As I have intimated, this tradition, weird and unjust as it may now seem to us, had some continuing authority on its own. It seemed to tell us where these unconscious urges we wanted yet did not want came from; and it told us why, though created by a loving God, we all—good and bad alike—sin and then die. And yet this seeming inevitability did not infringe our own essential or created freedom; we are not here subject to an original, irreducible, and a permanent fate. Its cause had been the free act, the conscious rebellion, of Adam and Eve—and hence it was an act whose consequences on us could be repealed by grace. As Augustine argued, if sin had been a part of creation, of our nature, it would have been unredeemable; but it was grounded in a historical act, and so it could be revoked by another historical event, a Second Adam who rescued us from the consequences of our common sin. All this could be credible not only on Biblical and ecclesiastical authority, but because at each step of the logic of the story it corresponded to our own experience: of our inability to control our own freedom, of our unwanted yet wanted acts of self-destruction, of our inescapable remorse at what we had done, and our continually experienced hope for redemption through grace—and our inescapable death. Our own daily sins against one another, of which we are all too well aware, are thus partly explained by the original sin that we have inherited as children of Adam, and from which we are redeemed or saved by the person and the work of Christ. In experience as in dogma, there seems to be 'sin' lying back of our specific acts of sin, 'original' both in time and as the act of the first pair, and 'original' in prominence as the taint (like the Hindu *maya* or the Buddhist *desire*) bringing our own specific sins into being.

This is the classical doctrine that Niebuhr both accepts and refashions. He accepts it (over against Pelagius) as expressing symbolically and hence making intelligible the presence of an undertow, a strong bias, an unconscious determiner of our conscious acts on the surface of experience: our thoughts, our intentions, and our plans, decisions, and external actions. These are in large part subject to our wills; they are conscious; many of them are or can be deliberate. On this level we are apparently free, at least inwardly. Yet experience of ourselves (and especially of others!) shows that these actions are themselves pushed, driven, impelled, forced to be more self-concerned, more unjust and insensitive, more unloving, than we claim or want to think of ourselves as being. As I have noted, many modern views accept such an unconscious yet determining factor on our intentions, our judgments, and our behavior. Marx saw it as class consciousness, Freud as neurosis, modern biology as an animal inheritance, and modern sociobiology as "the selfish gene." Thus this concept is not at all absurd in modern eyes. For Niebuhr all of these modern alternatives are too deterministic, and they do not explain our deep sense of repentance at even this level. "There is less freedom in the actual sin and more responsibility for the bias towards sin than moralistic interpretations understand" (ND 1:250).

There is, then, an underlying determiner or shaper of our conscious life, yet one that is a part of that life, conscious and yet unconscious, an aspect of our freedom. To this our experience both of incapacity and of remorse attests. So far Niebuhr is Augustinian: our wills are in bondage, and the cause of that bondage (original sin) is a strange, paradoxical mixture of freedom and necessity.

Niebuhr, however, differs completely and dramatically with Augustine—and with the entire pre-Enlightenment tradition—in his analysis of the 'cause' of that experienced bias or undertow. For that tradition the cause, as I have noted, had been the free and deliberate act of Adam and Eve; added to that act were the unexpected and fatal consequences of that act:[6] the condemnation by God not only of the unfortunate pair but of all of their descendents. This condemnation had several elements: (1) the inheritance of concupiscence by Adam's descendants through the act of conception; (2) the loss of *caritas* and faith for all of Adam's race; (3) the inevitable termination of the life of all descendants in death (what Augustine called "the first death," the death of the body); and (4) the condemnation for eternity for all those who do not receive the grace of redemption (what Augustine termed "the second death").[7] With some changes this general view was continued in the Reformation and in Protestant ortho-

6. Augustine, *The Trinity* 4.3.

7. Augustine argues that because this is historical and not an ontological cause—i.e., coming after creation and in history via a historical act of the historical creature Adam—it is not a *necessitating* cause, as is our bodily need for food. Thus it can be redeemed. Niebuhr and the other neo-orthodox deny (as did Pelagius), as we shall see, this role of Adam as a historical cause of our ills, and yet they seem unaware that this denial might push them into an ontological necessity, i.e., that the results of the fall are the consequences of creation.

doxy.[8] Note that all but the last (eternal condemnation) are continually experienced:[9] the presence of concupiscence, the loss of love, and the inevitable coming of death. Hence, as I noted, the doctrine seems to be continually revalidated in experience.

I have gone through this brief explanation of the classical doctrine of sin to make clear how dramatically Niebuhr has refashioned this doctrine. As he clearly states, all "literal" elements of the story are now gone. With the drastic change in our understanding of the past history of the cosmos, of the long-developing history of prehuman life, and of human prehistory, this story of a creation six thousand years ago and of an act of the first cre ated pair has become, as Niebuhr names it, a "literal" account that cannot be accepted. Adam and Eve are now for him *symbols* of the human condition, not any longer *causes* of that situation. The Fall thus has ceased to point to a historical event in the past and has become a *symbol,* a description of our perenially disrupted state, and one that discloses to us the deepest levels of that state: "The literalism of the Augustinians [and of Augustine himself] . . . converted [*sic*] the doctrine of the inevitability of sin into a dogma which asserted that sin had a natural history" (ND 1:260). As Christian tradition has always suggested, he continues, the truth, on the contrary, is that Adam's sin is symbolic: "the representation rather than the historical cause of Adam's sin" (ND 1:261). That literalistic conversion from a representative symbol into a historical cause was for Niebuhr fatal. It made our proneness for sin into a necessity of our birth, and it moved all the involvement of freedom in sin and the responsibility for it onto the shoulders of Adam and Eve. As Kierkegaard had already argued, this move separates Adam from all the rest of humanity;[10] correspondingly, it puts us under a necessitating fate from which he did not suffer. The paradox of freedom and necessity involved in the experience of sin has thus in the tra-

---

8. For example, the inheritance of concupiscence drops out of Protestant discussion, and unbelief, pride, and self-love (rebellion) remain central. However, the piety that felt sensuality to be the main component of inherited sin survived in Protestantism, especially in Calvinism.

9. One notes (with relief) that this last result of sin begins to disappear in the seventeenth century and continues to decline in the eighteenth century, especially among those who can be called "liberal" Protestants: Platonists, Deists, Rationalists, etc. See D. P. Walker *The Decline of Hell* (Chicago: University of Chicago Press, 1964). Little mention is made of eternal damnation in the liberal theologies of the eighteenth century and even less in the theologies that followed Schleiermacher and Ritschl. Nor does it appear in even the most fierce of the neo-orthodox.

10. See Søren Kierkegaard, *The Concept of Anxiety,* chap. 1, 1.

dition been split asunder: freedom has gone to Adam and Eve, necessity to us (see ND 1:262–63). Hence, Niebuhr argues, the only way to proceed is to recognize the paradox and explore it as a symbolic and paradoxical disclosure of our own deepest experience. There can be, I believe, little question that these are excellent theological arguments.

There are a couple of comments, however, that are appropriate at this point. In the first place, it seems to me ingenious on Niebuhr's part to write as if this literalization, this conversion to a historical cause, unfortunate as it may have been theologically, was a kind of latter-day perversion of a doctrine that in its original form and essential structure was symbolic and not historical. There is every indication that to both the Biblical tradition itself and certainly to its theological interpreters—including Paul and Augustine—Adam and Eve were our real (not merely symbolic) historical progenitors, that their unfortunate action and its results represent historical events, and that those historical events had a grievous effect on all of us, their descendants.

These events, however, although historical, were to them also *more* than merely historical. Clearly for the entire tradition these historical events were in many ways very special indeed. They represented the action of our original progenitors; the latter thus 'stood for' or represented and so affected all the rest of us in ways the actions of our other later ancestors did not. These acts of Adam and Eve possessed, therefore, a strange 'double level' significance at once historical and yet much more than historical. This double significance was at first conceived Platonically; Adam represented 'Man'. Later, with Augustine, this act became the historical cause of the contagion of concupiscence. In either case it was a uniquely transcendent event in history that qualified all the rest of history. But such historical and more than historical events have not been unusual in the tradition of Biblical theology. For example, for the entire past tradition, the same was true for the creation event itself, now the Fall, later the Incarnation, the Atonement and Resurrection, and for the promised End of all things. All of these were taken as representing *both* particular historical events *and* events of transcendent significance for the rest of history, and in that sense they are theologically symbolic.

What is important about modern theological interpretations, and especially Niebuhr's, is that the historicity of some of these events, as literally depicted, is denied (Creation, Fall, and End, especially), and their transcendent significance as "representations" or as symbols is retained. But my point is that this conversion or transmutation from historical event to symbol represents a definite break with tradition. Prior to the Enlightenment these were not 'symbols' unattached to any past historical event; that was as inconceivable to the traditional mind as a universally significant Incarnation or Atonement unrelated to a historical event is inconceivable to most modern biblical theologians. This same criticism applies to Niebuhr's interpretation of all "Biblical myths": to him these myths have always really represented only their symbolic content. Hence their literalization (into 'primitive myth') was a kind of perversion of their genuine meaning.

In fact it is ironic that on this particular point Niebuhr was much closer to Pelagius than he was to Augustine. Like Niebuhr, Pelagius rejected Augustine's view that Adam's historical fall was the cause of all our ills, and he suggested in place of this view that Adam would be better seen as a symbol of those present ills, namely as one who deliberately and so freely sinned against a known law.[11] Niebuhr, of course, both agrees (unconsciously) and disagrees (consciously) with this; for him Adam is not a historical cause but a symbol of our situation. However, the situation of which Adam is a symbol is different markedly for Niebuhr from what it is for Pelagius. For Pelagius, on the one hand, Adam is a symbol of our continuing and ever-present *freedom* to choose either good or evil and of our vulnerability to the dire consequences of our free choices. For Niebuhr, on the other hand, Adam is a representative, not of our freedom to choose either good or evil, but rather of our falling through unbelief and pride into a state of *sin* that renders us unable to choose the good we would choose. That Niebuhr speaks on this point only of his disagreement and not of his agreement with Pelagius (on the *symbolic* role of Adam) is interesting indeed; I shall comment later on some of the grounds for this.

If Adam is a symbol of our bondage and not its historical cause, how are we to understand this situation? What now is 'original sin'? Or, put another way, what is the cause of our ills that replaces the historical Fall?[12] Of course, as Augustine pointed out, there is no cause of our sin in the sense

11. Augustine, *On the Grace of Christ and on Original Sin* 2.11.

12. This question is relevant to all modern neo-orthodox theology, namely all those who seek as Niebuhr did to reinterpret and represent the classical Biblical doctrines of creation, of fall, and of eschatology, and to do so without affirming a specific historical component. See e.g., Emil Brunner, *Man in Revolt,* trans. Olive Wyon, (Philadelphia: Westminster Press, 1947); Paul Tillich, *Systematic Theology,* vol. 2 (Chicago: University of Chicago Press, 1957); and the later classic of Paul Ricoeur, *The Symbolism of Evil* (New York: Harper & Row, 1967).

of an external factor that necessitates it, as a material cause necessitates an effect. We sin through our will and thus somehow freely; we could love (and avoid sin) if we willed to do it, but we do not so will it, even if we wish we could. Something, therefore, is awry. Our wills are not themselves; and though it is our will that is at fault, we cannot seem to do anything about it. What is amiss?

Niebuhr's answer—which is also traditional—is that the prior 'sin' driving us to the actual sins we each commit concerns our relation to God. In effect that underlying sin (original sin) consists in a break in that central relationship to God. In the literal story, of course, that break was established by Adam's act; now it is shifted into our own spiritual depths where the self establishes itself.

> But the self lacks the faith and trust to subject itself to God. It seeks to establish itself independently. . . . By giving life a false center, the self then destroys the real possibility for itself and others. Hence the relation of injustice to pride. . . . The sin of inordinate self-love thus points to the prior sin of lack of trust in God. . . . The anxiety of freedom leads to sin only if the prior situation of unbelief is assumed. That is the meaning of Kierkegaard's assertion that sin 'posits itself'. (ND 1:252)

"Original sin," the sin that precedes, undergirds, and compels our sins on the surface of life, is thus for Niebuhr a lack of trust in God, which represents the break in that relationship that constitutes our humanity. This lack of trust, therefore, sets everything off-kilter. It spurs our anxious contingency to secure itself; in effect it causes us to make ourselves the center of our world; and thus it drives us to be unjust to others. This is, says Niebuhr, the "unbelief" that leads to pride. Pride in this case is pride in relation to God, the claim to be self-sufficient and in no need of the divine. And this pride over against God, 'defiance of God', leads to pride in its other forms, pride of power, intellectual pride, and moral and spiritual pride. Hence this 'original sin' is at once unbelief (lack of trust), rebellion, and idolatry; replacing God with the self or with its group, in effect, the creator with the creature. Therefore, original sin is the defiance of the first commandment to love and honor God alone and not the creature; and its consequence is the breaking of the second commandment, to love our neighbor as ourselves. The unbelief and rebellion that in the tradition were associated with Adam's historical act of defiance are now moved forward to characterize the inner and fundamental relation of each person to God. For Niebuhr we are each as close to original sin as were Adam and Eve; they are symbols of what we do.

Let us note the new and radical interpretation here of idolatry. Idolatry is no longer the explicit worship of material idols—which most Christians in history have been careful not to do. Rather, now, idolatry is the inner worship of the creature, the "idols" of self, nation, class, race, and church—which all Christians, and certainly all Christian communities, including the Church, had regularly done. Idolatry is here universalized into a principle of personal and social interpretation of unlimited scope.[13]

Note here as well how in Niebuhr the Pauline-Augustinian-Reformation mode of piety has been expanded. This piety had emphasized faith versus unbelief and rebellion, trust in God versus trust in self, and repentance and humility versus pride. In the tradition, this form of piety had been largely confined to specifically 'religious matters' and hence to matters of the individual soul's conscious relation to God. Now in Niebuhr this Reformation piety unites itself in a quite new way with the Social Gospel concern for justice and care for the other, with, that is, social and political issues. As Niebuhr said, the vertical dimension of sin is unbelief (the first commandment) resulting in idolatry and pride; and the horizontal dimension of sin is injustice (the second commandment). This reinterpretation of idolatry as central to the injustice and conflict of social existence in turn becomes the major principle for Niebuhr's theological analysis of society and its practices, an aspect of what Tillich called a 'theology of culture'.

As a consequence, the theological grounds for the pursuit of justice in the world have significantly shifted. Liberalism had based Christian social action on the confidence in 'building the kingdom' in the future, and so ultimately on a theory of historical progress under God. Niebuhr has now based social action on a theology of sin and grace, on sin as unbelief, re-

---

13. Idolatry has here become, one may say, symbolic or analogical. Not that the object of idolatry is symbolic; the nation or race is very real and historical indeed. Rather that these may be 'idols' is symbolic or analogical, and they function in a person's or a group's life as an idol (or a god) is purported to function: as the center of their existence, a center of ultimate concern to them, and so to be served with absolute devotion. Luther understood the first commandment in this sense, as referent to our 'god', whatever that object of devotion might be, and not just to an actual idol. The neo-orthodox loved to remind us of this usage. In the *Larger Catechism* (1529), Luther, in answer to the question What is God? says, "A god is that to which we look for all good and in which we find refuge in every time of need. . . . For these two belong together, faith and God. That to which your heart clings and entrusts itself is, I say, really your God" (First Part: The Ten Commandments, The First Commandment).

bellion, and inordinate self-love leading to injustice, and on grace as the gift of forgiveness leading to repentance, humility, and renewed trust, and all of these making newly possible love and care for the other. And the motive for social action is not confidence in creating a morally cleansed future, but a responsible obedience to the implications of faith, the commitment to a relative justice, and the confidence that thereby suffering may be decreased. In this new interpretation of sin as rebellion and subsequent pride, and faith as leading to the pursuit of justice, lies the main theological bridge between Reformation and Renaissance, between Pauline theology and social gospel, a synthesis that Niebuhr promised and that has dominated most subsequent twentieth-century theology.

Original sin as unbelief, as a rebellion that replaces God with self at the center of existence, is in Niebuhr laced with freedom. It is an act of the will not as the will makes its choices for this or for that, but as the will chooses itself, forms itself, or constitutes itself. Note how fundamental for Niebuhr's analysis—as it was for Tillich's—is Kierkegaard's insight that in existing as real selves and as individuals we choose ourselves, we forge a "synthesis before God of the eternal and the temporal," which synthesis constitutes ourselves.[14] This too is an act of our freedom, and it is the most decisive use of our freedom or spirit, shaping fundamentally all the spirit's other thoughts, attitudes, and acts.

We should also note—what the existential rhetoric in all these authors is apt to obscure—that this act of self-constitution represents an *analogical* act. In some sense it is an act of freedom, of self-constitution, lying behind our ordinary daily actions; but we should recognize it is not an 'act' just like any of these other acts; the words have shifted some of their meanings. Niebuhr locates this (not too helpfully, I think) as "the self in contemplation as opposed to the self in action" (ND 1:255–60). This self-constitution of our self is surely an aspect of our self and so of our free self, the deepest conscious/unconscious level of the self, not beyond our freedom but also not part of our ordinary self-awareness. It is difficult if not impossible to locate, in that act of self-constitution, that 'decision against God', or that 'act of centering the self around itself' to which reference is here made. We know vaguely what it is to which these words refer; but it is misleading to speak of them as we do of ordinary deliberations and ordinary acts. As Niebuhr says, they seem to be already there—not as necessitating but as the depths of our own spiritual exis-

14. Søren Kierkegaard, *Sickness unto Death,* pt. 1, chap. 1.

tence, of who we are, the vertical dimension to God through which we are our own selves.

∞

Niebuhr has frequently remarked that there is a double level of insecurity here: the primal insecurity of the contingent creature who is anxiously aware of its contingency, and the subsequent insecurity of the creature who has denied that anxiety, sought to overcome it, and deceived itself about both:

> The insecurity of sin is always a double insecurity. It must seek to hide not only the original finiteness of perspective and relativity of value which it is the purpose of sin to hide, but also the dishonesty by which it has sought to obscure these. (ND 1:256)

Hence the self desperately hides its real situation from itself. Acknowledgement of both its finitude and its guilt thus would expose it to a host of both old and new terrors: its vulnerability and contingency, its inordinate self-concern, its deception in hiding both. The most difficult achievement of all, therefore, is the recognition by the self of its own alienation and guilt. Sin hides itself from itself and as a consequence always blames the other:

> The fury with which oligarchs, dictators, priest-kings, ancient and modern, and ideological pretenders turn upon their critics and foes is clearly the fury of an uneasy conscience. (ND 1:256)

This unbelief leading to pride, self-love, and deceit takes innumerable forms: economic, social, political, moral, and religious. For sin at this level is universal, and frequently the subtlest, most spiritual forms of sin are the worst (ND 1:258). Hence "the saints' awareness of sin is no illusion": all are involved, there are none that are righteous, and only the real saint has the grace to recognize this. This implication of the symbol of original sin—namely that the universality of its application points even or especially to us, to ourselves—is thoroughly affirmed by Niebuhr, as well as by Tillich. Sin is present as pride and self-love even among the brilliant and the righteous; and the hardest task of all—especially for these forms of spiritual pride—is to recognize this fact. Hence there follows the final paradox:

The ultimate proof of the freedom of the human spirit is its own recognition that its will is not free to choose between good and evil. (ND 1:251)

We cannot escape the ultimate paradox that the final exercise of freedom in the transcendent human spirit is its recognition of the false use of that freedom in action. Man is most free in the discovery that he is not free. (ND 1:200)

And with this final burst of Augustinian rejection of Pelagianism, we leave for the moment Niebuhr's explication of sin and of original sin, and concern ourselves now with his understanding of history that grows out of this analysis of human nature.[15]

15. As is evident, I have omitted Niebuhr's analysis of sin as sensuality. I find this analysis very provocative and helpful, although it is more commonly criticized than is the analysis of pride, etc. I have omitted it for want of space and time, and because it is not so brilliantly argued as is the one just rehearsed. Nor does it function as importantly either in his own view or in subsequent theological discussion. To me, Tillich's analysis of 'concupiscence' is more on the mark. See *Systematic Theology,* vol. 2, pt. 3, 1C.

CHAPTER 8

The Understanding of History

Niebuhr wrote a great deal about history because, as we have seen, history stood directly at the center of his thought about cultures and their interpretation, about religions and their depth and coherence, and especially about the Biblical viewpoint for which he argued. History is, as a consequence, a very wide and complex subject in his theology.

I shall divide my examination into three general sections, corresponding to the three following chapters. Chapter 8 will deal with the general comprehension of history, its intelligibility and meaning and the modes of understanding both (myth). Since for Niebuhr the interpretation of history is central to all cultures and constitutes the heart of the religiosity of each culture, this chapter will spread out far beyond the Biblical-Christian perspective. It represents Niebuhr's most fundamental way of understanding the secular world around him and the other cultures different from his own Western culture. Then in chapter 9 comes his interpretation of the Biblical view of history, clearly the complement to chapters 5, 6, and 7 on the Biblical view of human nature and sin. Finally, in chapter 10 I shall deal with two subjects that are both important in Niebuhr and also somewhat obscure, namely (1) eschatology, the 'end' of history, its culmination and the fulfillment under God of its meaning, and (2) the kind of meaning Niebuhr thought the sovereignty of God—in which he thoroughly believed—gave to the course of history.

In Niebuhr's earlier political writings two 'theological' subjects steadily seemed to gain prominence: the nature of human being on the one hand and the character and meaning of history on the other. These two questions are for him deeply intertwined: if we would undergird the hope for justice in an unjust world, we must understand the sources for the pervasive patterns of human social behavior in the structure of human being. Hence the necessity for a careful analysis of the nature of human being. Correspondingly, if we are to know what the prospects of justice are in such a world, we must articulate a vision of history and its meaning.[1] The question of social justice—Niebuhr's abiding passion—involves immediately the questions of the nature of human being and the nature of history; in the context of justice, neither can be explored without the other. I believe it fair to say that these two issues represented, for very obvious historical reasons, the pressing 'secular' questions that dominated theological reflection in the first half of the century. Niebuhr's great significance is in part due to the fact that he addressed these issues head on.

The relation, therefore, between these two issues in Niebuhr's thought is extremely close and very complex. Certainly the question of the prospects for justice in social history is his "ultimate concern"; and that means that the prospects for good in history stand at the forefront of his thought. Also, for Niebuhr's generation the modern faith in a redemptive history, in progress, had been dissolved by events in the first half of the twentieth century, leaving, as Niebuhr repeatedly said, a religious vacuum at the heart of modern spirituality. Primarily because of that devastating demise of progress, optimistic, modern interpretations of human being are a prominent object of Niebuhr's sharpest criticism. On the other hand, it is also clear that Niebuhr could comprehend the precipitous demise of a progressive interpretation of history only by means of his own developing 'Biblical' understanding of human being. It is the anthropology he developed in his earlier writings and in the first volume of *Nature and Destiny* that gives structure and content to his subsequent discussion of history and human destiny in volume 2 and in *Faith and History.* A good example of this mode of understanding the obscurities of history through the understanding of the paradoxes of human being is on the first page of volume 2:

1. That Niebuhr can conceive and articulate a vision of history and its meaning—even if, as we shall see, that meaning is "by faith" more than by comprehension—is most interesting. The important role of faith rather than of philosophical understanding in explicating history's meaning is indicative of Niebuhr's conscious stance against "modernity" with its empirical and rational understanding of history as progress. But the presence of his confidence in an overarching meaning to history, even if by faith and even if grounded in God, indicates Niebuhr's separation from the sensibility common to the end of our century, seemingly a vast difference between Niebuhr in the 1930s and 1940s and the so-called postmodern culture of the 1980s and 1990s. I shall discuss this point further both in this chapter and in chapter 11 below.

Man's ability to transcend the flux of nature gives him the capacity to make history. Human history is rooted in the natural process but it is something more than either the determined sequences of natural causation or the capricious variations and occurrences of the natural world. It is compounded of natural necessity and human freedom. Man's freedom to transcend the natural flux gives him the possibility of grasping a span of time in his consciousness and thereby knowing history. It also enables him to change, reorder and transmute the causal sequence of nature and thereby to *make* history. (ND 2:1; see also FH 35, 55)

The understanding of history, then, is fundamental for Niebuhr, and the understanding of history is achieved through his Biblically shaped reflections on human nature. It is, moreover, by means of this dual mode of interpretation that Niebuhr proceeds to interpret, and make intelligible, the wide range of human cultures. That is, it is in terms of their assessment and interpretation of *history* that Niebuhr classifies cultures: classical, oriental, and modern (e.g., FH 16–17). It is in terms of its relation to history that Niebuhr describes 'classical' (i.e., Hellenic) culture: as identifying history with the recurrent cycles of nature and hence finding a notion of redemption or salvation 'beyond history' or 'separated from time and flux' in eternity (e.g., ND 2:11; FH 14–15, 58, 64). For this reason he denominates classicism as 'ahistorical' (ND 2:11). Furthermore, it is through their relation to history and its meaning that for Niebuhr the essential characteristics of each religion can be grasped (ND 2:2, 4, 5), namely as historical—those that find meaning in history and so in time—or as ahistorical, those that find meaning only in a timeless eternity beyond history.[2] It is hard to imagine at the end of this century, with its radical and positive reappraisal of mystical religion and its new awareness of the crucial importance, value, and integrity of nature, that this attitude toward history would be felt to represent the single most important clue to the nature and value of a culture or a religion.

Closer home theologically, it is in terms of its relation to history that Judaism is defined. The twofold center of Judaism is the covenant and the messianic promise; the first, in which the divine enters history decisively, leads essentially to the second, which discloses the meaning under God of the historical process (ND 2:15–34). Niebuhr distinguishes three types of messianism: (1) nationalistic (the victory of the nation), (2) ethical (the victory of the good over the evil), and (3) supraethical religion, expressed

---

2. Note the similarity to Tillich here, who also distinguished religions and cultures as 'historical' and 'ahistorical.' See e.g., *Political Expectations,* edited by James Luther Adams (Chicago: University of Chicago Press, 1971), 140–54.

in prophetism (ND 2:18). The significance of prophetism is also historical: in prophetism the chosen nation, as well as its enemies, is brought under divine judgment, disclosing the first case (for Niebuhr) of the transcendence of culture and so the reality of divine revelation into history from beyond history (ND 2:23, 27, 43).[3]

Finally, it is its message for history—its claim to understand at last the true meaning of history—that characterizes Christianity and its truth:

> The claim (with which Christianity entered the world) was that in the life, death and resurrection of Christ the expected disclosure of God's sovereignty over history, and the expected establishment of that sovereignty had taken place. In this disclosure of the power and will which govern history, both life and history had found their previously partly hidden and partly revealed meaning. (ND 2:35; see also ND 38–43, 68, 152)

> As the revelation of the paradoxical relation of the divine justice and mercy He [Christ] discloses the ultimate mystery of the relation of the divine to history. This revelation clarifies the meaning of history: for the judgment of God preserves the distinction of good and evil in history; and the mercy of God finally overcomes the sinful corruption in which man is involved on every level of moral achievement by reason of his false and abortive efforts to complete his life in history. (ND 2:68)

As is here abundantly clear, for Niebuhr the center of Christian faith (as of each religion) lies in its disclosure of the structure and meaning of history and of individual life as lived in the wider context of history. The point of faith, therefore, is not to disclose the deeper reality of nature (nor even our obligation to preserve nature); nor is it to help us to reach beyond history into a transhistorical realm. It is to provide us with an understanding and a trust that allows us to live creatively in social history, which thereby helps us to establish a wider and so more secure justice. In this sense, as he recognized, Niebuhr is 'modern' (emphasizing history and not a supernatural destiny) and, as he might not have recognized, 'liberal' (concerned with the relation of religion to social history). As he could not then have known, however, in this concentration on history he was not for us

3. Niebuhr's interpretation of the importance of prophetism is quintessentially modern and liberal. As he notes here, prophetism represents the initial divine incursion into history—the beginning of Special Revelation—because through the prophets God judges Israel's historical sins (social sins), and hence, as Niebuhr says, indicates that God transcends Israel and history, and so can judge both. Here 'God' is no mere extension of Israel's power and pride. This is modern and liberal because prior to the Enlightenment the prophets were of theological interest mainly as giving us foreknowledge of Jesus Christ, i.e., as *prophets*.

fully 'contemporary', for now there is a clear emphasis on our relation and obligations to nature. The historical events of his age represented a crisis in *history,* a crisis that dissolved the modern faith in progress. And these events forced his theological generation to concentrate on the question of history, just as the ecological crisis in the latter part of the twentieth century prodded theological concern to attend to the question of nature.

As is evident from the quotations above, what concerned Niebuhr about the question of history was the issue of *meaning* in history, that is, the meaning of individual and social life in its span of history, and—inevitably involved in that—the meaning of history as a whole.

> The problem of history is the impotence of the good against the evil forces in history. The momentary triumph of evil in history is seen as a threat to the meaningfulness of history and this threat is overcome by the hope of the coming of a Messianic king who will combine power and goodness. (ND 2:19)

Obviously, reflection on history can deal with many issues: causality in history, continuity and novelty in history, patterns of development and disintegration in history, the question of the knowledge of history, and so on. Although Niebuhr is interested in these and writes intelligibly about them, clearly what he means when he speaks of 'the problem of history' is the question of the meaningfulness of history, and when he refers to 'historical' cultures or religions, he means those that find meaning in historical life. And, as he says here, that question of meaning involves the interrelations of good and evil, of well-being and suffering, of fulfillment and disintegration, and, above all, for him, of justice and injustice in history. If, then, religion is essentially involved with the question of meaning in this sense, it is clear that Niebuhr's understanding of history is centrally a religious or theological, rather than a merely philosophical, understanding of history.

It is, perhaps, noteworthy that Niebuhr (as I noted above in chapter 4) seems to have assumed, almost without question, that history does in fact have a meaning. However obscure that meaning may be—and he argued, against the optimism of the modern consciousness, that history was in fact very obscure—he never drew the conclusion from that obscurity that there might in fact be no meaning to history at all.[4] Hence he frequently argued that if a culture viewed history as having no meaning, then its only recourse was to find meaning in an eternity beyond time (e.g., ND 2:13,

---

4. For examples of this latter view, see the works of Albert Camus, especially *The Myth of Sisyphus* (New York: Alfred Knopf, 1955), and the plays of Samuel Beckett.

289). And he frequently implied that a view that found no point in historical life was thereby simply found to be false. Thus the 'nihilistic' alternative, so vividly present in the last decades of the past century, that history has in fact no meaning and that, therefore, life must be lived in recognition of that sober truth, did not seem 'real' to him—much as the category of sin had not seemed real to many in the nineteenth century.

Niebuhr was convinced that life could not be lived in any creative sense without a deeply ingrained principle of meaning: "It is difficult, if not impossible, to live without presupposing some system of order and coherence which gives significance to one's life and actions" (FH 153). As Niebuhr sees it, the question is not whether life participates in a wider scheme of meaning, but what sort of scheme it is in which it does participate—and his apologetic is that, of all the alternative views of history, the Biblical understanding fits best the strange, paradoxical facts of historical life.

This assumption that individual life, social existence, and so history as a whole must embody some overarching scheme of meaning was, therefore, apparently natural to Niebuhr. And surely this is intelligible. As all his writings show, he lived in a cultural atmosphere quite dominated by one such scheme: that of progress through reason, science, technology, and democracy. Across the globe was another apparently powerful universal scheme: Communism. These two myths about history, both of which Niebuhr viewed as held by faith, gave purpose, meaning, and so vitality to the majority of those then-active communities of world culture. From our present perspective much of this seems to have evaporated, and these two myths now seem to be relics of a vanishing era, one of them apparently now quite evaporated, and the other remaining only in pockets of Western society—albeit important pockets (e.g., the commercial and the political communities, and the scientific academic communities). Niebuhr lived, so it now seems, at the end of an era, when some mode of order and coherence in history was assumed, whether it was ascribed to the symbols of traditional Christianity (which Niebuhr seeks to remold and revive), confidence in progress (which, for example, contemporary process theology adheres to), or the 'science' of Communism.[5] Niebuhr sees clearly the flaws in each of these latter two myths, with their superficial optimism on the one hand and their idolatrous character on the other. But he shared with them, and with the entire Enlightenment and post-Enlightenment world, the assumption that history has a meaning. And it was the 'Biblical' meaning of

---

5. For a further discussion of the evaporation of this confidence in a coherent order or meaning in history, see the author's description of "secularity" in *Naming the Whirlwind* (Indianapolis: Bobbs-Merrill, 1968), chapter 2, esp. 66–71.

history that he sought to articulate. One must add that despite the vanishing of these myths, the contemporary vigorous resurgence almost everywhere of fundamentalist or orthodox religion possibly validates his point that some wider scheme of meaning is utterly necessary for historical life.

One consequence of this assumption of the necessity of meaning is that for him the loss of meaning signaled a major spiritual disaster, an important void in the spiritual substance of social life. Hence in passage after passage the universal temptation to idolatry—that is, the temptation to establish local and partial schemes of meaning as absolute—is by him ascribed to the terror of meaninglessness, or, as he frequently puts it, the alternative specter of despair.[6] For the Reformation, the twin alternatives to real faith had been self-righteous pride on the one hand and deadly remorse on the other. So for Niebuhr's modern reinterpretation of Pauline theology, idolatrous schemes of meaning on the one hand and stultifying despair on the other represent the twin alternatives to a sense of meaning in history grounded in a sounder faith. For, as we shall see, every vision of meaning in history, idolatrous or valid, is based on faith: "Man's historic existence can not have meaning without faith" (FH 57). And so, granted that history is to be comprehended only by faith, we are led to the important question of the *method* of historical understanding; that is, how are we usefully to approach the question of faith and its relation to the meaning of life and of history?

∞

As I have sought to demonstrate throughout this volume, Niebuhr's hermeneutic of philosophies, of cultures, and of religions is theological. That is, he is looking for and articulating the religious center of each philosophy, each culture, and each religion, and such a task is, in the most general

6. Here Niebuhr is to me both in agreement with Tillich and yet different. In close touch with the post–World War I European mood, Tillich said that the dominant form of modern anxiety was concerned neither with mortality nor with guilt, but with meaninglessness. Niebuhr agreed that that was a major and universal threat; but at home in a still-optimistic America in the 1920s and 1930s, Niebuhr was more conscious than was Tillich, who had recently arrived from the Europe of the thirties, of the dominant cultural answer to that threat, namely historical progress, than he was of an actual presence of a debilitating meaninglessness. In this, as many readers of both have felt, Tillich represents a much more contemporary, post 1950s and 1960s, and thus disenchanted, postmodern mood; see Paul Tillich, *The Courage to Be* (New Haven, Conn.: Yale University Press, 1952).

terms, a theological one. In his discussion of human nature, he is primarily interested in the principles of good and of evil, of creative love and of destructive violence, that are found in human beings, and so of the grounds for optimism and of pessimism in each view of human being and of society. Now he is concerned with the wider religious question flowing out of that discussion of human nature—namely, the principle of the meaning of life, individual and social, as it is expressed in every vision of history and in each religion, 'historical' or 'ahistorical'. It is, Niebuhr believed, this question of meaning that leads us to the heart of each culture and each religion, and hence to all the philosophies, theologies, and ways of life that express them. Since this study is concerned, then, to uncover and articulate what Tillich called the "religious substance" embedded in any given culture, my enterprise is a part of the theology of culture and its method most appropriately is theological in character.

1.   Niebuhr is convinced that all interpretations of history have presuppositions that are not established by the historical inquiry in question. As a consequence, any knowledge of history is itself based on some mode of prior understanding. These presuppositions are varied. Some are roughly 'metaphysical': what is real and effective, and what is unreal and ineffective, in the sequences of historical events, that is, what causes what; what is the principle of continuity or order, and what is the principle of novelty or change, and how they are related, and so on. As we have seen, Niebuhr has established most of these categories concerned with the structure of history through the development of his anthropology. Hence in this discussion we will revisit many of the ways Niebuhr describes the nature of human being. These presuppositions, however, also include categories concerned with meaning, and it is with these that our present inquiry will primarily deal. And the question of meaning, especially the meaning of history, invariably encompasses the whole of that 'history' or sequence of events that is said to have or to lack meaning, be it a life, or a society's history, or history as a whole. But the whole cannot be known intelligibly, that is, 'scientifically', from a particular point of view in its flowing course. The whole can be envisioned only by an imaginative sweep that can never be proved.

Hence any interpretation of history—in fact any knowing of history, and *a fortiori,* any affirmation of history's meaning—not only eludes proof by inquiry; even more it is the result of 'faith', a faith in a vision of meaning that promises to secure and fulfill the self and its community.

> There is, in short, no possibility of preserving the sense of universal history except by faith, even in a highly sophisticated culture commanding all the resources of modern historical science. (FH 112–13)

> But insofar as men, individually and collectively, are involved in the tempo-
> ral flux they must view the stream of events from some particular locus. A
> high degree of imagination, insight, or detachment may heighten or en-
> large the locus; but no human power can make it fully adequate. . . . None
> of [the above] can obviate the necessity of using a scheme of meaning for
> the correlation of the observed data of history, which is not the conse-
> quence but the presupposition of the empirical scrutiny of historical data.
> The more the whole panorama of history is brought into view, the more
> obvious it becomes that the meaning which is given to the whole is derived
> from an act of faith. (FH 118)

Faith, then, is necessary for both the knowledge and the wider understanding of history. The finite character of the human mind means that
any comprehension of the whole is also finite and partial. Nonetheless, the
need for meaning drives the anxious self or community precisely to comprehend itself in the light of a whole it can barely envision. Hence the
temptation to idolatry, the making absolute one's own finite and partial
perspective, is always present. A finite creature's need for meaning breeds
idolatry as certainly as a vulnerable creature's need for security breeds idolatry, a condition I explored earlier in this discussion.

And hence the need (once again, see chapter 4) for a principle of comprehension—of comprehension of the whole—that is beyond our comprehension, beyond the limits of our partial vision so that we may
recognize these limits (see esp. FH 101). Hence, finally, since all interpretations have a given faith as their basis, it is not only necessary but also legit-
imate to ground our own interpretation of history and its meaning on a
particular faith.

> This is to say, merely, that there can be no interpretation of history without
> specific presuppositions and that the interpretation which is being at-
> tempted in these pages is based upon Christian presuppositions. (ND 2:6)

Also, Niebuhr describes his own work as "our analysis of the human situation in light of Christian faith" (ND 2:157).[7]

7. Niebuhr here is a particularly creative and interesting example of a mode of
theological argument common in those decades. Almost no one argued on rational
or 'scientific' grounds for the Christian faith. They admitted freely, as he had done,
that their position had unprovable presuppositions, was based on faith, and even was
an example of a historically relative mode of thinking. Instead, however, of abandon-
ing argument with the positions of others, they used these seemingly subversive
principles to persuade others that alternative positions were even less rationally defensible than were theirs. That is, they argued that other views were also based on un-
proved presuppositions (faith) and were also historically relative, imaginative

As will become evident when I examine Niebuhr's understanding of the Biblical faith in history, the general term 'faith' as he here uses it does not have its full or particular Christian meaning. In the later Christian context, faith implies a sharp experience of the word of judgment and so of our responding repentance, a hearing of a Word of forgiveness and so a responding trust in divine mercy, and finally a new sense of obligation as of a renewed capacity to do the good we should do—all continually and deeply present in response to a very particular Word addressed to us. The faith in progress and in the Marxist dialectic—or in a nation, race, or family—shares some of these characteristics but by no means all. What is in common are personal participation in a faith shared by the community (i.e., inward assent), inner agreement with the 'doctrines' about history implied there (i.e., 'belief'), assent to a set of norms with regard to one's obligations to the community, and so on. Niebuhr is clear, however, that this sort of 'secular' or general faith lacks two characteristics necessary for a truly valid faith: a permanent principle of self-criticism or of judgment precisely on ourselves and on our own group, and a transcendent source of meaning beyond the tragic possibilities of any life for either an individual or a community—lest the lurking perils of idolatry or of despair overwhelm that faith.

2. In Niebuhr's analysis of the human situation, there is, moreover, another element in understanding history than the faith that gives structure and meaning to the whole, namely the appeal to historical experience, to the 'obvious facts of the human situation', as he likes to call them. In Niebuhr's thought about history, experience, especially social experience, has an astounding and rare authority for a theology based on faith and its correlate revelation. Certainly few of his continental 'neoorthodox' colleagues recognized that authority as openly as he did:

> Repentance does initiate a new life. But the experience of the Christian ages refutes those who follow this logic without qualification. The sorry annals of Christian fanaticism, of unholy religious hatreds . . . offer the most irrefutable proof of the error in every Christian doctrine and every

---

analogies or 'myths' used to encompass a whole that remained a mystery. In short, they made 'theologies' in the formal sense of all alternative philosophies of human being or of history, and having brought them into their own ring, so to speak, they were then prepared to tangle successfully with them. Hence, surprisingly, one finds that emphases on the presuppositions and the historical relativity of all thinking, apparently principles at first subversive of theological statements, were exceedingly common in theological thought. Needless to say such modern principles would in truth have been subversive to all premodern theology.

interpretation of the Christian experience which claim that grace can remove the final contradiction between man and God. (ND 2:122)

In this case, historical experience sharply refashions many treasured
theological doctrines. The continuity of sin in the life of the redeemed is
not only a Biblical word; even more this crucial element in Niebuhr's theology of history is validated over and over for him by historical experience. For him, therefore, sanctificationist or perfectionist interpretations
of grace, however purportedly Biblical or traditional, are refuted by the
facts of historical and personal experience.

Other important elements in his vision of history have a similar experiential base, that is, in the common, observable experience of history. It is
useful to name just a few of these important assertions grounded in historical experience. Niebuhr held a conviction (a) that "there are no limits to be
set in history for the achievement of more universal brotherhood, for the
development of more perfect and more inclusive mutual relations" (ND
2:85) and that "it was the genuine achievement of modern historical science to discover that human culture is subject to indeterminate development" (FH 2; see also FH 15). Niebuhr recognized (b) the permanent
ambiguity of history despite its processes of radical change; this permanent
contradiction between the actual reality and the ideal in history is, as I shall
show, also symbolized by important Biblical categories: original sin, Last
Judgment, the Antichrist, etc. But clearly this permanent contradiction,
can, for Niebuhr, also be known by an open and wise look at the facts of
history, especially twentieth-century history (see ND 2:51, 80, 89, 167,
240; FH 98–100). As good develops, so the possibilities and hence the actuality of evil develop alongside it (ND 2:95, 155, 166–67; see also FH 94):

> The twofold possibility of creativity and destruction in human freedom
> accounts for the growth of both good and evil through the extension of hu-
> man powers. The failure to recognize this obvious fact [sic] in modern cul-
> ture accounts for most of its errors in estimating the actual trends of history.
> (FH 123)

As his political works illustrate, there are also (c) permanent aspects of
social existence that can be seen if the historical experience of societies is
examined openly and seriously. Among these is the necessity of power if
any social unity is to be achieved (and anarchy avoided) (ND 2:20–21,
260). Correspondingly, there is the permanent ambiguity of precisely that
unifying power, which is the necessary agent of what harmony and order
the community possesses (ND 2:262). This ambiguous power unifies the

community and yet is potentially destructive of its justice and its peace, and can be seen in the behavior of every ruling class; each such class brings essential order to the community, yet it also dominates and frequently oppresses other elements. This ambiguity is present as well in the behavior, once they are themselves established, of each once-rebellious group in the community—and always in community there is the latent peril of tyranny (ND 2:21, 260; and esp. FH 228).

Experience shows that every nation and each established or rising class within a nation finds itself both blessed and challenged by a special mission (FH 79; ND 2:30)—and hence each is prone to idolatry. And finally, because of the continual appearance of novelty in history, and so of new forms of order, history is permanently unstable, with indeterminate possibilities of good, but also ever newer possibilities of disorder and of conflict between the old established forces and the new advancing ones—all of which have the deep temptation to idolatry, to seeing their mission to preserve a given order or to establish a new one as the ultimate answer to history's meaning (ND 2:30). These constituent elements of power, ambiguity and idolatry in all of history have, for Niebuhr, been especially visible in the turbulent experiences of the twentieth century. As we have seen, these elements represent for him clearly 'visible facts'; but they are easily obscured by the manner in which our false myths dim our eyesight:

> We have, or ought to have, learned, particularly from the tragedies of contemporary history, that each new development of life, whether in individual or social terms, presents us with new possibilities of realizing the good in history; that we have obligations corresponding to these new possibilities; but that we also face new hazards on each new level and that the new level of achievement offers us no emancipation from contradictions and ambiguities to which all life in history is subject. We have learned, in other words, that history is not its own redeemer. (ND 2:206; see also FH 7–8)

Finally, there is (*d*) the 'common sense of mankind', which agrees on many matters essential to an understanding of history: for example, that we are all responsible for our actions because we are in part free, that our actions are ambiguous because our selves are divided between warring tendencies, and that we (as individuals or as communities) seek to avoid the remorse or guilt resulting from our responsibility and our waywardness by evasion, by excuses, and especially by self-deception or rationalization (cf., e.g., FH 96–97, esp. 99–100). Biblical symbols (like Calvin's 'spectacles')[8] certainly open our eyes in new ways to these obvious facts.

8. John Calvin, *The Institutes,* 1:6.

Nevertheless for Niebuhr these facts are there in experience to be seen if only the false interpretations that hide them from us can be eliminated. Experience, then, provides the other major element besides faith and its implications to the understanding of history.

3.   The third ingredient to an understanding of history—besides faith and a careful look at historical experience—is the *myth* through which, as we saw in chapter 4, the structure of history as a whole and its meaning are conceived. Faith for Niebuhr is by no means blind; it enshrines a meaning within the deeper mystery of temporal and historical passage. Each faith is, therefore, intentional; it intends a definite referent. What each faith refers to is a coherent structure of symbols through which the mystery of history is structured and its meaning articulated, that is, a myth.[9] The Christian understanding of history is only one of these myths. So also are the contemporary examples of historical understanding dominant in Niebuhr's world, namely the vision of progress of the bourgeois/democratic societies and the Material Dialectic of communism (FH 210–11).

These myths in turn are composed of symbols or analogies drawn from central aspects of group life, those which for that group sustain, defend, and further the deepest interest of the group. Thus these symbolic stories can be concerned with fishing or agriculture, kingship or political rule, commerce or the military, or, in the modern scene, science, technology, and politics on the one hand, or economic relations and class on the other. In each case these crucial and so central aspects of common social experience are taken to be clues to the structure and meaning, not only of their own particular life, but of the whole of history of which their life is but an aspect.[10] Hence these clues or analogies in the myth are enlarged, magnified,

---

9. Ahistorical religions and cultures by definition do not have central myths about history, myths expressing what is to them the meaning of history. However, they do have myths (stories) of the history of the individual soul, perhaps in a cycle of transmigration, as in classical Hinduism or Buddhism, or perhaps in its descent into history and its release again out of it, as for example in Plotinus. Such stories or narrations concern (1) the relation of eternity and time, (2) the enshrinement of the possibilities of meaning resident in present human existence, and (3) the promised release or salvation at the end—either in release from the wheel or in unity with the One of eternity. And these stories, like historical myths, are composed of symbols, structured so as to express this religious meaning, symbols taken from the ordinary space-time experience to express that which transcends, in various degrees, the realm of ordinary experience.

10. Obviously, "the whole of history," whose meaning is reflected in the myth, will encompass as much of history (and nature) of which the group is then aware. In early societies this is—from the perspective of this discussion—not very much; as consciousness grows, this "whole" will, of course, itself enlarge.

and given universal scope, power, and meaning. Each myth 'fits' the cultural group that holds it to be true; the structure and meaning enshrined in the myth is correlated with the particularity, individuality, and success of that group's life.

Clearly, as Niebuhr admonishes, such myths referent to the structure and meaning of the whole are to be taken as symbolic and not as literal; that is, as referent merely to particular facts, events, and causes (ND 2:250, 289)—what Niebuhr elsewhere called "primitive myth." But it is also clear, as Niebuhr seemed not to recognize, that in the premodern history of the Christian community these myths or narratives were taken as sharing in both literal references and universal symbolic power. The union between particularity of reference and universality of meaning was generally achieved by locating the particular event of which the myth speaks at the "origin of all things" or at the "final end," and thus giving their particularity also, so to speak, a universal reference. Mythical symbols are analogies drawn from group experience—in which context they do have a literal referent—and then enlarged with symbols in order to give structure and meaning to the whole of experience.

In any case, the relation of mythical visions of the whole—which every group possesses—to the particularity embodied in that group's life and enshrined in the myth, gives the myth its grasping and persuasive power for the community that holds it. But that same particularity also makes the group and its myth continually subject to the temptation to idolatry, to interpreting universal history in the light of its own partial story.

> Since the beginning of ancient civilizations history is interpreted, not pluralistically but in terms of false conceptions of universal history. The culture which elaborates the scheme of meaning makes its own destiny into the false center of the total human destiny. (FH 115)

And this idolatry of the early tribe and nation repeats itself, ironically, even in those sophisticated cultures that see so clearly this parochial character of their historical predecessors:

> The inability of any age, culture or philosophy to comprehend the finiteness of its perspective and the limit of its powers always produces a presumptuous claim to finality.
>
> There is a curious pathos in the fact that modern interpretations of history almost invariably exhibit this tendency. . . . They identify their own age and culture, or even their own philosophy, with the final fulfillment of life and truth and history. . . . It is not possible for any philosophy to escape this error completely. But it is possible to have a philosophy, or at least a

theology, grounded in faith, which understands that the error will be committed and that it is analogous to all those presumptions of history that defy the majesty of God. (ND 2:167)

One might sum up Niebuhr's point by noting that one of the major myths of modernity was the illusion that it was quite free of myths, and so that it was only modernity that for the first time saw history as it really was.

As this discussion implies, for Niebuhr the only hope of escape from this universal idolatry and its destructive results resides in our awareness that the principle of meaning to which the myth points is transcendent to our partial and finite understanding—that it be, as he said earlier, a principle of comprehension beyond our comprehension (cf., e.g., ND 1:52; FH 101). If our life is not centered on such a transcendent principle, it will inevitably center itself on what we can comprehend, namely the principles of structure and meaning in our common cultural life. And then once again the relative and the partial will be rendered absolute.[11] Such transcendent principles of understanding manifest themselves as transcendent insofar as they lead to the criticism as well as to the support of the group that embodies and lives through them. The appearance in the prophets of criticism directed at Israel, as it had been at Israel's enemies, signaled for Niebuhr the genuine process of transcendence, and the "beginning of revelation" (ND 2:25). The interesting and ever-present relation between relativism (the partiality of every recipient) and the transcendent (the need for a word from beyond our relative works) is transparently clear in this discussion.

As this discussion has also made clear, not all myths have the same structure. Some are ahistorical; some are purely historical—like the two modern myths. And some combine in paradoxical ways the historical with what transcends history, time, and eternity; that is, transcendence with the historical realm that is transcended. Such for Niebuhr is the Biblical myth: it is unique in uniting time and eternity, transcendence and our historical world, in paradoxical language. Hence Biblical myth provides the structure through which a transcendent judgment and transcendent grace can be mediated to us. Thus in principle—if not in fact—Biblical myth (like Biblical faith) guards against idolatry on the one hand and despair on the other.

---

11. One notes again the assumption in Niebuhr that the greatest spiritual (and political) danger consequent on the relativity of all things cultural and historical is idolatry, that a partial vision or myth will be made absolute, *the* meaning of all of history. To him the danger is not that history will be felt, because of its relativity, to be meaningless, to be a void in which no coherence or fulfillment is possible. On the contrary, the great danger to him is that an idolatrous meaning of history will be held by the group.

Although all myths are "beyond our comprehension" and held by faith, these symbols interpretative of history may be tested by experience. "A truth of faith is not something that stands perpetually in contradiction to experience. On the contrary, it illumines experience and is in turn validated by experience" (ND 2:63, also 121, 206). There is, then, a negative and a positive proof of the symbols of faith in relation to experience despite the fact that these symbols are not induced from experience:

> The Christian gospel is negatively validated by the evidence that both forms of worldly wisdom [its philosophical alternatives], leading to optimism and pessimism, give an inadequate view of the total human situation. . . . There is [also] . . . a positive apologetic task. It consists in correlating the truth, apprehended by faith and repentance, to truth about life and history, gained generally in experience. (FH 164–65; see also 167)

In these passages, Niebuhr is referring to Biblical symbols dependent on Christian faith. However, this negative and positive validation shows that intellectual discussion among faiths and about their respective 'myths of meaning in history' is possible and fruitful. Each viewpoint has the task on the one hand of showing how alternative viewpoints are contradicted by recognizable contours of experience or leave out obvious and important aspects of social life, and on the other of showing the positive relation, the illuminating and unifying power of its symbolic vision, with other ranges of accepted knowledge. In this sense, Niebuhr's is in principle, as in fact, an apologetical theology, grounded on the criteria of coherence and of adequacy to experience.

As I suggested earlier, in Niebuhr's theology symbols provide the form of understanding and general experience its content. Without experience to be interpreted the symbols are empty; without symbols, the experience to be interpreted is for him blind, that is, misinterpreted and falsified, and in the end given a false absoluteness. Clearly this method of uniting symbols received from revelation with knowledge gained by general experience indicates that, for Niebuhr, there is a "point of contact" in human being that persists despite its finitude and its sin, namely the self-transcendence of each man and woman (ND 2:117).

> The finiteness of the human mind does not completely exclude the truth of faith for the reason that the finite mind is sufficiently free to transcend itself and to know something of its finiteness. It is this capacity for self-transcendence which gives rise to both the yearning after God and to the idolatrous worship of false gods. . . . Neither the finiteness of the human mind nor the sinful corruption of the mind or the 'ideological taint' in all human culture

can completely efface the human capacity for the apprehension of the true wisdom. (ND 2:63; also 64)

Although he has admitted that his own view of history is based on faith rather than either on careful scientific historical inquiry or on the possibilities of rational coherence, Niebuhr has not thereby consigned his view to an irrational irrelevance in reflective discourse. On the contrary, he has, so to speak, counterattacked his rationalistic critics by maintaining that all views of history, including their own—like all views of human being—presuppose some particular vision that is assumed intellectually and assented to existentially, and so cannot be proved. Further, these differing myths held by faith can argue with one another about validity by seeking to show the nonconformity to shareable experience of the alternatives and the correlation of one's own viewpoint with experience.

> Every larger frame of meaning, which serves the observer of historical events in correlating the events into some kind of pattern, is a structure of faith rather than of science, in the sense that the scientific procedures must presuppose the framework and it can, therefore, not be merely their consequence. The difference between structures of meaning is, therefore, not between supposedly 'rational' and supposedly 'irrational' ones. Supposedly rational frames of meaning may be irrational in the sense that an implicit and unacknowledged center and source of meaning may be inadequate to do justice to every dimension of human existence and every perplexity and antimony in the stuff of history. A supposedly 'irrational' framework of meaning may be rational in the sense that it acknowledges a center and source of meaning beyond the limits of rational intelligibility, partly because it 'rationally' senses the inadequacy or idolatrous character of centers and sources of meaning which are within the limits of rational intelligibility. (FH 119)

For Niebuhr the major alternative vision of historical meaning to what he calls the Biblical understanding of history was the modern vision: the myth of progress. To him, as I noted, classical culture (Hellenic and Roman) did not have a scheme of historical meaning:[12] on the whole, history was identified with the endless cyclical, recurrent, and so meaningless changes of nature in which repetition of fundamental forms of life repre-

12. Niebuhr recognizes that Rome did see itself as the center of history and viewed the "eternity" of Roman rule as the pivotal meaning of history with messianic overtones (ND 1:16, 17). Perhaps it is fair as well as accurate to say that Niebuhr's interpretation of "classical culture" as radically ahistorical applied more clearly to the Hellenistic culture (200 B.C.–400 A.D.) than to the Hellenic culture of the pre-Alexandrian city-states.

sented the only principle of coherence. In terms of the resolution of life's greatest problems, therefore, meaning was found only in an eternity beyond change (ND 2:5–11; FH 14–16, 37–39, 62–64). The other relevant vision concerning history to Niebuhr, the other modern historical myth, was of course the Marxist understanding of history. I have already gone over his changing interpretation of Marxism in his earlier writings; he does not add substantially to that assessment in the works now under consideration—though he has in the later period much to say about what was to him the grave political threat of Soviet Communism.

For this reason our present concentration will be on the modern faith in progress, the view of historical meaning that still dominated his world, the American world between the great wars.[13] From the vantage point of the 1990s, it is hard to feel, and certainly to credit, the dominance, the taken-for-grantedness in American intellectual life, of this view of history in the 1920s, 1930s, and 1940s. Niebuhr writes as if this vision or myth was for most of his readers "what is obviously the case," and hence the vigor and frequency of his arguments against it. My own experience as a youth during the same period indicates he was quite right in this.[14] I must note, however, that the relatively mild and positive reception of Niebuhr's later works in the early 1940s and the 1950s, compared to the shock and even violence of the reaction to *Moral Man and Immoral Society* and *Reflections on*

13. It is important to note that, while after the First World War, the vision of progress receded in Europe, its point of origin, it was nonetheless hardly challenged in post-World War I America or, I believe, in Great Britain. It was not until after the depression of the 1930s and the rise of Hitler—and the arguments of persons like Niebuhr—that it began to dissipate among intellectual circles in America and Canada (except, one notes that to this day it has not dissipated among many scientists and even among many social scientists).

14. I recall the textbook used in our lower grade school at the University of Chicago Laboratory School (roughly 1928–30); it portrayed human society as a steady progress from the early Egyptians (then regarded as the beginning of all civilization) through the Greeks and Romans, with a dip in the Dark Ages of faith, up to the splendid modern civilization of America with its miles of telephone lines, its numbers of refrigerators, its fast steamboats and trains, and its radios. (Not much mentioned was art, to be sure, but a great deal of time was given to commerce, industry, technology, and science—as, I noted, the centers of this modern myth.) I recall also at tea at our home on the University of Chicago campus in 1933 or 1934 hearing the faculty present there wonder in amazement at how this new Nazi persecution of the Jews, which was clearly then underway, could be comprehended: "How is it possible," said one faculty member, "that such things could happen in the twentieth century? With the Romans, yes; in the medieval world, certainly—but in modern civilized life? It is incredible." I doubt if anyone in the second half of the twentieth century would conceive of asking such questions.

the End of an Era in the 1930s, indicates that in the decade from 1933 to 1943 many changes associated with a progressivist understanding of history's meaning had begun to occur in the intellectual culture of the United States of America as well as of Europe. In any case, it will be with this alternative myth about history that I will be concerned before I deal in the next two chapters with Niebuhr's own Biblical understanding.

Niebuhr is clear that although this myth of progress is new, a child of the Renaissance and the Enlightenment, it is nevertheless itself also partly a synthesis of older elements or streams in our cultural inheritance, namely the Hellenic and the Hebrew or Biblical elements. From the Hellenic or classical inheritance, modernity (the spiritual center of which, for Niebuhr, is the myth of progress) took its predominant faith in reason. Reason is the chief source of virtue, and so moral problems are at bottom intellectual problems, in which the clarity about what is or is not the good and the expertise about how best to achieve it represent the principal sources of virtue (ND 1:1–54; FH 12). Correspondingly, evil comes from the 'irrational' substratum of human experience: matter for the Greeks, but 'nature', 'desires', 'our animal inheritance' for moderns.

> Modern thought accepted the classical conception that evil and illusion, the frustrations to the fulfillment of life and the confusion and cross purposes to the harmony of life, are all derived from the ignorance of a mind involved in nature, and from the impotence of a will involved in natural necessity. With classical thought it hoped for the fulfillment through the extension of reason . . . just as the evolutionary process in nature represents the gradual ascendancy of a cosmic mind over mechanism so the evolutionary process in history guarantees the gradual triumph of human reason over the ignorance of the undeveloped mind, the confused impulses of natural man and the bigotries and prejudices of primitive life. (FH 67)[15]

15. Niebuhr's sentence ("just as the evolutionary process in nature represents the gradual ascendancy of a cosmic mind over mechanism") reminds us that his familiarity with evolutionary theory—and note how readily he accepts that theory—is not quite up to date, even in 1940–42. At the turn of the century and well into the 1920s, theoreticians of evolution spoke of "laws of development" and, as he does here, the "cosmic mind"—e.g., Alexander, Bergson, Whitehead, and Julian Huxley, and his contemporary Teilhard de Chardin. By the 1930s and 1940s, however, this sort of language was noticeably vanishing among the Darwinian and neo-Darwinian biologists, and a view of cosmic and biological evolution (if the word is still appropriate to the cosmos) as *random* and so "blind" became predominant in scientific circles; see, e.g., George Gaylord Simpson, Ernst Mayr, and our contemporary, Stephen Jay Gould. One must note, however, that while the certainty of progressive development in *nature* may have disappeared from the scientific understanding of nature,

As is evident from the last part of this quote, something different, even alien, was added to the classical in modern culture, namely the sense of the linear and purposive character of temporal history. The sense that time moves forward, that history's events are unique and unrepeatable, and that this linear process is meaningful and headed toward its own culmination is for Niebuhr originally 'Biblical', derived from the religious concepts of creation, revelation, and eschatological end that dominate both Hebrew and Christian understanding. It is this conception of time and history that was expressed with powerful clarity by Augustine,[16] and that subsequently dominated the Western consciousness. As Niebuhr and others have pointed out, the linear and progressive character of time is perhaps the most important 'Biblical' element of the modern consciousness (ND 2:154).

Now the point is that in the modern vision the classical faith in reason is combined with the Biblical emphasis on the meaningfulness and purposiveness of history under God to create a quite new myth, namely the conception of history as an unlimited progressive development. The sources in the early modern period of this new idea of progress are multiple.[17] I agree with most commentaries, which state that the conception of immanent progressive development in history—and so in the unfolding of time itself—came from the exciting and transforming experience in the seventeenth century of the new science and of the new and apparently limitless technological power that emanated from that new scientific knowledge. Niebuhr agrees, although this is hardly what is usually called "the Renaissance":

---

nonetheless it has not noticeably diminished in the realm of history. The belief in historical progress is still present in most of the scientific community. And, as an even greater surprise, the question of a "cosmic mind" and so of immanent purpose has returned as a question, with regard now to the development of the cosmos; it is now debated among astronomers and physicists if it is not at all debated among biologists. See the debate over the so-called cosmic anthropological principle, e.g., J. D. Barrow and F. Tipler, *The Anthropic Cosmological Principle* (Oxford: Oxford University Press, 1986).

16. For further amplification of this Biblical and Augustinian inheritance, see my own *Reaping the Whirlwind* (New York: Seabury Press, 1976), pt. 3, chapter 7, a book heavily indebted to Niebuhr's thought.

17. See the excellent study by J. B. Bury, *The Idea of Progress* (1932; reprint, New York: Dover, 1955). One of the great values of this work is that the British author (in 1932) firmly believed in the idea of progress; to him it was by no means a 'myth'. And he writes of its history as the history, not of how an idea was generated historically, but of how a 'truth' was discovered—much as historians of cosmological science speak of the history of the discovery of the expanding cosmos. In fact the volume was dedicated to Saint-Pierre, Condorcet, Comte, and Spencer, and "other optimists mentioned in this volume."

The chief agent of this development was undoubtedly the new confidence in developing reason, or cumulative knowledge and experience and in the rational conquest of nature. For this historical trend the classical confidence in rational man was disassociated from the historical pessimism of classical culture and made the instrument of historical optimism. . . . The guiding principle of the philosophy which underlies the idea of progress is that of an immanent logos which is no longer believed to transcend history as an eternal form, but is thought of as operating in history, bringing its chaos gradually under the dominion of reason. (ND 2:164)

In modern culture the idea of progress was substituted for the idea of providence a full century before the concept of evolution was substituted for the idea of creation. The historic development of human institutions and the emergence of novelty in historic time was more obvious and therefore more quickly discerned than the fact that the forms of nature were also subject to temporal mutation. (FH 36)

Hence for modernity "the 'laws of nature' and the 'laws of reason' are its surrogates for providence and grace. They give meaning to the whole of history, for they guarantee its growth" (ND 2:162).

In this modern vision the passage of time is itself redemptive, for the law of temporal growth and development gradually empties nature and history of its confusions, ambiguity, and evil (see FH 304):

This new view of a moving, a growing, a developing world seemed to resolve every perplexity about life and to hold the promise of emancipation from every evil. . . . History was the story of man's increasing power and freedom. . . . The obscurity which evil introduces into history ceased to be a problem because modern culture returned to the classical view of history as an intrusion of natural chaos into the rational ends of history; but, unlike classical culture, it found the possibility of the growth of reason to be limitless. It therefore interpreted history as a movement toward the final triumph of rational order over the primitive chaos. (FH 30; see also FH 68)

As Niebuhr notes, the astounding accumulation of knowledge and of new technical power resulting therefrom gave the modern age an extraordinary sense of increasing, almost limitless, freedom, that is, freedom to control the forces which we now understand, and so now can manipulate. Hence increasing knowledge represents power and freedom: the freedom to manipulate nature and the potential to manipulate society and even ourselves as we wish. As Francis Bacon said, knowledge is power, the power to do now what we wish to do; and an unlimited expansion of knowledge thus signifies an unlimited growth of freedom. Or, as John

Herman Randall, Jr., said in a Columbia University class in 1946, commenting on modern progress, "We now know how to know—and so there is nothing, almost nothing, we cannot do."

Moreover, modernity not only identified knowledge and power and power and freedom; even more it identified freedom and virtue. Were not the sources of virtue an objective mind and a trained intelligence, just the traits characteristically provided by an advancing science? Hence as a freedom based on trained intelligence grows, so correspondingly does relevant goodness—the objectivity, the elimination of bias, the eradication of selfishness, in short "virtue"—grow. As the ignorant, biased, technologically incapable, self-seeking, and ideologically (or religiously) prejudiced human being of the historical past recedes, a more knowing, understanding, technically capable, and benevolent human future lies ahead. Scientific and technological development may represent the saving factors in this process, but its culmination will be the approximation to the ideal: a harmonious commonwealth of moral persons. Such was the idea of progress, a faith shared by liberalism and communism alike.

> The triumph of virtue is more or less guaranteed because historical development assumes both the increasing priority of reason and the efficacy of its scientific techniques. This error of identifying increasing freedom with increasing virtue is primarily responsible for the false estimates of history by contemporary culture. The increasing evils which arose with increasing power could be neither anticipated nor comprehended within the terms of these presuppositions. (FH 90)[18]

What is essentially modern about this vision, distinguishing it sharply from Greek rationalism, is the conception of radical novelty combined with the affirmation that that novelty is better, a step forward. This is, as I noted, partly classical (the victory of rational order) and partly Biblical (the appearance of the new); but taken as a whole it is different from both.

> The radical contrast between the two views (the classical and the modern) lies in the modern emphasis on the emergence of novelty in both the

18. At the end of the twentieth century, this progressivist vision seems to be extravagantly incredible, one of the least likely of myths. However, the intellectual circles of democratic America of the 1920s and 1930s and the apparently antithetical vision of history affirmed by communism both held progress to be not only plausible but certain—and in amazing harmony with all the 'available facts'. I can testify that the liberal form of this vision was assumed and taught in my youth at such "hardheaded" intellectual centers as the University of Chicago. Niebuhr gives many quite bizarre examples of this amazing confidence in the future and our ability to control it (see FH, chapter 5).

> historical and the natural process, leading to the conviction that duration means the invention and creation of forms, the continual elaboration of the absolutely new (Bergson). (FH 41)

The Biblical sense of a new (a revelation, an incarnation, an appearance of the spiritual, an eschaton) that enters and transforms history is here united with the classical confidence in rationality as the ground of new virtue. Hence the experience of cumulative development in scientific knowledge and technological power, that is, of a cumulative freedom, led to the identity of the new in history with an increasing good, with the elimination of old ignorance, disharmony, and violence. The passage of time manifests continual novelty, and novelty manifests the growth of understanding and order: this is progress, and in believing in it, a community can and does have confidence in its vocation, its future, and so in the meaningfulness of its historical existence. Niebuhr once remarked that the myth of the fall became meaningless to moderns not so much because that myth had now through science become *incredible* as because it was, in the light of modern optimism about human being, finally *irrelevant*. One could well apply that result to the Christian myth of salvation through God's grace and God's providential sovereignty, namely that it was now not so much incredible as it was rendered irrelevant by the belief in history's rational and moral progress.

Despite the implicit criticism embedded in his description of the modern myth of progress, Niebuhr is very clear that this modern understanding of history is not thereby entirely in error. On the contrary, it contains for him a most important truth, namely that history manifests a dynamic thrust into novelty, that new possibilities of different modes of order appear continuously, or, as he usually puts this, that there are indeterminate possibilities in history for new and for even higher forms of cultural and social life.

> It was the genuine achievement of modern historical science to discover that human culture is subject to indeterminate development. (FH 2)

> To deny this is to be oblivious to an aspect of historical existence which the Renaissance understood as well: that life represents an indeterminate series of possibilities, and therefore of obligation to fulfill them. (ND 2:190; also 192)

And these are not merely indeterminate possibilities of change, of new forms of individual or of social life; they are indeterminate possibilities of a better, or higher, or more harmonious, equal, and free form of social life. Niebuhr here seems nearly to embrace a concept of progress:

There are no limits to be set in history for the achievement of more universal brotherhood, for the development of more perfect and more inclusive mutual relations. All the characteristic hopes and aspirations of Renaissance and Enlightenment, of both secular and Christian liberalism are right at least in this, that they understand . . . the agape of the Kingdom of God as a resource for infinite development towards a more perfect brotherhood in history. (ND 2:85; see also ND 2:246)

Clearly these indeterminate possibilities of the new, of radical change in the forms of social and cultural history, are grounded in the continuing freedom of human being to transcend the present, given forms of order and to create new forms—and then in turn to break those and to create ever newer ones. History is essentially creative and essentially unstable precisely because it is the 'nature' of human being to be at once temporal and dependent and yet free. As always, the understanding of history is correlated closely with the understanding of human being.

Niebuhr's agreement with the modern vision of history is, however, only partial. Despite these indeterminate possibilities of advance, there is no *moral* progress. And the reason is that each advance toward higher forms of order, toward new possibilities of harmony, brings with it a corresponding advance in possibilities of chaos, of disorder, and of destruction:

> If we examine any individual life, or any social achievement in history, it becomes apparent that there are infinite possibilities of organizing life beyond the centre of the self; and equally infinite possibilities of drawing the self back into the centre of the organization. The former possibilities are always the fruits of grace, . . . yet the possibility of new evil cannot be avoided by grace; for so long as the self, individual or collective, remains within the tensions of history and is subject to the twofold condition of involvement in process and transcendence over it, it will be subject to the sin of overestimating its transcendence and of compounding its interests with those which are more inclusive. (ND 2:125; see also 51, 166–67, 240)

As I pointed out earlier, freedom has the twin possibilities of the creative fashioning of the new, and even of the better; but it has the concurrent possibility of inserting the self into the center of each new achievement. Hence the possibilities of evil rise with the advancing possibilities of good:

> The twofold possibility of creativity and destruction in human freedom accounts for the growth of both good and evil through the extensions of human powers. (FH 123)

As freedom develops, both good and evil develop with it. The innocent state of trust develops into the anxieties and fears of freedom; and these prompt the individual and the community to seek an unjust security at the expense of others. (ND 2:95)

Human history is indeed filled with *endless possibilities;* and the Renaissance saw this more clearly than either classicism, Catholicism or the Reformation. But it did not recognize that history is filled with endless possibilities of *good and evil.* . . . It did not recognize that every new human potency may be an instrument of chaos as well as of order, and that history therefore has no solution of its own problems. (ND 2:159)

For Niebuhr, of course, it was the social experiences of the first half of the twentieth century that formed the empirical background for this understanding of development as the development of possibilities of both good and evil (e.g., FH 77–79, 84). First, there was the reality of the class wars of the 1920s and 1930s; and second (FH 182, 89), there was the reality of the two national wars in the midst of the advanced scientific, technical, and democratic civilization of the West; and, as one legacy of the Second World War, the development of the atomic bomb was at once the pinnacle of scientific advancement and the source of a new terror in history. And, of course, there was the ultimate terror of the Holocaust. Niebuhr's denial of essential progress amid his assertion of indeterminate advance is perhaps best summed up in the sentence, "Where there is history at all, there is freedom; and where there is freedom there is sin" (ND 2:80).

The obvious facts of contemporary life were, however, obscured for most modern intellectuals by their faith in progress, showing the power of any deeply held myth to reshape our experience of history.[19] This had been a familiar theme in Niebuhr's early political writings, and in his discussion of modern optimism with regard to human nature. And now, as before, the juxtaposition of optimistic myth in relation to the growing grimness of the facts leads to one of Niebuhr's major ironies:

The history of mankind exhibits no more ironic experience than the contrast between the sanguine hopes of recent centuries and the bitter experiences of contemporary man. Every technical advance, which previous

19. An indication that this confidence in the concurrent growth together of knowledge and virtue has not vanished altogether, albeit it recognizes it no longer dominates the intellectual scene, is found in the title of Carl Sagen's last book, *The Demon-Haunted World: Science as the Candle in the Dark* (New York: Random House, 1996).

generations regarded as harbingers or guarantors of the redemption of mankind from its various difficulties, has proved to be the cause, or at least the occasion, for a new dimension of ancient perplexities. (FH 1)

And back of this irony about history's developments lies another about human nature. The culture that based its optimism on our growing knowledge of natural laws, and so of the subservience of human being and autonomy to causal determinism, has on that precise ground—namely of the power that this knowledge of determinism gives to us—come forward with the promise of the most extravagant growth of freedom imaginable. Because we know, and know how to know, there seems to be nothing we cannot do:

> The thesis is that man's increasing freedom first emancipates him from subjection to natural necessity but finally makes him master of historical destiny. . . . The traditional debate between voluntarism and determinism in the history of thought has been aggravated in modern culture by the fact that modern forms of determinism have annulled human freedom more completely than Christian ideas of Providence; and modern forms of voluntarism have asserted the freedom of man more absolutely than either classical or Christian theories. (FH 79; see, e.g., chap. 5)

Thus not only does the vision or myth of progress lead to the denial rather than the illumination of the facts of historical experience; just as damaging, it contains an unresolved contradiction of determinism and freedom at its center. It represents, in other words, a naturalism in which a reason thoroughly embedded in nature, yet inexplicably rises to a point where that reason can dominate nature and even free itself from nature (cf. FH 70–71). This represents Niebuhr's 'negative validation' of the Biblical view, namely by showing the way alternative views both deny the facts and contradict themselves, a method he had carried on in the first chapters of volume 1 of *Nature and Destiny*.

This unexpected union of modernity's 'indeterminate possibilities' and the Pauline-Augustine and Reformation assertion of the continuity of sin even in the life of the redeemed, represented, as Niebuhr recognized, a new synthesis of heretofore opposing religious and intellectual traditions. And quite deliberately he proposes just that synthesis: a union of the truth of the Renaissance with the truth of the Reformation. This synthesis will omit, as he believes, the central error in each tradition: the belief in simple moral progress in the Renaissance, and the pessimism about history and culture—the 'obscurantism' as he called it—of the Lutheran Reformation:

A new synthesis is therefore called for. It must be a synthesis which incorporates the twofold aspects of grace of Biblical religion, and adds the light which modern history, and the Renaissance and Reformation interpretations of history have thrown upon the paradox of grace. Briefly this means that on the one hand life in history must be recognized as filled with indeterminate possibilities. There is no individual or interior spiritual situation, no cultural or scientific task, or no social or political problem in which men do not face new possibilities of the good and the obligation to realize them. It means on the other that every effort and pretension to complete life, whether in collective or individual terms, that every desire to stand beyond the contradictions of history, or to eliminate the final corruption of history, must be disavowed. (ND 2:207; see also 205)

As it promises here, this synthesis is in effect the 'Biblical understanding' of history that Niebuhr himself proposes. It is, therefore, incumbent upon us to embark now on its articulation.

CHAPTER 9

The Biblical Understanding
of History

With this subject, the Biblical understanding of history, we reach, so I believe, the center of Niebuhr's theology. The understanding of history is for him the most fundamental of theological issues, in fact, of all the issues of human reflection. As I have shown and will demonstrate again, Niebuhr's elaboration of his view of history is dependent throughout on the understanding of human nature that he first articulated. Nonetheless the full scope of Niebuhr's theology of human nature becomes clear only when that subject moves into the comprehension of history: here the parameters implicit in the doctrine of human existence are vastly enlarged to the Beginning and on to the End; the relation to God, central as it was to Niebuhr's doctrine of human being, is nonetheless now made much more explicit and is much more thoroughly articulated. In short, now the symbols of creation, revelation, incarnation, atonement, and kingdom are fully and explicitly discussed, and the symbols of God on the one hand and grace on the other—so to speak on the periphery of the discussion of human nature—now move center stage. Thus the popular 'secular' interpretation of Niebuhr, as having a brilliant and realistic understanding of human nature and society and little else, shows its deep inadequacy when we move to the subject of Niebuhr's Biblical understanding of history.

As noted, the structure implicit within the doctrine of human being becomes quite explicit here in the understanding of history. This structure is the vertical relation between God and human nature, between eternity and time, between divine transcendence and divine involvement, expressed symbolically and paradoxically in the categories or symbols of creature, image of God, and sinner. This essential structure of human existence in relation to God also represents for Niebuhr the real structure of historical reality, in terms of which alone "the heights and the depths" of history, its possibilities and its problems, can be measured and understood. Hence history can be properly understood only if it is seen as a drama of the encounter of God and men and women in which God, and not human power, overcomes the deepest problem of history, much as the understanding of God resolves the deepest puzzles about history. The "God-centered" character of Niebuhr's theology—its Biblical character—thus now becomes plain.

> The drama [of the human story] is, in essence, not so much a contest between good and evil forces in history as a contest between all men and God. In this contest God has resources of power and mercy finally to overcome the human rebellion. (FH 125)[1]

> Ultimately the rebellion of man against God is overcome by divine power which includes the power of the divine love. The 'foolishness of the Cross' as the ultimate source of wisdom about life consists precisely in the revelation of a depth of divine mercy within and above the 'wrath' of God. By this love God takes the evil and sins of man into and upon Himself. (FH 28)[2]

It is God alone, as creator, judge, and now redeemer, whose actions make possible the redemptive meaning of historical existence and so who clarifies the deep mystery of history's life.

From this fundamental character of the drama to which the Biblical message witnesses—as a dialectic between eternity and time, divine transcendence and divine involvement, a drama of the encounter of God with men and women—flows the character of the Biblical symbols themselves

---

1. We note with some amusement when we read this passage—a "contest between all men and God"—that there is another issue that comes to mind besides the ever-present 'man' and 'men' in Niebuhr. We (or at least I) immediately think of the angry and omnipotent God contesting and so oppressing innocent and helpless humans—such is the power of the modern consciousness in all of us, "the easy conscience of modern man." We must recall, therefore, that in this sentence 'man' is not at all innocent, the helpless victim of evil; but for Niebuhr humans are the agents of the untold suffering of their fellow human beings and so are the beings responsible for the evil and tragic character of history. Hence in this contest, all goodness is on the side of God, as the next quote clearly shows.

2. In these moving passages that unequivocally present God and God in Christ as central to the understanding of history, we see how dramatically, for Niebuhr and his generation, nature is relegated to a place that lies quite outside this central drama. As Barth once put the same point, for the Biblical consciousness, nature is the stage on which the drama between man and God is played out. It is not that the Biblical message so interpreted was against nature; it is just that it left it out.

and so in the end the nature of Biblical understanding. These symbols, says Niebuhr, are essentially paradoxical. They speak of the relation of eternity to time, of God to history, and in such a relation nonparadoxical language is not possible. Direct language exclusively about the temporal (e.g., naturalistic philosophy, possibly Process thought) is misleading as it fails to witness to the divine that transcends the temporal—and thus it has no possibility of assessing and understanding the "heights and the depths" of human existence. Correspondingly, philosophical language about eternity falsifies Christian witness since, in order to maintain coherence, such language must fail to speak of the divine relatedness to the temporal, a relation that, for Niebuhr, provides the only means by which we can speak of God at all. Like Schleiermacher, Niebuhr can speak of God only in relation to history and to our experience of history. What valid theological language must do, therefore, is speak, and speak paradoxically, of eternity in relation to time and so in the language of time. Hence Biblical discourse speaks of God in terms of time, the *form* of its language being temporal (i.e., mythical, a story in temporal categories) and yet the *content* of the language pointing speech and reflection beyond the temporal to the eternal. Thus does Biblical language distinguish itself from ahistorical mystical discourse on the one hand and naturalistic discourse on the other. It is analogical and paradoxical; it presents myths about the relation to eternity in the language of time.[3]

The paradoxes—which abound in Niebuhr's work—are thus there in Biblical understanding for two reasons. First it is because relations to God concern relations between apparent linguistic contraries: eternity/time, unconditioned/conditioned, aseity/dependence, Creator/creature, and so on. Hence apparent contraries are brought together in the same categories and propositions: creature and image of God, necessitated and free, grace and freedom, and so on.

Second, these paradoxes exist because one term of the apparent contraries is relatively, so to speak, "out of sight." Niebuhr's whole point is that neither human existence nor historical communities can be understood if their essential relatedness to the divine is omitted; that is, if no place is given to what transcends our relatively clear and intelligible understanding, our very useful, appropriate, but limited ordinary rules of coherence. Hence, as we have seen repeatedly, if we seek to understand either human

---

3. See Langdon Gilkey, *Maker of Heaven and Earth* (Garden City, N.Y.: Doubleday, 1959), esp. chap. 10, for a Niebuhrian interpretation of Christian theological speech concerning creation as mythical and paradoxical. Also note the absence in that volume, written in 1956–57, of any sustained attention to nature.

being or history in creaturely terms alone—or in terms of their mystical negation—we will misunderstand them. We must understand them in light of a principle or principles that 'transcend our comprehension'— only then can we understand their "heights and depths."

This transcendent principle is, however, not pure mystery; it can be dimly known in ordinary experience, and it has disclosed itself in part. There is meaning in the mystery of God, meaning by faith. But this meaning remains a mystery to our simpler understanding, and hence our propositions about it are not only based on faith rather than on full comprehension, but they are also paradoxical in form. Paradox here represents a linguistic recognition that the mode of coherence of these terms ("necessary and yet free," "universal sin and yet responsible") is beyond our comprehension, that in each of them we are dealing precisely with a relation to transcendence and so to mystery, something quite beyond our full and precise comprehension. As a consequence, it is faith that sets each term beside each other term, that unites them in terms of meaning; but that union by faith fails to unite them in terms of either empirical or rational coherence. Their point of unity is precisely transcendent to our comprehension, that is, in the relation to God. Hence are they 'foolish' to the Greeks, that is, absurd to rationalists. But here the mystery is *constitutive* of real existence (which is related to transcendence) and thus is a part of our experience. As a consequence these paradoxes turn out to make more sense of the contradictions and puzzles of actual experience (which puzzles also arise from this relation) than do the coherent systems that delight the mind.

> In the same manner the social and historical sciences may give constantly more accurate accounts of cause and effect in the wide field of human relations. But without relation to Christian truth they finally generate structures of meaning that obscure the profounder perplexities of life, offer some plan of social enlightenment as the way of redemption from evil, and lose the individual in the integrity of his spirit to the patterns of cause and effect which they are able to trace. (FH 167)

We humans are "in yet out of" time, necessity, conditionedness; we are creatures yet self-transcendent. This 'out of' aspect of our nature is, of course, in us; it is, says Niebuhr, our self-transcendence, the imago dei. But it is more than an attribute of ours; it reflects our relatedness to God, to what transcends us infinitely, to the mystery that is over against us, to the mystery of God. We, therefore, cannot 'see' the other side of this relation, nor can we see how this other and we fit coherently together; we must witness to this relation, therefore, in paradox. This relatedness quite beyond ourselves in mystery is true of our creaturely nature, of our necessity and our freedom, and also of our universal sin for which we are still responsible. And the mystery, paradoxically, becomes ever more evident when our relation with God is reestablished through grace. Here for Niebuhr the relation to God is real but nonetheless quite beyond our clear understanding: it is "I, yet not I"; it is Christ and yet also I; it is grace and also our freedom. If either side is taken alone, the relation is misunderstood and disaster follows. The paradox of grace is continuous with the other paradoxes in Niebuhr; yet it seems (to me) to be more intense even than the paradox of inevitability and yet responsibility that dominated my discussion of human nature.

As Niebuhr makes abundantly clear, these paradoxes expressing our relation to God must not only be thought, though that is important. They must also be embodied in our existence, our life, and our actions; they point to the presence of grace as well as to the disclosure of truth. And hence this paradoxical relation to God takes on a slightly different though still paradoxical form when we ask how *we* as existing persons are related to this divine presence, perhaps the most fundamental question of Christian faith. Here the paradox is expressed neither in sheer negation on the one hand (There is no grace or truth) nor in sheer possession on the other hand (We have grace and we have truth). Again, it must be embodied 'paradoxically'; that is, as a 'having and a not having' that corresponds to the Pauline "I, yet not I, but Christ in me." As we shall see, this 'having and yet not having'[4] is Niebuhr's way of speaking of our positive relation to God's redeeming presence (whether as grace, as truth, or as the presence of justice), just as the inevitable and yet not necessary, the universal and yet responsible, character of our sin expressed the 'break' in or warping of our relation to God. In both cases, these are relations to that which we cannot fully comprehend, to God and to God's grace. Hence if we seek too easily to comprehend these relations or to possess them, we quickly and fatally distort them.

> Reason was bound to find difficulty in understanding that the faith and the grace by which we stand beyond the contradictions and ambiguities of history is no simple possession: that is, it is a having and a not having; and that claimed as a secure possession, it becomes the vehicle of the sin from which it ostensibly emancipates. (ND 2:147)

On the basis of the paradox of a having and a not having of both grace and truth, it is easy to see why Niebuhr's thought is led inescapably to find

---

4. Niebuhr credits Emil Brunner with providing the original form of this fundamental paradox: of having and yet not having grace (ND 2:124).

justification by faith, or as he prefers, justification by grace through faith,[5] as perhaps the crucial symbolic expression of the Christian message and of Christian existence. Something has been given: the relation to God is a reality, and it has been reestablished to us and in us. Yet if we claim to possess it—either as truth or as sanctifying grace—not only do we lose it, even more we distort it, and it turns into its opposite, into falsehood and even into deeper sin. Thus we are 'justified' by the grace of mercy: we are not fully in the truth, nor are we fully virtuous; it is God's mercy that makes this up. And we hold to this by faith, not by sight and understanding. Neither truth nor grace is our possession to use as we will, and the moment we claim either one to be ours, we lose it.

Niebuhr rightly sees this point as central to the Reformation consciousness. And it is this paradox of mercy and faith that, as we now begin to see, he uses to interpret the relation of God and God's redemption to ourselves and to our human story, and so as the fundamental principle of the meaning present in and to history. In life, *coram deo,* in the presence of God, we experience a having and a not having, and we can affirm and we can bear this relative incomprehension and this relative nonconsummation because we know in faith of the divine mercy and of the divine promise that will "complete what is incomplete in our existence" and "purge us of our false and vain efforts at self-completion" (ND 2:57; cf. also FH 150, 170).[6] Niebuhr (like Tillich) has expanded the principle of justification by faith beyond the religious relation of individual sin to redeeming grace, expanded it outward to everything within the creative dynamic of culture, to issues alike of truth and of justice. Thus has he united in a new synthesis Reformation and Renaissance, the continuity of sin and the divine mercy on the one hand and the indeterminate possibilities of historical creativity on the other.

As in the Reformation, moreover, the paradoxical form of this disclosure of the Biblical message expresses not only the transcendence of its major terms and so its "irrationality" to rationalism—a characteristic this message shares with mysticism. Even more it represents a challenge to human self-sufficiency, to the pride of a self-sufficient reason and the pride of a self-sufficient virtue:

> It is as difficult for a rational man to accept the possibility and necessity of such a disclosure as for a virtuous man to accept its specific content. Its spe-

5. See the brief comment to this effect in the footnote in ND 2:186–87.

6. We note here how the essential nature of grace as forgiveness and mercy, and of our relation to grace as one of *non*possession, leads inexorably to eschatology, to a final fulfillment beyond our imperfect life and history.

cific content challenged the virtues of the virtuous; its form and dimension challenged the self-sufficiency of human reason. (FH 145)

> The specific content of the revelation, on the other hand, challenges man as a sinful creature, whose alternative methods of bringing history to a meaningful conclusion always involve some pretension which is revealed in the light of the Cross to be a false conclusion. (FH 142)

We saw earlier that every vision of the structure and meaning of history, every myth, required something like faith for it to be held as true. We must, as Tillich would say, "be grasped" by each myth, not just in our minds but with our entire being. And Niebuhr showed that this 'grasping' was characteristic of both the major secular 'faiths' of his time, the myth of the Material Dialectic and that of historical progress. Now we see that this requirement of faith continues with regard to the Biblical understanding of history, except that in this case the meaning of 'faith' has vastly deepened and has been reshaped into the particular and unique form of *Christian faith*. Faith here, therefore, has on the one hand the form of repentance at the sharp experience of divine judgment on our pride, and on the other hand the transference of our trust from ourselves and our own to the power and the mercy of God. Faith here does involve the activity of the conscious self, and so the hearing and understanding of a message, the Word. But it is much more than an intellectual matter, more than correct belief; it is thoroughly existential, a character of our existence as persons. It involves inner repentance and inner trust, a transformation of our personal being more than a transformation of our thought.

Only through such inner transformation is the idolatry of self-sufficiency (with its injustice to the neighbor) broken and a new mode of confidence, in God and not in our partial and defensive selves, made possible. Our reception of the Biblical vision of history is, therefore, a deeply existential matter; it is not the substitution of one intellectual concept for another, but a dramatic change in the orientation, in fact the very centering, of the self, a "dying to self in order that we can live to Christ."

> In this experience man understands himself in his finiteness, realizes the guilt of his efforts to escape his insufficiency and dependence and lays hold of a power beyond himself which both completes his incompleteness and purges him of his false and vain efforts at self-completion. . . . This fundamental disclosure of the meaning of life in terms of its dependence on the divine judgment and mercy is not simply some truth of history which is comprehended by reason, to be added to the sum total of human knowledge. It must be constantly apprehended inwardly by faith, because it is a

truth which transcends the human situation in each individual just as it transcends the total cultural situation historically. (ND 2:57; see also 61)

The Christian interpretation of life and history is rooted in a faith prompted by repentance. It will not be convincing except to the soul which has found the enigma of existence not in the evil surrounding it but in itself. There is, therefore, no simple Christian "philosophy of history" which could be set against a modern or a classical one in such a way as to prove its superior profundity through rational comparison. Yet it may be possible to prove its relative rationality, even as it has become possible to make a rational analysis of the limits of a theory of history's rational intelligibility. (FH 101; see also 125–26, 140, 149, 151, 170, 198)

Faith, in the sense Niebuhr uses it here, is, therefore, a response to the presence of the divine judgment and the divine mercy. It is thus the work of grace, and it occurs only through genuine repentance and genuine trust. Such an understanding of the self and of history cannot, therefore, be proved, but it can be shown to make more sense of the baffling contours of life than any of its alternatives.

∞

Now let us turn from the issue of the form of Biblical understanding to its content. How for Niebuhr does the Christian faith understand the meaning of history? Niebuhr begins to construct his own vision with what he calls Prophetic Messianism. In the prophets, God's word is spoken against Israel as well as against Israel's enemies. Thus all nations are seen as in actual rebellion against God. Hence "the problem of meaning in history is not how the good can gain power over the unrighteous but how history can be anything more than judgment" (ND 2:27). Put another way, granted the universality of sin, how can there be any fulfillment of meaning at all for anyone? (See ND 2:27–30.)

The answer is that, because all are unrighteous, "the consummation of history can only be in a divine mercy which makes something more of history than recurring judgment" (ND 2:29). Granted the unrighteousness of even the righteous, the victory of one group over the other, or even the utopian hope of a perfect ruler or society combining power and justice, remains futile. Both in the end lead to the idolatry of one ruling group and its dominance over others. Niebuhr has carefully laid the foundation for these judgments in his political writings and his study of human nature:

the facts of history witness to the universal presence of sin, to the destructive consequences of all claims to imperial virtue, and to the danger of the delusion that our society represents or will represent a union of perfect justice with unchallenged power. Every nation sees "itself as given a special mission" (ND 2:30); each age sees itself as embodying history's fulfillment (ND 2:167); and both examples of communal pride result in the end in the catastrophes of injustice and conflict.

The question of the meaning of history has thus for Niebuhr radically shifted. If this be the problem of history—that *all* are unrighteous—then the resolution of the problem is immediately taken quite out of human hands. If there is an answer at all, it must lie in the hands of God alone (see ND 2:30–35, 43–46). This radically new understanding of the human situation, as we saw, is for Niebuhr the result of revelation, of the appearance with the covenant of a special disclosure of God to Israel. Our ordinary questions, also addressed in Hebrew religion, namely how our enemies are to be overcome or how the good we represent is to be victorious over the forces of evil surrounding us, have become other, quite different, questions: How is the evil in us all to be overcome? And correspondingly, how is this evil to be overcome by God?

> The distinction between the righteous and the unrighteous disappears in the discovery that "all our righteousness is as filthy rags" and that "we are all as an unclean thing." The assurance that God will complete history by overcoming the ambiguity of the momentary triumph of evil yields to the question of how God will complete history by overcoming the perennial evil in every good. (ND 2:30)

> The final enigma of history is therefore not how the righteous will gain victory over the unrighteous, but how the evil in every good and the unrighteousness in the righteous is to be overcome. (ND 2:43)

The solution is as radical as the questions themselves. It is found in another departure: the disclosure of the divine mercy and suffering rather than the manifestation of the divine wrath and power. Here sin is overcome by forgiveness rather than by simple judgment, a forgiveness that itself is paradoxical and so received only by repentance and faith. It is in fact a paradoxical disclosure of the divine powerlessness, precisely the abdication of the almighty power of the creator and ruler of all things. For Niebuhr the agape of God—the divine mercy that transcends the divine law, and the divine suffering that bears and overcomes our sin—is "thus at once the expression of both the final majesty of God and of His relation to history" (ND 2:71; see also ND 2:92). In effect the divine powerlessness, the paradoxical vulnerability and consequent deep suffering of God, is the only way sin can be overcome rather than encouraged. And for Niebuhr this is the main disclosure of the meaning of both Jesus' life and his death, of his refusal to defend himself and his acceptance of death:

> It is impossible to symbolize the divine goodness in history in any other way than by complete powerlessness, or rather by a consistent refusal to use power in the rivalries of history. For there is no self in history or society, no matter how impartial its perspective upon the competitions of life, which can rise to the position of a disinterested participation in these rivalries and competitions. It can symbolize disinterested love only by a refusal to participate in the rivalries. Any participation in them means the assertion of one ego interest against another. (ND 2:72)

The powerlessness of God in Christ is therefore necessary as a manifestation of the divine love in relation to history. It is also alone efficacious in the overcoming of sin. For it discloses the divine mercy (that Christ died for us while we were yet sinners) in the midst of divine judgment—for it was because of our common sinfulness that Christ, who refused to participate in power, died. It represents, therefore, the mercy that comes to us precisely through judgment: a judgment that appears and encourages our repentance at the same time that the mercy that it also embodies elicits our trust. Above all, it was the clear sign that it was God—in the love incarnate in Christ—who suffered here and thus bore our sins. It is God alone who has here acted, God alone who is to be praised and worshiped. This familiar 'monotheistic' note in all forms of Biblical religion makes its appearance at the center of Niebuhr's theology. I shall articulate this further in Niebuhr's concept of the Atonement. For the moment, however, let us note how it is for him the divine mercy and the divine suffering in tandem that overcome our sin. The presence of the divine activity in the life and death of Christ is central to Niebuhr; it is the love of God, not just the transparent goodness of Jesus, that is present and disclosed here and that effects the breaking of sin.

> It is God who suffers for man's iniquity. He takes the sins of the world upon and into Himself. This is to say that the contradictions of history are not resolved in history; but they are only ultimately resolved on the level of the eternal and the divine. . . . Thus Jesus' own interpretation of Messianism contains the two offensive ideas that the righteous are unrighteous in the final judgment and that God's sovereignty over history is established and his triumph over evil is effected not by the destruction of the evil-doers but by his own bearing of the evil. (ND 2:46)

Clearly for Niebuhr God's presence and action in the event of Jesus are crucial: it is God's judgment and God's mercy that are disclosed there, and it is God's bearing in suffering of the consequences of sin that represents this combined disclosure of judgment and mercy. Thus the divine love in the form of mercy and in the divine suffering for the life of others, both present and visible in Jesus, is not merely the agape of Jesus, though it is importantly that (as the norm for us all). Even more, it is the *divine* love that is present and so disclosed there.

As in classic Christologies, therefore, Jesus the Christ is both fully human and fully God. For Niebuhr this paradox is not usefully expressible in ontological categories (of divine substance or nature on the one hand and human substance or nature on the other). Niebuhr held that to express these paradoxes in ontological categories led to intellectual contradiction rather than to paradox and can be 'believed' without repentance and faith (ND 2:60–61).[7]

The divine aspect in this decisive event of the Christ is for Niebuhr the *love* resident and active in Jesus; and the recognition of and assent to this love as divine is of the utmost significance for Christian faith and understanding. As in a number of twentieth-century Christologies,[8] Niebuhr centers his theological concerns on the decisive and ultimately unique "divine event" of the Incarnation, Atonement, and Resurrection, and understands those events as the presence or manifestation of the divine love (through the Spirit) in the human person, Jesus of Nazareth.

> To declare, as Jesus does, that the Messiah, the representative of God, must suffer, is to make vicarious suffering the final revelation of meaning in history. But it is the vicarious suffering of the representative of God, and not of some force in history, which finally clarifies the obscurities of history and discloses the sovereignty of God over history. (ND 2:45)

> The perfect love which his life and death exemplify is defeated, rather than triumphant, in the actual course of history. Thus, according to the Christian belief, history remains morally ambiguous to the end. . . . For the Christian faith the enigma of life is resolved by the confidence that this same love has more than a historical dimension. This love is a revelation of a

---

7. Tillich also held that the juxtaposition of divine nature and human substance or nature in the incarnation represented an "impossible contradiction" and not, as it should, a paradox; and so he too reinterpreted the mystery of the incarnation: It is the presence, he said, of essential God-manhood in existence that represents the divine event, a presence effected by the Divine Spirit in that event. See Paul Tillich, *Systematic Theology,* vol. 2, pt. 3, chapter 2, and pt. 4, chapter 2, B, esp. 3 and 4.

8. Perhaps most expressive of this way of doing Christology was Donald Baillie, whose *God Was in Christ* (New York: Charles Scribner's Sons, 1948) represented a classic of this period.

> divine mercy which overcomes the contradictions of human life. Suffering innocence, which reveals the problem of moral ambiguity in history, becomes in the Christian faith the answer to the problem at the point when it is seen as a revelation of a divine suffering which bears and overcomes the sins of the world. (FH 135)

Clearly the presence and manifestation of God, of God's love, is absolutely crucial to Niebuhr's view. This is by no means an extremely liberal or a humanist Christology, portraying Jesus as the greatest teacher of truth about God and the most evident human example of his own teaching—even if for Niebuhr he was both of these. It is because it is God's love and God's wrath that are present and manifested there that there is hope that sin can be overcome, insofar as it is overcome. Briefly, we can accept the divine judgment on our sins, recognize those sins as a consequence of our own freedom, and inwardly repent of them only if we know as well the divine forgiving mercy that accepts us despite them. In turn the mercy is effective in its conquest of our self-centeredness only if it comes not as a benediction to our self-centeredness but as a divine challenge to it. Judgment and mercy, as in the Reformation, appear together or not at all; and both appear only if each is taken 'by faith' to represent the judgment and mercy of God. And finally, since grace as gift is permanently characterized by grace as forgiveness and mercy, clearly the 'overcoming of sin', the purging of our waywardness, which for Niebuhr is an aspect of faith, is eschatological. A theology of justification, just like a theology of sanctification, leads inevitably to eschatology however much the historical character of Christian faith is emphasized (FH 140).

This intertwined, dual manifestation of divine judgment and divine mercy, with the latter clearly dominant at the beginning and at the end, is disclosed for Niebuhr in the event of God's suffering, in the Atonement:

> The Pauline doctrine really contains the whole Christian conception of God's relation to human history. It recognizes the sinful corruption of human life on every level of goodness. It knows the pride of sin is greatest when men claim to have conquered sin completely. . . . It proclaims no sentimentalized version of the divine mercy. It is possible to appropriate this mercy only through the Christ, whose sufferings disclose the wrath of God against sin, and whose perfection as man is accepted as normative for the behavior by the same faith which sees in Him, particularly His Cross, the revelation of the majesty of the divine mercy triumphing over without annulling, the divine wrath. (ND 2:104)

> Thus the suffering of the guiltless which is the primary problem of life for those who look at history from the standpoint of their own virtues, is made

into the ultimate answer of history for those who look at it from the standpoint of the problematic character of all human virtue. This suffering of the guiltless one was to become in Christian faith a revelation of God's own suffering. It alone was seen to have the power to overcome the recalcitrance of man at the very center of man's personality. . . . It alone was also the final dimension of the divine sovereignty over human history. To make suffering love rather than power the final expression of sovereignty was to embody the perplexity of history into the solution. (FH 142–43)

If mercy can only be appropriated inwardly by repentance, by resigning the claim—now or in the future—to grace as a possession and thus understanding grace as a continuing mercy or forgiveness for our continuing self-centeredness, if this be the situation of "faith," then clearly grace is, as Niebuhr, has said, a having and a not having, an aspect of the self (I) only if it continually criticizes itself and so points beyond itself. Equally clearly the relation to God's acceptance is based on God's mercy and not our goodness; it is a justification by grace (forgiveness) through faith and not through works or through the sanctifying presence of grace as renewing power. If for Niebuhr we once forget this continuing dependence on the grace of forgiveness and begin to conceive of grace received as a possession and ourselves as the unambiguous instruments of God's work, then not only is the transcendent mercy of God lost, but so is our hope of renewal: we have then merely created a new idolatry precisely out of that given by grace to eliminate it.

> To understand that Christ is in us is not a possession but a hope, that perfection is not a reality but an intention; that such peace as we know in this life is never purely the peace of achievement but the serenity of being "completely known and all forgiven"; all this does not destroy moral endeavor or responsibility. On the contrary it is the only way of preventing premature completion of life or of arresting new and more terrible pride which may find its roots in the soil of humility, and of saving the Christian life from the intolerable pretension of saints who have forgotten they are sinners. (ND 2:125–26)

> They prove that just as sin is the corruption of man's creative freedom, so also the ultimate form of sin is a corruption of man's quest for redemption. (FH 205)

There is, however, genuine renewal in history if the paradox of grace is understood and maintained, if in truth we know we are forgiven but not yet sanctified, or better, are partially sanctified insofar as we know we are forgiven.

> When followed consistently, the Biblical faith must be fruitful of genuine renewals of life in history, in both the individual and the collective life of man. These renewals are made possible by the very humility and love, which is derived from an awareness of the limits of human virtue, wisdom and power. (FH 215)

The Atonement here is utterly central; it is, says Niebuhr, "the significant content of the Incarnation" (ND 2:55). Here "in the epic of this life and death the final mystery of the divine power which bears history is clarified; and with that clarification, life and history are given their true meaning" (ND 2:55).

> The wisdom apprehended in Christ finally clarifies the character of God. He has a resource of mercy beyond His law and judgment but He can make it effective only as He takes the consequences of His wrath and judgment upon and onto Himself. . . .
>
> The wrath of God is the world in its essential structure reacting against the sinful corruption of that structure; it is the law of life as love which the egoism of man defies, a defiance which leads to the destruction of life. The mercy of God represents the ultimate freedom of God above His own law; but not the freedom to abrogate the law. . . . The divine mercy cannot be effective until the seriousness of sin is fully known. The knowledge that sin causes suffering to God is an indication of the seriousness of sin. It is by that knowledge that man is brought to despair. Without this despair there is no possibility of the contrition which appropriates the divine forgiveness. It is in this contrition and in this appropriation of divine mercy and forgiveness that the human situation is finally understood and overcome. (ND 2:57)[9]

Thus it is the Atonement that institutes repentance and new life—if the paradox of grace is maintained. In this event of Christ's death the judgment of God on our common sin is starkly revealed, the love of God for even sinners is manifest, and, above all, the suffering of God because of our sins and so out of love for us is disclosed. Faith apprehends this judgment,

---

9. One can see clearly here the way in which the traditional "Anselmic" and Reformation conception of the atonement as a dialectic of divine justice and divine mercy is united in Niebuhr with an even stronger "Abelardian" conception, namely the importance of the effect of the atoning death of Christ on the consciousness and "heart" of the believing Christian. For Niebuhr it is not at all that the sacrifice in Christ the Son has "satisfied" the Divine Father's wrath; rather it is that in the atoning death of Jesus, God manifests at once God's judgment, God's transcending mercy, and God's suffering in agape for humans. This judgment/mercy and suffering/agape together effect the transformation of our proud and stubborn self-centeredness into a reality of repentant trust.

this mercy, and this suffering love and responds in contrition and gratitude and in a new trust in the mercy and providence of God. And God, we now know, will complete our incompleteness and purge our continuing corruption. As we noted, faith in the Atonement and mercy lead in the end to eschatological hope.

Above all, for Niebuhr, in and through its message of overarching mercy—the final pinnacle of the divine sovereignty—the importance of the judgment of God, that is the importance of the distinctions of good from evil, is maintained. The law of life, the structure of historical existence according to which all that is not love ends in destruction of neighbor and so of self, remains. Thus, as Niebuhr says, these distinctions between the just and the unjust, between liberation and oppression, between peace and violence, are "the stuff of history." Within each of these pairings, the predominance of the former (which are creative) over the latter (which are destructive) gives meaning to historical life, individual and social. Hence the pursuit of justice remains all-important, an aspect of our obligation to the will of God as to our neighbor and ourselves. It represents the work of love in a world not yet free of sin and self-concern. For a vision of history that finds history and a life of action in history as meaningful, it is supremely important to pursue justice, to do what good one can, and to shun as much evil as possible.

Niebuhr is clear on the need for the pursuit of righteousness and never relaxes his insistence upon it. The paradoxical difficulty is that in the end we all remain unrighteous—and if we are at all wise, we know this. Thus even the 'saints' depend on the mercy of God to all—and surely they above all must know that they, too, are sinners. Hence at the end of the day, the distinctions between good and evil that make historical life meaningful themselves drop out. This is, for Niebuhr, the central paradox of historical life, and correspondingly it is the central paradox of the Atonement. The Atonement reveals God's judgment on our sin and God's wrath at our defiance of justice and our oppression of others; hence it emphasizes the distinction between good and evil—sin is, as Niebuhr says, ultimately serious even to God. But in and through the same disclosure of judgment comes the light of the divine mercy—and so even we are enabled to experience a renewal of life and return to our task in the world.

> The Christian doctrine of the Atonement, with its paradoxical conception of the relation of the divine mercy to the divine wrath is therefore the final key to this historical interpretation. The wrath and the judgment of God are symbolic of the seriousness of history. The distinctions between good and evil are important and have ultimate significance. The realization of the

good must be taken seriously. . . . On the other hand, the mercy of God, which strangely fulfills and contradicts the divine judgment, points to the incompleteness of all historic good, the corruption of evil in all historic achievements and the incompleteness of every historic system of meaning without the eternal mercy which knows how to destroy and transmute evil by taking it into itself. (ND 2:211–12)

∞

After this discussion of the Atonement, let us pause for a moment to note the appearance of Niebuhr's final and perhaps most unexpected paradox. This is his surprising statement that "the agape of God is thus at once the expression of both the final majesty of God and of His relation to history" (ND 2:71). We here have reached Niebuhr's culminating definition of divine transcendence, not as ultimate power or unconditioned being but as agape or divine love. Transcendence was the theme with which our study of Niebuhr's theology began, and now with this discussion we reach what is for him the final sign of the divine transcendence. This paradox becomes even sharper when we find Niebuhr in turn defining agape in terms of powerlessness (ND 2:72), a powerlessness symbolized and enacted historically in the event of Jesus' suffering on the cross. What can Niebuhr mean by this juxtaposition of divine transcendence and majesty with powerlessness, radical vulnerability, and sacrificial death?

This theme of love transcendent over law and over power began almost as soon as Niebuhr initiated the discussion of God's redemptive action in history. As we recall, prophetism had for Niebuhr shifted radically the understanding of the nature of this redemptive action. No longer was it conceived as the appearance of divine power on the side of the righteous, since the prophets saw that all, including even Israel, were unrighteous. Hence the only meaning of redemption, of the divine achievement of meaning in history, now could be through the mercy of God for all who are unrighteous:

> The final enigma of history is therefore not how the righteous will gain victory over the unrighteous, but how the evil in every good and the unrighteousness of the righteous is to be overcome. (ND 2:43)

The redemptive, fulfilling action of God in history is thus grounded in the divine mercy rather than in the divine sovereign power enacting and defending the divine law. As we have seen, for Niebuhr the divine law represented the orderly structure of reality (especially human reality), the logos character of all creation. Insofar, however, as all are sinners—and this is where we started—all must, in the validity of the divine judgment, be condemned. Hence the hope for any re-creative redemption, rather than a devastating judgment, is grounded in the triumph of the divine mercy over the divine law—a theme central to the gospel from Paul on. Mercy and forgiveness thus transcend logos and power as representing the profoundest and most mysterious depths of the divine nature. Divine agape, love, rather than divine law—and back of that divine power—has in Christ and the cross become, as Niebuhr said, on the one hand the final character of the divine transcendence, towering, so to speak, above logos, order, and law, and on the other the crucial key to the relation of God to history:

> The significance of the affirmation that God is revealed in Christ, and more particularly in his Cross, is that the love (agape) of God is conceived in terms which make the involvement in history a consequence of precisely the divine transcendence over the structures of history. The final majesty of God is contained not so much in His power within the structures as in the power of His freedom over the structures, that is, over the logos aspect of reality. This freedom is the power of mercy beyond judgment. (ND 2:71)

The final level, so to speak, of divine transcendence, the furthest reach into the divine mystery, is the divine mercy. God's agape, which comes to us beyond and over the law (as the final expression of that law) represents the grace of forgiveness. As Niebuhr has made plain, this transcendence of mercy over law and judgment—and over power—abrogates neither the divine logos and the judgment based upon it, nor the power of the divine being. In fact, as we have argued, he understands Atonement precisely as the means through which God establishes both God's mercy and God's judgment on our sin, and does so precisely by taking the suffering due to us as sinners upon God's self. The 'Atoning work' of Christ is precisely that, namely that in the self-sacrifice involved in Christ's death, God takes the suffering of the world, and deserved by the world, on God's self. As Niebuhr reiterates, it is thus necessary theologically that Jesus be the Christ, the representative of God, and not just a valiant and noble servant of God, and that as a consequence, "the sacrifice of Christ" is at the same time the bearing of the consequences of our sins by God's redeeming love.

In this interpretation of the cross, Niebuhr provides not only an interesting and original understanding of the Atonement. At the same time, he gives us his Christology, in the sense of his interpretation of the relation of the divinity and the humanity of Jesus the Christ (see ND 2:71ff., esp. 72–75.) As is evident, both are related to and spring from his under-standing of human nature, of sin, and especially of the ambiguous (creative yet fallen) character of social history. This intimate relation in Niebuhr be-tween social theory, political ethics, and "high theology" (Atonement and Christology) is nowhere more evident than in Niebuhr's discussion of 'powerlessness', the powerlessness and so the ultimate vulnerability of Jesus as the Christ. Here the agape of God, which represented the pinnacle of the divine transcendance and mystery, becomes in historical enactment the apparent opposite of transcendence, its paradoxical partner, *power-lessness* and *vulnerability*. In the divine love the ultimately unconditioned becomes the absolutely conditioned. And this paradox of unconditioned majesty and radically conditioned vulnerability, of ultimate power and ab-solute powerlessness, is for Niebuhr the center of the Christian gospel and of the Biblical message. As the following shows, this theological interpre-tation is entailed directly by his interpretation of political history:

> The final majesty, the ultimate freedom and the perfect disinteredness of the divine love can have a counterpart in history only in a life which ends trag-ically, because it refuses to participate in the claims and counterclaims of historical existence. . . . It is impossible to symbolize the divine goodness in history in any other way than by complete powerlessness, or rather by a consistent refusal to use power in the rivalries of history. For there is no self in history or society, no matter how impartial its perspective upon the com-petitions of life, which can rise to the position of a disinterested participa-tion in those rivalries and competitions. It can symbolize disinterested love only by a refusal to participate in the rivalries. Any participation in them means the assertion of one ego interest against another. (ND 2:72)[10]

Thus directly in relation to his earlier analysis of social history as self-interested and hypocritical, as a conflict of 'rivalries and competitions', and so, as he later termed it, 'sinful', has now arisen his Christology of di-vine participation in the event of Jesus' sacrifice and death, and his inter-pretation of the Atonement as the inescapably 'powerless' revelation of the transcendent divine agape. This understanding of society—albeit in very different philosophical and theological terms—had begun with *Moral Man*

---

10. As I noted some years ago (1959) in *Maker of Heaven and Earth,* Thomas Aquinas makes much the same point about the union of divine transcendence, or omnipotence, and divine mercy: "God's omnipotence is particularly shown in shar-ing and having mercy because in this it is made manifest that God has supreme power, namely that He freely forgives sins. For it is not for one who is bound by the laws of a superior to forgive sins of his own free choice" (*Summa Theologica,* pt. 1, question 25, art. 3).

and Immoral Society. Now enshrined in quite different theological ("Biblical") categories, it reappears as central to his understanding of christology and Atonement. In a history saturated with self-interested power, the divine can only appear—precisely as transcendent to this 'war of the finites'—as powerlessness.

∞

The central thrust of Niebuhr's argument concerning grace and redemption in history is, one may legitimately say, that only God can accomplish redemption and hence establish and fulfill the meaning of existence. Most of the discussion of redemption I have traced has centered on the need for both judgment and mercy, and vis-à-vis grace with the dialectic of empowerment and mercy, sanctification, and forgiveness for continuing sin. We should not, however, miss the strong antihumanist thrust of Niebuhr's thought: if humans take their own salvation as the fulfillment of meaning in their life into their own hands, the inevitable result is idolatry, pride, and destruction on the one hand or despair and enervation on the other. Only God can provide a sufficient and creative meaning for life; this is the meaning of Christ and of grace. And it is precisely the role of faith to recognize and assent to this.

> Every facet of the Christian revelation, whether of the relation of God to history, or of the relation of man to the eternal, points to the impossibility of man fulfilling the true meaning of his life and reveals sin to be primarily derived from his abortive efforts to do so. The Christian gospel nevertheless enters the world with the proclamation that in Christ both 'wisdom' and 'power' are available to man; which is to say that not only has the true meaning of life been disclosed but that resources have been made available to fulfill that meaning. . . . Grace represents on the one hand the mercy and forgiveness of God by which He completes what man cannot complete and overcomes the sinful elements of all of man's achievements. Grace is the power over man. Grace is on the other hand the power of God in man. (ND 2:98–99)

The main subject of this passage is, to be sure, the twofold character of grace as forgiveness and as sanctifying power. Nonetheless, behind this dialectical duality clearly lies an even more fundamental motif: God alone can accomplish this, and the first rule of faith—implicit in both repentance and trust—is to recognize and assent to this.

Despite its major concentration on an empirical look at human social behavior, on the real characteristics of political existence, and on the actual shape of the contours of history, Niebuhr's theology is, therefore, a "God-centered" theology and not a humanistic or naturalistic one. As a consequence it cannot possibly be understood—as many have sought to do—as primarily brilliant social commentary with the pious icing, so to speak, of theological or Biblical rhetoric. Such an interpretation is clearly untrue to Niebuhr's texts; but even more, it completely falsifies what he wished to say in every line he wrote. Without God—and God's judgment and mercy—there are only the possibilities of idolatry and destruction or despair and enervation; without God, therefore, there is hope of neither meaning nor renewal in life or in history. Without God—and the agape of Christ—mutual love, descending rapidly into the self-interested calculation of survival, remains our only 'norm' and the secure establishment of the self and its community our only moral ideal. This is the view that he labeled 'cynicism' and that he steadily and rightly contrasted with his own view. We are able to face the present ambiguity of our actions, and the certain prospects of the continuing ambiguity of these actions, and still try to hold to our moral norms only if we count on neither our own virtue nor on our own power but on God's judgment and mercy.

Because of the centrality of God and of God's grace in Niebuhr's understanding of history's meaning, it is no wonder that those who found his theological language merely 'rhetoric' always thought of him as 'gloomy'. Not able or willing to credit that so brilliant a commentator on history could actually believe in God, they discounted this entire discussion as Niebuhr's 'traditional piety'—and were hence left either justifying an uncritical self-interest or, to their horror, an existence without hope. This is why Niebuhr's theology is as important in understanding him as are his political and ethical insights, and why I have devoted this volume to this aspect of his thought.

∞

God, then, is the center of this theology and so of the meaning of life and of history that the Christian faith promises. Essential to this, of course, is the reality of God. Niebuhr does not to my knowledge discuss this point; he assumes it. In Niebuhr's theology, God cannot be a projection, a human ideal shone outward onto the cosmos, an ideal made transcendent by the creativity of human self-transcendence (though many of his statements in his early writings seemed to imply this view).

Such a deity would for the mature Niebuhr be the creation of ordinary and all-too-common human idolatry, a product of a finite and so partial cultural imagination and so no more transcendent than any other cultural artifact. Here then there would be no judgment beyond self-judgment and no hope beyond the hope our own powers and ideals may give to us. The proof of Niebuhr's belief that only God gives meaning to human history is his repeated identification of criticism of the prophets' own nation with the genuine transcendence of cultural limitations and with the appearance of revelation, and so the unquestioned presence of an authentic and not an idolatrous divine voice. This clear Niebuhrian identification of judgment with transcendence over culture and of hope with a power not our own necessitates the primordial identification of the transcendence of God with the ultimate reality of God. Like both Luther and Calvin, Niebuhr characteristically avoided ontological language; but as in so many cases in his thought as in theirs, beyond the personal and historical (mythical) symbols about God which he used the most, lay the ontological assumption that God represents ultimate reality, or properly put, that God is Being itself.[11]

This ontological assumption, latent in all that Niebuhr says about transcendence, is clear in the following:

> The idea of a source and end of life, too transcendent to the desires, capacities, and powers of human life to be either simply comprehended by the human mind or easily manipulated for human ends, represents the radical break of Biblical faith with the idolatrous tendencies of all human culture. (FH 103; see also ND 2:22)

And Niebuhr continues in a passage already quoted in chapter 4 above:

> The idea of a God choosing Israel as an act of grace, since Israel has no power or virtue to merit the choice, represents a radical break in the history of culture. It is, in a genuine sense, the beginning of revelation; for here a nation apprehends, and is apprehended by the true God [sic] and not by a divine creature of its own contrivance. The proof of the genuineness of His majesty and of the truth of His deity is attested by the fact that He confronts the nation and the individual as the limit, and not the extension, of its power and purpose. (FH 104)

11. See Langdon Gilkey, *Maker of Heaven and Earth* (Garden City, N.Y.: Doubleday, 1959). This early Niebuhrian book represents a study of the symbol of creation. Largely inspired by Niebuhr's theology, it came to the above conclusion: according to ex nihilo (a favorite symbol for Niebuhr) God is the source of all existence and hence the "ultimate reality," creator of all things whatsoever. Here Niebuhr and Tillich, despite their fundamental linguistic differences, are thoroughly in accord.

The clear implication of these passages is the 'objective' reality of the God who 'confronts' Israel and is accordingly apprehended as judging as well as choosing the nation. Hence it is evident that Niebuhr does not affirm that God is here a human projection in the sense of an imagined and then hypostasized illusion, a symbol that has no ontological referent in a universe void of deity.

What, then, could he have meant by the language of projection, language which he used in his early work and also, if infrequently, in his mature thought? Niebuhr agreed that the Hebrew and the Christian communities conceived of the God "they apprehended" in human images taken from their cultural, social, and personal lives. From these they formed the symbols in terms of which they spoke of God. Hence their words and symbols could have been called 'projection', and he so named them. As we have seen, however, these projected images and symbols were for him a *response* to the presence of God, whom they apprehended and who apprehended them. The fact that persons conceive and speak in terms of their images does not at all entail, for Niebuhr, the unreality of that of which we speak. In short, Niebuhr seems here to put himself among the "critical realists."

One can also note in passing that the Biblical 'break with reason', which is the disclosure of a transcendent and universal reality within and through a single and merely finite event, a particular and so 'positive' event (Lessing's "wide, wide ditch")[12] now makes, as Niebuhr argues, genuine sense and not *non*sense. The universality of God or of our concepts of God cannot be grounded on the universality of the notion of God within our experience, nor even on the universal coherence of that notion with the structures of our rational understanding. Such universal rational principles, and any coherent system based on them, are, in the end, for Niebuhr, cultural products and so culturally relative. God's universality is based on the divine transcendence over all that is partial and relative, including the rationality and coherence discerned in all experience by a particular cultural reason. And that transcendence in turn is grounded in the ultimate reality of God as the universal source of everything creaturely, including our own most universal principles of comprehension.

> The 'scandal of particularity' in the Biblical interpretation is a necessary point of revelation and Biblical Faith. The mysterious divine power, which expresses the beginning, the present order and the final end of history, represents a depth of mystery and meaning which is not fully disclosed by

12. Gotthold Lessing, *Über den Beweis des Geistes und der Kraft,* vol. 10. See Kierkegaard's extended comments on this issue, *Concluding Unscientific Postscript,* pt. 1, chapter 2, "Theses Possibly or Actually Attributable to Lessing."

the obvious coherences of nature and sequences of history. Yet Biblical faith is not identical with agnosticism. It believes that God does disclose His purposes. The disclosure takes place in significant events in history. (FH 105; see also 113)

It is, moreover, the transcendent power of God as well as God's mercy that is disclosed in the events to which the Biblical message witnesses. The sovereign power and transcendent love in God are not separated (as in the Reformers), but both together appear essential to the redemption I have articulated. The divine power is manifested both in the existence and vitality of all creatures and in the structure of order that gives coherence and pattern to their motion, their behavior, and their creative action. The divine power or sovereignty is on the one hand the being of the beings and on the other the logos, or order, that rules their existence. Power as logos in ordering creation thus establishes limits to what creatures can and cannot do; it sets bounds to the rebellion of which a free creature is capable:

> The drama [of history] is, in essence, not so much a contest between good and evil forces in history as a contest between all men and God. In this contest God has resources of power and mercy finally to overcome the human rebellion. He asserts his sovereignty partly by the power which places an ultimate limit on human defiance and partly by a resource of love and mercy which alone is able to touch the source of the rebellion in the human heart. (FH 125; see also 126)

> Ultimately the drama consists of God's contest with all men, who are all inclined to defy God because they all tend to make their own life into the center of history's meaning. An outer limit is set for this human defiance of the divine will by the fact of God's power, revealed in the structures of existence, which leads to the ultimate self-destruction of forms of life which make themselves into their own end by either isolation or dominion. . . . Ultimately this rebellion of man against God is overcome by divine power, which includes the power of the divine love. (FH 27, 28)

The divine sovereign power that limits the destructiveness of human rebellion effects, however, only a 'rough justice'; and the bounds it sets to sin cannot finally deal with the inwardness of sin. Hence the need for the sharper disclosure of the divine judgment in the law and for the final revelation of the divine mercy in the covenant and in Christ, whose joint culmination in the Atonement I have already articulated. Sin remains wherever freedom remains; the disclosure of meaning in history effects renewal of meaning, but also it awaits the fulfillment of meaning at the end of history.

> History, in short, does not solve the enigma of history. There are facets of
> meaning in it which transcend the flux of time. These give glimpses of the
> eternal love which bears the whole project of history. . . . Faith (therefore)
> awaits a final judgment and a final resurrection. . . . But the clue to the mys-
> tery is the agape of Christ. It is the clue to the mystery of Creation. . . . It is
> the clue to the mystery of the renewals and redemptions within history.
> Since whenever the divine mercy is discerned as within and above the
> wrath, which destroys all forms of self-seeking, life may be renewed indi-
> vidually and collectively. . . . Whatever provisional meanings there may be
> in such a process, it must drive man to despair when viewed ultimately, un-
> less they have discerned the power and the mercy which overcomes the
> enigma at its end. (FH 233)

There are, therefore, renewals in life through God's power and God's
grace; these renewals are effected in and through the experience of a judgment leading to repentance and of grace leading to renewed faith. In this
experience there is a shattering of the old self-centered self on the one
hand and a new confidence or trust in a forgiving power not our own on
the other, a confidence in the fulfillment God will achieve through us and
for us—so long as we know that that judgment and mercy do not cease but
remain necessary to our end. Repentance and faith in response to God's
judgment and mercy represent the continual possibilities of new life in
history. They are the only guard against idolatry, the only motivation for a
life devoted to increased justice, and the only way to avoid despair. At the
center again is the paradox of grace, the "I, yet not I, but Christ," and of a
having and yet not having:

> On the one hand, there is the possibility of the renewal of life and the de-
> struction of evil, whenever men and nations see themselves as they truly are
> under a divine judgment, which is as merciful as it is terrible. On the other
> hand, the life of each individual as well as the total human enterprise remain
> in contradiction to God; and the final resolution of this contradiction is
> by God's mercy. . . . Life may be reborn, if, under the divine judgment
> and mercy, the old self or the old culture or civilization are shattered. (FH
> 125–26)

All grace is of God, and only of God, as we have seen. Nonetheless, its
presence establishes once again the 'real self', now truly free of the self-
centering that distorts it and ultimately destroys it: "This new self is the
real self; for the self is infinitely self-transcendent; and any premature centering of itself around its own interests, individual or collectively, destroys
and corrupts its freedom" (ND 2:110). This is the real self, and so the free

self. Hence as free and self-directed, as autonomous, the self must participate in this dramatic new birth; it cannot for Niebuhr remain a passive on-looker to its own renewal. It must 'choose itself' even in this new situation of the presence of grace:

> The real situation is that both affirmations—that only God as Christ can break and reconstruct the sinful self, and that the self 'must open the door' and is capable of doing so—are equally true; and they are both unquali-fiedly true, each on their [*sic*] own level. Yet either affirmation becomes false if it is made without reference to the other. (ND 2:118)

Niebuhr has here, so it seems to me, expressed very vividly what Tillich labeled *theonomy*. This is the conception of the true or essential self that on the one hand is utterly dependent on God and on the other at last free to be fully itself. The true self is the self that finds itself freely in its depen-dence on God. Then its infinite self-transcendence finds its true home in the divine mystery, and its anxious creaturely existence finds its real secu-rity in faith in the divine power and love. It is fully itself because its creative spirit is finally rooted in God. It is now fully autonomous, free now to choose itself because its existence through faith is in fact theonomous, de-pendent on God in all that it is, including its virtue and righteousness. Clearly in this, both Tillich and Niebuhr are dependent on Kierkegaard and his insistence that the self must choose and so constitute itself.[13]

∞

Niebuhr conceives of the divine sovereignty, expressed in the divine judg-ment and the divine mercy, as the principle of meaning and of hope not only for the individual but also for the collective life of human beings, that is, as the basis for meaning in wider history. Nonetheless, we recall his con-tinual insistence that this disclosure of the divine action in historical life can be received or known only by the deepest inwardness, by genuine and inward repentance and "the shattering of the self" on the one hand, and a responding and personal confidence or trust in the divine power and mercy on the other.

---

13. Kierkegaard described the self as a synthesis of eternity and time, a relation-ship that establishes and effects itself, in relation to an other—the Other that has es-tablished both; see *Sickness unto Death*, 1:a:a.

As a consequence, we are led inevitably to a puzzling question. Is such a deeply existential interpretation of the divine sovereign power of God in history really relevant to the question of the destiny of human collectives, to the actions of communities as well as to the lives of individuals, and so to the careers of justice and injustice in history? Were not the Lutheran Reformation, and Augustine, finally right that the gospel of salvation by grace *alone* and its correlate justification by grace through faith could be applied only to the personal life of individual men and women and not to their political and public existence? We have seen how Niebuhr (and Tillich) expanded the paradox of justification by grace through faith, a having and a not having, from the realm of personal religious justification to the wider cultural realms of truth and of justice: we have the truth and we can hope to be just only if we do not claim either one too proudly or too confidently. But now we are asking a deeper question: Can we speak of *collective* renewal—either with regard to truth or to justice—in categories apparently dependent or inward, and so individual, repentance and inward trust? Kierkegaard said that each individual appropriated grace only by inward decision and so 'one by one', and not in crowds.[14] Is Niebuhr the existentialist able so thoroughly to break with Kierkegaard on this issue?

Niebuhr clearly recognizes the problem of a translation, so to speak, of an existential and inward resolution into the public, historical sphere, and he seeks to deal with it (FH 221–30). There are, he says, structures of 'common grace' in history that mediate creative renewal to public life. Prominent among these structures is the need of each community for unifying rule, for the minimal harmony and order that make creative social life possible. This collective harmony is, of course, of interest to the self-concern of each ruling class, especially as it comes to power; but it is also of great value to the wider community. This 'coincidence' between the interests of a ruling group and the interests of the whole community—a "righteousness that is not our own"—is, says Niebuhr, by virtue of a grace of providence (FH 220–23). And there are many such 'structures of common grace' in history, namely communal social structures erected by both creativity and self-concern, that nonetheless mediate harmony to the entire community (e.g., ND 2:192, 248; FH 174–75). Second, there is in history the continual possibility that when an established order is challenged, the ruling group may be driven to see the limits of their collective pretensions, and, if not repent, at least desist from their determined resis-

14. Kierkegaard, *Concluding Unscientific Postscript,* e.g., chapter 3, "Real or Ethical Subjectivity—the Subjective Thinker."

tance to that challenge.[15] Here the consequences of their pride of power in terms of injustice begin to be visible, the threat of endless violence and destruction is heeded, and, therefore, a new kind of 'repentant enlightenment' may begin to occur. Of course, if this new challenge is met by "patriotism," that is, ever more extravagant claims, then only renewed conflict will ensue.

> The death and famine in the life of man's social institutions and cultures is thus never so much the fruit of a natural mortality as a consequence of the vain delusion which seeks to hide the contingency and mortality of every power and majesty in human history.
>
> But there is fortunately another possibility in history. . . . Sometimes the competitive challenge serves to moderate the idolatrous claims. Judgment leads to repentance. There is not as clearly defined an experience of repentance in the life of communities and social institutions as in that of individuals. Yet there is a possibility that old forms and structures of life may be renewed, rather than destroyed by the vicissitudes of history. These experiences establish the validity of the Christian doctrine of life through death for the collective, as well as for the individual, organism. (FH 226; see also 229–30)

Niebuhr finally ends this discussion with a Biblical, even an Augustinian theme; namely, the role of the community of faith in collective renewal:

> Ideally the Christian Community is the "saving remnant" which calls the nations to repentance and renewal without the false belief that any nation or culture could finally fulfill the meaning of life or complete the purpose of history. (FH 230)

This was certainly in Niebuhr's mind the ideal vocation for the church, as it was the reality of much of his own preaching. It seems to imply, as I noted above, a kind of "Augustinian" solution in which a social history dominated by sin is until the end continually renewed by the presence of

---

15. Quite possibly Niebuhr here had in mind the belated realization by Great Britain—and other colonial powers—that ultimate and endless resistance to the demands for national autonomy by India, Indochina, Algeria, etc., was useless and self-defeating, a realization to which America came—equally slowly and just as unwillingly—many years later in the period 1969–73.

the Word of judgment and of mercy borne by the community of grace, the church.[16]

Niebuhr maintained, however, that despite this hope, the fact is that with the church as with the individual, sanctifying grace and even social wisdom are present in 'principle but not in fact'; that is, in earnest and promise but all too frequently not in reality. Hence the church too is justified only by the grace of forgiveness and not by its own secure possession of sanctification or of truth. Thus the church must be 'prophetic' before it is 'priestly'; it begins with repentant self-criticism, and only then can it become a medium of renewing grace to history. This Niebuhrian 'prophetic' understanding of the church and its role in history is, I believe, in its critical distrust of the established church fully equal to that of the French Enlightenment and to the later 'secular' criticisms of religion, for example, those of John Dewey. Both of these secular critiques saw clearly the continuing danger of absolutism in a community built on its relation to the absolute; for them it is religion per se, in itself, that introduces absolutism and all its woeful consequences into historical life. Somewhat surprisingly, Niebuhr agrees that the great danger to the justice and peace of history is precisely the claim to the absolute, to possess it, to represent it, or to be its instrument. This is precisely what he calls idolatry or intellectual, moral, and spiritual pride. His disagreement with these secular critics is, of course, that the only antidote to this tendency to claim an absolute authority and virtue, which is the quintessence of sin, is repentance and faith, that is, the presence of a transcendent judgment that includes criticism even of our own obvious wisdom and virtue. And thus this judgment limits and reduces our common pretensions.

Niebuhr agrees with the secular critics of religion, moreover, that while every group or community is tempted by whatever eminence it possesses to make such pretentious claims, it is explicitly religious groups that are especially prone to this destructive idolatry. And among religious groups, it is precisely those that are most concerned with redemption from sin— and especially those that claim to have overcome sin through redeeming grace—that must struggle hardest with this temptation. Hence his criti-

16. For my articulation of Augustine's view of history under providence, see Langdon Gilkey, *Reaping the Whirlwind* (New York: Seabury, 1976), chapter 7. See also in another thoroughly Niebuhrian volume my early exploration of the role of the churches in modern American society; Langdon Gilkey, *How the Church Can Minister to the World without Losing Itself* (New York: Harper & Row, 1964).

cisms of the church—through history as in the present—are breathtaking in their depth and in their scope. Let us now see how this criticism of the very religious 'means of redemption' unfolds, and what it may mean about Niebuhr's understanding of history.

> The sad experiences of Christian history show how human pride and spiritual arrogance rise to new heights precisely at the point where the claims of sanctity are made without due qualification. (ND 2:122)

> It becomes increasingly apparent that human self-esteem resists the truth of the Christian gospel almost as vigorously within the bounds of a faith which has ostensibly accepted it, as it was resisted by the pre-Christian ages. (ND 2:127)

> It [the Catholic structure of faith] seeks for a place in history where sin is transcended and only finiteness remains. In seeking for that place it runs the danger of falling prey to the sin of spiritual pride and of illustrating in its own life that the final human pretension is made most successfully under the aegis of a religion which has overcome human pretension in principle. (ND 2:144)

Eight years later (1948–49) this critique of the pretensions of religion, and especially of the Christian religion, Catholic or Protestant, has only increased in intensity even as, paradoxically, Niebuhr's theology has become more centered on revelation and on the gospel of grace:

> They [Catholic and Calvinist efforts to overcome moral ambiguity] prove that just as sin is the corruption of man's creative freedom, so also the ultimate form of sin is a corruption of man's quest for redemption. . . . If the effort of modern culture to make history itself into a false Christ is to be refuted, the Christian faith must allow modern culture to bring its evidence against Christianity itself, wherever Christian life or thought has created false Christs of political power. (FH 205)

> It is obvious, in short, that the church may become involved in a more grievous error than the world, precisely because it is a bearer of a Gospel according to which all human truths and virtues are rendered problematic. One may question whether any fragment of the modern church understands as well as the prophets of Israel understood how severe the judgment of God falls upon the community which is the bearer of the judgment. (FH 242)

Any confidence that the church can become the bearer of the meaning of history is, therefore, for Niebuhr, disastrously misplaced. Human religion and the church are prime offenders when it comes to idolatry and its destructive consequences. So far Niebuhr is, as he recognized, a child of the Renaissance even more than the Reformation, which agreed on this about the sacramental, apostolic Catholic church but failed to see that the same criticism applied to the evangelical church that claimed to bear the Word of God.

In this sharp criticism or self-criticism, however, Niebuhr has by no means capitulated to the Enlightenment or to its modern naturalistic and pragmatic descendants. He agrees with their critique of religion, but he broadens that critique to the 'secular' life of human beings, whose emergence they prophesied and in whose promised freedom from religion and so from all absolutism they firmly believed. Idolatry, says Niebuhr, is a problem for religion, even, or especially, for profound religion; but it is much more than that. It is the central problem of being human, and hence it will appear in just as violent form in the communities of secular culture, but without the potential limitation that a gospel of judgment and of grace might bring to it.

> The enemies of religion do not, of course, understand that they are dealing with a more fundamental problem than anything created by this or that religion; that it is the problem of the relative and the absolute in history; that the problem is solved by Christian faith 'in principle'; that Christian faith may aggravate the problem if it claims more than that; but that alternative solutions, as they are evolved in secular culture, present us with either the abyss of skepticism or with new fanaticism. (ND 2:220)

And here, as in the above, Niebuhr speaks as if his own mind were itself a synthesis of the Enlightenment (modernity) and the Reformation, presenting to us this quite new vision of the ambiguity of history and of the transcendent hope that gives meaning to history. Again the Reformation principle of justification by the grace of judgment and mercy received by repentance and faith is made the principle for understanding the meaning of our common life, both secular and religious:

> This is the final enigma of human existence for which there is no answer except by faith and hope; for all answers transcend the categories of human reason. Yet without these answers human life is threatened with skepticism and nihilism on the one hand; and with fanaticism and pride on the other. For either it is overwhelmed by the relativity and partiality of all human perspectives and comes to the conclusion there is no truth, since no man

can expound the truth without corrupting it; or it pretends to have absolute truth despite the finite nature of human perspectives. (ND 2:149)[17]

The communities and institutions of history remain ambiguous to history's end. The only hope, therefore, lies in the understanding and recognition of this ambiguity and in a new repentant confidence in the power and love of God—that is, as Niebuhr says, by faith and hope. He ends, therefore, consistent with his understanding of the paradox of grace: There are renewals in history; there is a growing treasury of truth; there are hidden possibilities of more justice. These fragmentary meanings are there, and they give life its confidence and hope. But they are there only so long as we recognize humbly that they all remain relative, that we do and will corrupt them, and so that we mortals live by faith and hope and not by the conviction we possess either truth, justice, or security, or that we can— even through our own faith and hope—purge or complete our incompleteness (ND 2:57; FH 150, 170). And we can recognize this relativity and our corruption of it only if we know a divine judgment transcendent to our own achievements. And we can bear this recognized relativity, incompleteness, and ambiguity only if we have faith in a transcendent fulfillment in God's promise.

Because of Niebuhr's sharp realism, even about things he treasured the most, it is important to stress the many significant things in which he did believe—lest he be pictured as the cynic he always deplored. To this catalog of his beliefs I shall now turn in our final chapter on eschatology.

17. One might add that modern, pragmatic naturalism, e.g., that of John Dewey, would dispute this older dichotomy and maintain that science recognizes its truth to be relative and that democracy recognizes each perspective to be relative—and yet neither one falls into Niebuhr's predicted despair of skepticism on the one hand or the danger of idolatry on the other hand. Niebuhr would reply that while scientific conclusions may be held to be tentative, the faith in science as "the only way to know" has become a modern dogma and that similarly in a world of competing ideologies, democracy itself may well make itself absolute, and has done so. I should add that Niebuhr seems also to be right when he says that it is by no means easy to bear serenely the relativity of truth and of moral and political commitment envisioned by Dewey and pragmatism. As our present situation demonstrates, in such a culture absolute forms of religion appear quickly enough and show that the "problem of the relative and the absolute" remains at the center of history's enigmas.

CHAPTER 10

The Enigma of History and Eschatology

History

As this volume attests, Niebuhr's consciousness of sin, of its lurking, its continuing, and its destructive presence in all of human life, is so heavy, and his depiction of it so persuasive, that a careful student of his thought cannot help but ask: What, then, did he believe in? What sort of theological, that is, reflective and grounded, basis was there for the pervasive themes of confidence and hope that run through his work? Granted the near certainty of continuing sin on every level of human achievement, even in the religious community and even to history's end, what is it that for him makes history—as he surely thought it was—meaningful and not meaningless?

Clearly the first and most obvious thing Niebuhr believed in was the creativity of men and women. This creativity is on the one hand intrinsic, an essential and ineradicable capacity of the human, and it is virtually limitless. Here Niebuhr is—as he suggested—a thoroughly modern observer of the human scene, imbued with the sense of the novel possibilities latent in each next moment of history. Creativity here is the human capacity to create the new, to refashion what is given into something genuinely novel or, as Niebuhr puts it, to break through older patterns of order, older forms, and establish new forms in their place. Though he does not say so, Niebuhr agrees with Whitehead and Hartshorne that human freedom entails the capacity to be 'cocreator' with God, to introduce new forms into temporal sequence that had not been there before.

This intrinsic capacity is deeply built into the essential structure of human being, namely the self-transcendence that Niebuhr calls the 'image of God'. For Niebuhr it is because we are self-transcendent that we can become critical of given forms, break through their hegemony, and imagine and establish new forms: new forms of material artifacts, of social life, of ideas, of truth, of moral obligation. We note at once his immense, and surprising, approval of a developing technology as well as of a continuingly transformed social existence. This is, moreover, for him an 'autonomous' capacity latent in what we are as humans, a part of "human nature." We are not creative through participation in the divine ground, as in Tillich; nor do we even need to envision the realm of 'not-yet' possibilities represented by Whitehead's Primordial Nature of God, in order conceptually to comprehend novelty. On the contrary, novelty here seems to spring forth 'naturally' or 'immanently' from our innate imaginative powers as a part of our native self-transcendence. In being creative, men and women seem in Niebuhr, therefore, to be 'over against' God, a bit on their own. God surely limits God's self and God's power here, or (as Kierkegaard says) "steps back," so to speak, in order to give the creature room to be creative on its own and in its own way.

In this sense, despite his heavy antihumanist themes, Niebuhr has absorbed a very great deal of the enthusiasm about the creative capacities of the human from modern humanist culture. Humans are here radically 'autonomous', creative themselves of their own creativity as they are creative of their own rebellion. There is, therefore, little intimation in Niebuhr of any identity between humans and God; their relation is always a *relation,* crucial to human being but nonetheless imaged as of one between two relatively independent beings. It represents, as he frequently puts it, an *encounter* between God and women and men, an encounter in which we must personally and autonomously participate in the inwardness of repentance and faith. We choose ourselves and autonomously constitute ourselves as selves, even in our relation to God. In this sense we are free 'over against' God; Niebuhr is here Arminian to the core. We are *autonomous* in and through the dependence of faith on God, just as we are as free creatures utterly dependent ontologically on God.

Of course the moment these latter points are made, they must be qualified by the paradoxical affirmation that God is the Creator and Preserver of men and women, and hence none of their capacities, even to be autonomous creatures, are or could be at all without the continuing power of God's creative being. In this sense there is no ultimate autonomy, independence, or equality here. Men and women are utterly dependent on God for their entire being, for their continuity in time, and for the fulfillment—as opposed to the self-destruction—of their self-transcending creativity. They are and they remain dependent creatures, even in their creativity. Nor does the obvious transcendence of God in Niebuhr's thought, not least in this matter under discussion, negate the necessary immanence of God's power and order throughout creation, or of God's judgment and grace throughout history. Nonetheless, despite their obvious dependence, humans are creative, and hence, as Niebuhr reiterates, does history have unlimited possibilities of indeterminate development. For Niebuhr, as for Augustine, the paradoxical requirement of human existence is that one's autonomy and independence of spirit represent, through the autonomous freedom of inward faith, a *spiritual dependence* on God (i.e., faith) and hence reflect thereby the *ontological* dependence on God that our creaturely existence illustrates. Then in the radical dependence on God of faith (reflecting our ontological dependence), our equally radical autonomy (reflecting our freedom) is fulfilled. Autonomy, creativity, and freedom are in Niebuhr established, fulfilled, and perfected by the relation of dependence on God, which is faith. Thus just as autonomy requires rather than challenges the transcendence of God, so in Niebuhr freedom is realized and completed and not compromised in a dependent relation to God. Niebuhr, in other words, and on his own terms, is a *theonomous* theologian.

As I have noted, this divine transcendence in Niebuhr does not at all imply the smothering of human autonomy or uniqueness, as Nietzsche feared. It is God's power that grounds but does not stifle our creativity. Further, as we recall, it is God's transcendence that gives 'room' for the infinite self-transcendence of the human spirit. Our capacity to challenge and to criticize every apparent coherence and to move creatively beyond it—that is, our capacity to transcend ourselves and our every coherent achievement indefinitely—is precisely what required the ultimate transcendence of God as the mystery beyond our partial meanings. God's transcendence is thus the ground of the infinity of our creativity, not its antithesis or even its limitation.[1] This is a modern, 'humanist' understanding of divine tran-

---

1. Recall the essential role of the infinity of human self-transcendence and the transcendent mystery of God: "We must comprehend ourselves in terms of a principle beyond our comprehension" (ND 1:125). See the discussion of this theme in chapters 4, 6, 8, 10, and 11. Granted that autonomy, creativity, and freedom are, in Niebuhr, established, fulfilled, and perfected by the relation of dependence on God—which is central to human being and which is expressed inwardly in us in faith—autonomy, nevertheless, requires rather than challenges the transcendence of God. In Niebuhr, freedom is realized and completed, not compromised, in relation to God.

All three errors of most estimates of man, therefore, point to a single and common source of error: man is not measured in a dimension sufficiently high or deep to do full justice to either his stature or his capacity for good and evil or to understand the

scendence based on the infinity of human aspiration and creativity. Correspondingly, God's transcendence—and the corresponding transcendence of agape—does not limit the possibilities of historical development but lures each development on and gives each one room. For Niebuhr, creaturely creativity is so vast that there are no assignable limits to its scope; and God is so conceived as to ground, encourage, and celebrate the novel forms that this creativity brings forth in time.

Niebuhr says all of this over and over—and then admonishes us to remember that each new act of creativity also represents the temptation to regard it as final and ultimate, and so it represents also the ever-present danger of idolatry and sin with their evident consequences of injustice, conquest, violence, and suffering. That admonishment is so relevant and persuasive in the light of each day's news that we can easily forget the very great confidence in creative human powers that it presupposes. Niebuhr, then, believes in human creativity—but he does not believe it resolves the problem of human meaning, because there is also and always sin. And sin is not gradually eliminated by creativity as most of modernity believed; on the contrary, sin is encouraged by creativity, a condition that modern history illustrates.

> The increase of human freedom over nature is like the advancing season which ripens both wheat and tares, which are inextricably intermingled. . . . History, in short, does not solve the enigma of history. (FH 232–33)

The infinity of human creativity calls for the transcendence of God to make 'room' for the continuing outpouring of the new; correspondingly, the infinite capacity for sin balancing that creativity calls for the transcendence of God as the sole basis for the judgment, criticism, and healing of human pretensions.

---

total environment in which such a stature can understand, express and find itself. (ND 1:124; see also 1:122; also FH 49)

The rational faculty by which he orders and interprets his experience . . . is itself part of the finite world which man seeks to understand. The only principle for the comprehension of the whole . . . is, therefore, beyond his comprehension. Man is thus in the position of being unable to comprehend himself in the full stature of his freedom without a principle of comprehension which is beyond his comprehension. (ND 1:124)

Implicit in the human situation of freedom and in man's capacity to transcend himself and his world is his inability to construct a world of meaning without finding a source and key to the structure of meaning which transcends the world beyond his capacity to understand it. (ND 1:169)

And my comment: "The transcendence of God is correlated with, not antithetical to, the infinite self-transcendence and inescapable autonomy of the human spirit."

Let us also recall that, like the liberal tradition that preceded him, Niebuhr thoroughly recognized and affirmed the value of each human being. And like the liberals, he believed this estimate of human beings to be the major result of Jesus' teaching. By the value of each person is meant that person's value to God, to others, and also to herself—her 'worth' as an end in itself and never, as Kant said, to be considered a means to another's end. Niebuhr does not speak of this frequently, as he does of creativity or of sin; almost certainly he inherited this conviction from his own liberal, Ritschlian background.[2] But obviously he assumes it; I say "obviously" because this assumption is the absolutely necessary presupposition for his concern with justice. The suffering of others, the oppression and domination of others, the violence and cruelty to others—which are for him the essence and substance of evil in history and the important consequences of sin[3]—are evil if and only if the human beings so used are of value, in fact the center and focus of value. Finally, the love and mercy of God toward us "While we were yet sinners"—that is, while we have little or no virtue and no merits—shows that to God we nonetheless possess value, and hence, at the deepest level, value to ourselves and to others.

One of Niebuhr's most important distinctions is that between the *value* of a person and the *virtue* of that person. All persons are of value, even when they have little virtue—that is because God loves them and because they are autonomous persons, ends in themselves. The value of those who suffer remains and calls for our justice; but this presence of value in the oppressed does not mean that those who are oppressed are thereby virtuous or selfless. The justice of the cause of the proletariat, of the peoples occupied by colonial powers, of oppressed races, or of dominated women did not for Niebuhr at all mean the unalloyed virtue of any of these groups, as liberal sensitivities are inclined to assume. Hence their value as human beings remained the constant ground of the requirement on each of us of giving them both justice and love—even when, as is frequently the case, their lack of virtue becomes evident when they in turn gain power. In sum the value of each creature, and especially of each human creature, is for Niebuhr central to everything Christian faith wishes to say.

2. See Adolf von Harnack, *What Is Christianity?* (New York: G. P. Putnam, 1906), chap. 1.

3. The important consequences of sin for Niebuhr are not, as for most of the tradition, death on the one hand and eternal damnation on the other, nor are the consequences of sin mainly the self-destruction sin brings on each sinner; rather they are the destruction of the other, who as a consequence is assumed to possess her or his own infinite value.

Since, then, the value of each human being does not indicate their virtue, nor does creativity promise the reduction of sin, our question returns: On what grounds does Niebuhr have the hope he evidently had for meaning in history?

∞

The answer to this query is unquestionably that for Niebuhr hope for a meaningful life and a meaningful history lies in the power and in the love of God.

> The antinomies of good and evil increase rather than diminish in the long course of history. Whatever provisional meanings there may be in such a process, it must drive men to despair when viewed ultimately, unless they have discerned the power and the mercy which overcome the enigma of its end. (FH 233)

Of course to most moderns this radical dependence on God for meaning means there is in effect neither meaning nor hope—such expressions of dependence represent mere 'rhetoric'. Any forces in history that to them might realistically make life meaningful are the natural and historical forces that alone effect anything and so can alone justify a valid hope for meaning—forces of nature, patterns of immanent historical and cultural development, or the intellectual, moral, and spiritual capacities of men and women. If these cannot bring meaning, but on the contrary in seeking to bring meaning bring along with them new forms of sin and destruction, what hope is there? Niebuhr answers as clearly as possible: God. Since our generation has experienced even more vividly than his how new forms of technological and cultural creativity generate new and more serious dilemmas, his answer is at least relevant to us. Our further question, then, is, What does he really mean by his answer, if he means anything at all?

First, Niebuhr speaks, as we have seen, of the divine providence containing or limiting the rebellion of humans within prescribed limits; and he calls this a "rough justice." This means that the divinely established structures of nature and history are such that the inordinate pretensions of persons and groups (sin) have the consequence of creating and enlarging injustice, oppression, and consequent violence; such pretensions in turn breed radical discontent and goad oppressed forces to rebel; and in the end, if continued or increased, such oppressive domination will, therefore, inevitably result in the overturn, the downfall, of the oppressor. In breeding injustice, therefore, sin generates in the end its own self-destruction: "no human rebellion can rise so high as to challenge the divine sovereignty essentially" (FH 137). This 'natural law', so to speak, of historical life represents, so Niebuhr insists, one aspect of the judgment of God on human pretensions. It is the creative power and order of God (the Logos) that has instituted and upholds these patterns of social dynamics and thus prevents sin from overturning completely the good creation God has established. As always, Niebuhr illuminates the meaning of a theological or religious symbol (here: God's judgment in history) by showing its coherence with visible patterns of ordinary experience, and the relation of the latter to the divine activity. Theological symbols point to the presence and activity of God (transcendence) within the contours of ordinary experience.

This work of divine judgment or rule in objective history, however, is clearly not sufficient. There is an enormous amount of innocent suffering (it is only a "rough justice"); the perpetuators by no means pay all their bills; and above all such external limits or bounds—except in rare cases—do not lead to the kind of inner recognition of sin that alone can begin to diminish sin. Hence, as Niebuhr says frequently, on the one hand, the enigma of history is not resolved in history and so history waits for a final judgment; and on the other hand (and this is our present concern), other aspects of the divine activity in history must be present for any renewals of meaning in history to occur.

These other aspects of the divine activity represent, so it seems to me, a shift from the objective or the external to the subjective or the inward. The judgment of God through the 'natural law' (as described above) represents the work of an external divine judgment on an oppressing group by means of the objective social consequences of their actions; that is, the overthrow or the radical diminution of the power of the dominating group that a rebellion achieves—a judgment that occurs irrespective of changes in the inwardness of the oppressors. The "dominant minorities"[4] (the ruling groups) are overthrown, but not because they are repentant—there is no necessary inward renewal here. Like the human beings who help create history, history has for Niebuhr both an objective, or outward, and a sub-

---

4. The reference is to Toynbee's theory of the breakdown and disintegration of civilizations. For Toynbee, a minority in a larger community is creative at the start of a culture, in large part forms that culture and its mores, and gains thereby inordinate privilege. In the end, it becomes a "dominant minority," idealizing and idolizing its own resolution of past problems, defending its old order and its privileges against all criticism and revolt—and hence bringing about the breakup and demise of its own culture. This is, needless to say, a view remarkably like that of Niebuhr. See Arnold Toynbee, *A Study of History* (Oxford: Oxford University Press, 1939), vols. 4, 5.

jective, inward side. The objective side is what happens to the power or status of groups through events; the subjective is what happens to them through changes in their inner consciousness and self-consciousness. Clearly for Niebuhr for any real renewal there must be a renewal on both sides. Thus new patterns of divine activity are present to work on the inwardness of men and women. And these patterns represent an approach to the deep inwardness I articulated in describing repentance and faith in response to the Word.

These actions of God in history, actions 'among the nations' designed to instigate and inspire inner renewal, are described by Niebuhr as 'common grace.' I have mentioned a number of them (see chap. 9): generally in Niebuhr's texts they refer to essential structures of social existence that beguile or impel self-interest to enlarge itself into a wider interest inclusive of other persons or groups in the society. Niebuhr cites the need for the unity and harmony of the entire community that impels the 'coincidence of interest' between the ruling class and different and often competing vitalities and groups in the community. Such coincidence of interest pushes each group to temper its driving self-interest so that some social harmony may obtain.

Among other contemporary examples that might also have been in Niebuhr's mind, we might mention the following; in each case a wider self-interest appears that includes the self-interest of competing groups. It was in the apparent self-interest of the vastly weakened European colonial powers, especially perhaps England and Holland, to relinquish (willingly and yet unwillingly) their military, political, and economic control over their former colonies. They were certainly pushed by events and by the potential threat of revolution—as well as moral urging by many—to do so. But they could have refused this wider prudential and moral course and resisted with much greater force right up to a totally self-destructive end. Again, it was in the self-interest of America to contribute to the rebuilding of Europe and of Japan after World War II—even though this was, for many, also a strong moral obligation. Niebuhr invariably ascribes such a 'prudential' enlargement of immediate and narrow self-interest to include a wider communal interest and so a wider self-interest to 'common grace'. He also acknowledges in each case the work of a committed moral (prophetic) minority that calls on the entire community to take this wider view. Unexpected prudence is for him, therefore, a "righteousness not our own," the work of common grace and of prophetic grace.

One may well question this theological interpretation of such historical events. Why are these seemingly natural processes of social dynamics, which lead to the downfall of oppressors on the one hand and to greater prudence on the part of powerful groups on the other, asserted by Niebuhr to be the work of God and attributable to "common grace"? The general answer is that Niebuhr always discerned a deeper dimension at work in all historical processes, a dimension of divine activity he has tried to articulate in his theology of human nature and now of history. He clearly thought that the divine was acting in and through such sequences of historical events, either as judgment or as grace; and he thought that the contours of those events—just like the essential structure and the sin of human beings—could not be understood if that divine activity was omitted from consideration.

Ever since 1939 this sense of the divine dimension to history's sequences has made good sense to me. It makes sense, for example, to say that the onset of the Second World War represented the judgment of God on the major powers of Europe, Allied as well as Axis; I refer to all that each of the former did at the end of World War I and subsequently to repress Germany and to maintain imperial control of Asia. Such a judgment seems a true and illuminating assessment of the meaning of that period and the real factors at work there: anxiety, inordinate self-concern, self-deception, injustice, and in the end, horrendous conflict—in short, the judgment of God. Clearly sin in Niebuhr's sense was apparent in that tragic history of oppression by the Allies, revolt by the Germans, and vastly increased cruelty and violence by all parties. Clearly none of the great powers saw themselves as sinful nor even as contributing to this disaster; and yet the results were such that an understanding of the presence of common sin and of resulting judgment is necessary if one is to understand what really occurred. But to say this, as Niebuhr did, is not to deny the relevance or significance of the many historical factors—political, economic, psychological, and social—that led up to that war and through which the sins of men and women and the judgment of God worked. To call it "judgment" is to point to this presence of inordinate self-concern in their midst, to recognize the driving sense of insecurity and guilt, and to recognize the inevitable results of all of this—on innocent and guilty alike—in judgment.

In order to understand events in history, even in a scientific, technological, and industrial culture, we must recognize that freedom (i.e., the power to choose as we will to choose) is itself driven by an underlying force or power that *uses* our freedom, what Niebuhr terms *inordinate self-concern,* what the Buddhists term *desire,* what Tillich called *concupiscence.* If we leave this out, we do not understand at all what really happens. Correspondingly, to leave that dimension out, either as sin or as desire, and to omit the corresponding judgment is to misunderstand that grim portion of history between the wars. It is not enough for each of the participants to say, "We misjudged all this," or "We did not see these results coming," or, more probably, "We just did what we had to do." That is to excuse each of the participants and especially oneself, that is, to deny the driving anxiety and self-concern (desire), the self-deception, and the remorse. The same analysis could be made of the conquest of and near destruction of Native Americans and of the history of racial relations in America. To leave the dimension of sin (or of grace) out of any historical sequence is to miss perhaps the major driving force—along with creativity—that impels history on its course.[5]

Niebuhr had a very strong sense of the weight of the tendency to sin. Augustine said that the wrong sort of love (love of self and of the world) is like gravity: it pushes the soul despite itself down and down until it cannot of itself rise again.[6] Niebuhr agrees, as his discussion of mutual love shows. Left to itself without criticism and away from the lure of agape, a love based on mutuality alone will end in calculation, and mutuality will have vanished into undiminished self-interest—as case after case of broken marriages based on "mutual self-enhancement" shows. So it is with these aspects of common grace: for Niebuhr sin tends to overcome any 'natural' element that leads the self beyond the self. Prudence, the capacity of reason to reshape one's selfish interests to include the interests of possible competitors, is for Niebuhr a rare gift. It betokens an *already present* limitation on self-love, a sense of the legitimacy of the claims of the other as well as of one's own, and a touch of repentance. These latter alone allow me to see a limitation on my own self-affirmation not as naïveté or betrayal, but as 'wisdom'.

And so for Niebuhr it is by grace that self-love is through the 'natural' processes of social dynamics transmuted into a mutual concern with a common good. Something has to enter history if history is to be rescued from its own processes of self-destruction, if history is to become 'natural'. This rescue from self-interest into prudence is often, so Niebuhr avers, helped through a minority voice (a remnant) which does have the wider interest at its heart and so evokes the conscience as well as the potential

5. It is interesting to note that a modern Buddhist analysis makes the same point in different categories and even with a quite different worldview. In order, says Keiji Nishitani, to understand events in history, even in a scientific, technological, and industrial culture, we must recognize that freedom, the power to choose as we wish to choose, is *itself* driven by desire. If we leave this out, we do not really understand at all what happens in history. See Keiji Nishitani, *Religion and Nothingness,* trans. Jan van Braght (Berkeley and Los Angeles: University of California Press, 1982).

6. Augustine, *City of God,* 9:18.

prudence of the dominant majority. As our history from anti-slavery to the Marshall Plan to Civil Rights shows, without this help from an already-present and vocal moral conscience, self-interest would have triumphed and wisdom vanished.

Clearly, moreover, Niebuhr felt that in many areas of common life unexpected renewals constantly take place, where a creativity endangered by self-love and pretense would begin to right itself and become creative again. And in these he seems to see a more personal, if I may so put it, work of common grace. This more personal presence of grace in ordinary experience he calls "the hidden Christ" (ND 2:109, 123, 187). He is sure that groups of men and women who have never heard of the gospel message are led in various ways to a kind of genuine inner repentance and trust in a power not their own, and so are lured to a concern for others, even for other groups, beyond and even against their own interests. To him again such renewals in social history (analogical to renewals in personal life) are the work of grace, or in this case the work of an unknown and so "hidden Christ." In the strange contours of historical events, something like the gospel message of judgment and grace has been present and has led to a responding repentance and trust, and in effect to the appearance of facets of agape—that is, to some inner renewal—and this, he avers, is the work of God's sovereign love in history.[7]

There are, therefore, several elements or layers, so to speak, to Niebuhr's confidence in the ultimate meaningfulness of life and history. There is the ever-present and unlimited *creativity* of the humans whose spirit transcends

7. We see here the beginning—but only the beginning—of a new conscious concern about other religions, a consciousness that was to flower among theologians two decades later in interreligious dialogue on the one hand and theoretical 'pluralism' among religions on the other. Niebuhr shows no explicit consciousness of or interest in such a new relation between religions as expressed, for example, by the word *parity.* He had long relinquished any idea of divine judgment on nonbelievers, and he recognized doctrinally a knowledge of God outside the special revelation of Covenant and Incarnation. And here he intimates at a universal, almost revealing, and redemptive action of God throughout human experience, the "hidden Christ." The fact he thus labels this action as "Christ" shows that the Incarnation and Atonement remain for him the unique and decisive revelation of God of which there are other effective but incomplete manifestations. In this decisive event for Niebuhr, the agape of God is revealed. This is the agape of God that appears "hiddenly" or "incognito" through other religions. Hence he calls it the "hidden Christ." He is, therefore, what is now termed an "inclusivist," recognizing the relative truth and validity of other religions, but also recognizing their incompleteness when measured alongside the decisive Christian revelation. He does not at this point differ very much from Tillich, it seems to me, and he is to be compared with his younger Catholic colleague, Karl Rahner, S. J.

and remakes each established form of life; there is the ever-present and essential *value* of each human person, to God, to each other, and to themselves. There is the judgment of God in history, which limits and so controls within bounds the inevitable (though not necessary) *misuse* of these creative achievements in order to establish, possess, and secure these partial achievements at the expense of others. There is the continuing and also 'objective' work of *common grace,* which beguiles anxious self-concern in part away from its self-destructive path to harmonize itself with the needs, insecurities, anxieties, and interests of others in the wider community. And there is the hidden work of *redemptive love,* which uses historical events and crises to instigate repentance and a new humility—and so the possibility of a 'prudence'—which encourages a more harmonious and peaceful issue. In these ways God works continually in history to bring about renewals and new possibilities, renewals that mitigate the self-destruction introduced by sin, and new possibilities that can lead to higher levels of harmonious and just social existence. By these means, providence assumes and builds on human autonomy and creativity. It does not direct nor does it compel human autonomy. On the contrary, it lures and cajoles it, hiddenly but effectively, with the result that there are, as Niebuhr reiterates, genuine achievements in a contingent and anxious and vulnerable existence.

Meanings, therefore, do exist in history, and there are renewals of these that avoid catastrophe and build further on the past; there is development. But none of this is as final as its enthusiastic agents believe; none is ultimate, though it will claim to be so. The reiteration of this last, so typical of Niebuhr, should not blind us to its positive polarity—and these positive gains, as we see, are the cooperative work of human creativity and grace, of a temporal prudence and the intricate and sensitive work of divine providence:

> There are provisional meanings in history, capable of being recognized and fulfilled by individuals and cultures; but mankind will continue to see through a glass darkly and the final meaning can be anticipated by faith. . . . There are renewals of life in history, individually and collectively; but no rebirth lifts above the contradictions of man's historical existence. (FH 214)

Thus do providence and free will bring about provisional meanings and renewals. These, however, are ever vulnerable to idolatry, and sin is ever-present. Evil grows with each growth of good. Hence any faith in the meaning of history, any confidence in an established or final meaning not vulnerable to destruction and elimination, must be a confidence in the power and love of God—not in the precarious creations of human

intelligence and human morals. Niebuhr reiterates this point too: faith—
Christian faith, that is to say—a confidence in the divine power and meaning to complete what we cannot complete and to purge whatever is false
and destructive in our creativity, is necessary (ND 2:57; FH 150):

> In this experience man understands himself in his finiteness, realizes the
> guilt of his efforts to escape his insufficiency and dependence and lays hold
> of a power beyond himself which both completes his incompleteness and
> purges him of his false and vain efforts at self-completeness. (ND 2:37)

> This pinnacle of faith in New Testament religion is the final expression of
> certainty about the power of God to complete our fragmentary life as well
> as the power of His love to purge it of the false completions in which all of
> history is involved. (FH 150)

It is, then, God who establishes and completes the meaning of history.
Meanings are creatively undertaken by us and through us, as we have seen;
but in the end any fulfillment of them, any 'redemption', must be from beyond these efforts that continually fall short. Without this power and love
there would be few real meanings, fewer renewals, and the destructive
consequences of sin would overwhelm the reality and the hope of meaning in history. Hence for Niebuhr—as he said in the quotes above—the
precarious and incomplete meanings of history point beyond themselves
to the culmination and fulfillment of meaning with the end of history. A
providence which here in history can only assist a wounded and straying
creativity points beyond itself to eschatology. The final sovereignty of God
over history, a sovereignty pivotal to Niebuhr's understanding of the meaning of history according to Biblical faith, is thus necessarily expressed in eschatological symbols of the completion of that sovereignty:

> The light of revelation into the meaning of life illumines the darkness of
> history's self-contradictions, its fragmentary realization of meaning and its
> premature and false completions. But obviously such a faith points to an
> end in which history's incompleteness and corruption is finally overcome.
> Thus history as we know it is regarded as an 'interim' between the disclosure
> and fulfillment of its meaning. (ND 2:288)

A Biblical understanding of history, therefore, concludes with reflection on the 'eschata', the symbols that concern the end and fulfillment of
history. These symbols, for Niebuhr, express in significant ways the ultimate divine sovereignty over the meaning of a history that otherwise, because of the obscurity and even ambiguity of that sovereignty, would quite
fail to embody such meaning. But as we have seen, faith for Niebuhr is pre-

cisely the confidence that there is meaning within history, despite the mystery of existence. Eschatology is, therefore, utterly essential for Niebuhr's understanding of both faith and history.

Eschatology

History, we have seen, has a meaning that is disclosed but not fulfilled or completed. The fragmentary and transient meanings of history, utterly significant as they are for individual life and for collective justice, are not capable of giving to an individual or to collective life a secure and unambiguous meaning. On the one hand, they are too contingent and too corruptible to fend off cynicism and despair, or if affirmed with confidence, they can easily beguile us into idolatry. Hence any secure and creative meaning points beyond the continuing ambiguity of history to God and to history's end: to the fulfillment of meaning that faith knows and whose promise guards us against despair whenever frustrations or tragedy appear. This fulfillment and completion that faith affirms is expressed in and through eschatological symbols. This fulfillment is neither in history, as if some ideal society would give meaning to the entire process; nor is it quite beyond history in eternity, which is, as Niebuhr reiterates, to annul completely the meanings in history.

> Against utopianism the Christian faith insists that the final consummation of history lies beyond the conditions of the temporal process. Against other-worldliness it asserts that the consummation fulfills rather than negates the historical process. (ND 2:291)

Hence Christian eschatological symbols are paradoxical symbols that express this strange yet secure sense of history's meaning: the fulfillment of history genuinely includes what history has produced, yet this fulfillment lies beyond the scope of history.

> This promise of the fulfillment of life involves the rational absurdity of an eternity which incorporates the conditions of time: individuality and particularity. (FH 137)

And clearly here even more than in intrahistorical events, this fulfillment represents the work alone of God on whose ultimate sovereignty any genuine Christian faith depends:

> But nothing can happen in history to shake the confidence in the meaning of existence to those who have discerned by faith the revelation of the ultimate power and love which bears and guides men through their historic vicissitudes. (FH 136)

Eschatological symbols, then, are paradoxical expressions on the one hand of the final sovereignty of God over the dynamic and wayward stuff of history, and on the other of the final fulfillment of those fragmentary meanings through the power and mercy of God. The creation by God of an autonomous creature gives significance to history's variety and value and yet also provides the possibility of a divine sovereignty that secures history's meaning. So, correspondingly, the eschatological symbols establish at once the sovereignty of God that makes a fulfillment possible and the variety and value of achieved creation that makes history's fulfillment relevant.

We should note two things about these symbols besides their paradoxical expression of the divine sovereignty over history. First, they describe history—in the light of its end—rather than what lies beyond history. Niebuhr was characteristically wary of speculation about eschatology, whether via philosophical reason in metaphysical elaboration or in theological elaboration of the implications of scriptural passages. He urged "a decent measure of restraint in expressing the Christian hope" (ND 2:298). As we have seen, any theological affirmations he wished to make were essentially related to and validated in experience, though their forms, as I have argued, were given by revelation. In this he shows his empiricist, even his Schleiermachian, heritage. Hence speculation, either philosophical or scriptural, about what transcends time and space, and so ordinary experience, was out of the question for him. In a typical burst of humorous modesty combined with an appeal to serious experience, he said:

> It is unwise for Christians to claim any knowledge of either the furniture of heaven or the temperature of hell; or to be too certain of any details of the Kingdom of God in which history is consummated. But it is prudent to accept the teaching of the heart, which affirms the fear of judgment. (ND 2:294)

As a consequence, in Niebuhr's hands eschatological symbols do not describe eternity or even the character of the end of time outside of time. On the contrary, like the balancing symbol of creation,[8] they describe history but with regard to its culmination, fulfillment, and end; that is, how it is that the sovereignty of God completes history's fragmentary finitude,

---

8. Creation is a symbol describing nature, humans, and history with regard to their ultimate origin: that is, as dependent on God, as relatively autonomous, and as 'good'. As Augustine agreed, it does not say what "preceded" creation or time, or even how God did it. See Langdon Gilkey, *Maker of Heaven and Earth* (Garden City, N.Y.: Doubleday, 1959).

purges its waywardness, and fulfills its partial but real meanings. In fact what we find embedded in these symbols as bearers of their meaning are "general principles about history," which Niebuhr's theological analysis of human nature and history has uncovered.[9] The symbol of the Last Judgment means in part that each "heightened potency in human existence may also represent a possibility of evil" (ND 2:166), and that "history is a meaningful process but incapable of fulfilling itself and therefore points beyond itself to the judgment and mercy of God for its fulfillment. . . . [And] the wrath and the judgment of God are symbolic of the seriousness of history" (ND 2:211).

These symbols, therefore, point to general principles of historical passage uncovered by Niebuhr's analysis. Like other symbols to Niebuhr, they do not point or refer to particular events: a first moment of time, a particular last moment of history, an event of judgment, or a described state of blessedness, and so on. In fact Niebuhr makes plain that even Jesus misunderstood this point and made the 'error' of expecting the 'interim' that was history between disclosure and fulfillment 'to be short' (ND 2:49–50). This literalism was natural: the paradoxical relation of eternity to time is more easily conceived in literal terms as a point in time than as a symbol of their paradoxical relation. Hence we must reinterpret these symbols—as we have done already with Creation and Fall—as symbols expressing the dialectical and paradoxical relation of eternity and time, of God and the creaturely world. Or, as Niebuhr puts it, "It is important to take Biblical symbols seriously but not literally" (ND 2:50). Thus this reinterpretation is in Niebuhr in effect a translation from a literal interpretation in terms of an event at a point in time into a symbolic expression of certain significant general principles of historical existence, which principles represent what the symbol means in relation to the end and fulfillment of history. Or, in other terms, the symbol expresses certain aspects of the Christian faith with regard to history and history's end—that is, what faith holds those essential characteristics of history to be. However, despite the translation, Niebuhr is clear that it is important to retain, as he does, the symbol, and not to "demythologize" in toto. Like *creatio ex nihilo* or the Fall, this symbol embodies a paradox, in effect a paradoxical 'story', which appropriately expresses the relation of eternity to time in the language of time—and hence the symbol preserves the paradox and with it the mystery.[10]

9. For further examples of this use of general theological principles about history vis-à-vis eschatological symbols, see ND 2:166–67 and 211–13.

10. See also the discussion of these symbols in FH 235–37.

The 'return of the triumphant Christ' is, says Niebuhr, the dominant eschatological symbol. It "expresses the faith that existence cannot ultimately defy its own norm" (ND 2:290), or in more detail:

> The vindication of Christ and his triumphant return is therefore an expression of faith in the sufficiency of God's sovereignty over the world and history and in the final supremacy of love over all the forces of self-love which defy, for the moment, the inclusive harmony of all things under the will of God. (ND 2:290)

The symbol does not refer to *a* return, *an* appearance, and *a* triumph; it refers rather to the general truth that the power and love of God (i.e., "Christ") remain completely sovereign over history, its events and its meanings, and that as a consequence that power and love will "triumph"; that is, they will complete and fulfill our partial meanings in God's eternity.

The symbol of the Last Judgment enlarges on this theme of an ultimate divine sovereignty. It expresses, says Niebuhr, continuing his translation, "three important facets of the Christian conception of life and history."[11] The first is that "history is judged by its own ideal possibilities, and not by the contrast between the finite and the eternal character in God. The judgment is on sin and not on finiteness" (ND 2:292). Second, the symbol of the Last Judgment emphasizes the ultimate importance of the distinction between evil and good in history. This distinction, so crucial to historical life and especially to its pursuit of justice, is not erased at the end but recognized, not eliminated but incorporated into history's culmination. And the symbol of a final judgment on our acts, good and bad alike, underlines this relation of eternity itself to history's moral distinctions. In fact the distinction between good and evil is so serious, and the evil permeating history is so universal ("no man living is justified" [ND 2:292]), that the solution to history's meaning cannot finally be that of judgment at all. For there being no one who is righteous, an End in terms of judgment alone would imply that no meaning would remain in history at all. On the contrary, the only solution is the divine mercy: "For God cannot destroy evil except by taking it into and upon Himself" (ND 2:292).

The Atonement, in which God resolves the evil of history by taking it upon himself, thus becomes the central symbol illustrating the Last Judgment. Faith understands through the Atonement that the divine mercy overcomes sin by means of the divine suffering—and this overcomes at once the rebellion of sin and yet upholds the distinctions of good and evil.

---

11. Note, as we have said, that this symbol, too, illuminates the Christian conception of life and history, not some event of judgment at the end of history.

As in the personal life of the individual, the experience of judgment leads to repentance, and the experience of grace as forgiveness leads to faith and renewal, so at the Last Judgment, the knowledge of the divine judgment makes a consciousness of sin and so repentance possible, and yet, transcended by the atoning agape of God, divine mercy makes possible a newly confident faith. It is for Niebuhr through the Atonement that judgment and mercy, moral distinctions and forgiveness, unite. It is, therefore, in the Atonement that the paradox of a Last Judgment and a final mercy can be understood.

Third, as I noted, the symbol of the Last Judgment reinforces the inner sense known in repentance or remorse of our own serious and continuing ambiguity. Despite, Niebuhr says, the acclamation of many human judgments, and of our own confidence in our own virtue, our lives, even those of the best of us, represent a mixture of sin as well as of creativity. The Last Judgment reminds us of the seriousness and the validity of this uneasy and often repressed anxiety. There are no true and final judgments in history, either of goodness or of evil; each human judgment represents a particular locus, perspective, and 'interest', however objective it seeks or pretends to be. To recognize the relativity of all of these historical—that is, political and personal—judgments is necessary for individual sanity and courage, and for the sanity and openness of society. We know that life and its decisions are more serious than are the estimates, good or bad, that others make of us. To know there is a 'final' judgment beyond all these partial ones validates our own inner seriousness, our integrity, as it does our faith.

On the other hand, to accept without the hope of some final and valid assessment the total relativity of all our human judgments is to dissolve the moral fiber of existence entirely—and again to be untrue to our experience. Hence this symbol—recognizing, as it does, a final judgment superseding all our relative judgments—upholds the divine order and the moral center of existence, while in the Atonement it also points beyond this judgment to the mercy that includes it. And, to return to our first symbol, the fact that it is Christ that embodies the Last Judgment means the judgment is to be interpreted through the Atonement, and so in terms of the mercy and love of God that bears and transcends the judgment. It is through the love of God manifested in Christ that the judgment becomes a symbol of hope and affirmation—of a righteousness not our own that becomes our righteousness.

The Resurrection, I believe, is the central symbol for Niebuhr of the Christian hope. It expresses as clearly as any of the above the characteristic affirmations of Christian faith—in response to Christian revelation—about the nature of life and history. As he admits in an earlier work, when he was younger, it was this symbol that, as part of the creed, caused him the greatest intellectual and so spiritual difficulty:

> These closing words of the Apostolic Creed [I believe in the resurrection of the body] in which the Christian hope of the fulfillment of life is expressed, were, as I remember it, an offense and a stumbling block to young theologians at the time my generation graduated from theological seminaries. . . . We were not certain we could honestly express our faith in such a formula. . . .
>
> The twenty years which divide that time from this have brought great changes in theological thought. . . . Yet some of us have been persuaded to take the stone which was then rejected and make it the head of the corner. In other words, there is no part of the Apostle's Creed which, in our present opinion, expresses the whole genius of the Christian faith more neatly than just the despised phrase: "I believe in the resurrection of the body."
>
> The idea of the resurrection of the body can of course not be literally true. But neither is any other idea of fulfillment literally true. All of them are symbols from our present existence to express concepts of a completion of life which transcends our present existence. . . . It is no more conceivable that the soul should exist without the body than that a mortal body should be made immortal. Neither notion is conceivable to reason because reason can only deal with the stuff of experience; and we have no experience of either a disincarnate soul or an immortal body. But we do have an experience of a human existence which is involved in the processes of nature and yet transcends them. (BT 289–91; see also ND 2:294)

This is a most interesting account. It delineates not only Niebuhr's own theological development but the entire movement of modern theology from a literal interpretation of traditional creedal symbols (see also Creation and Fall) to a symbolic understanding of those symbols; and it shows, though that is not his point, how crucial Niebuhr himself was to that important development.[12] The liberal theology that he absorbed in his early student career was acquainted with these creedal affirmations only in their traditional, literalistic form; hence the young liberals discarded or ignored, or certainly found distasteful, these creedal affirmations as anachronistic and irrelevant; they translated the theological content of these symbols, particularly with regard to Creation, Fall, and Redemption, into the more modern and palatable progressivist terms of evolutionary language. As

12. Note the great span of years in Niebuhr's life covered in this reflection on the creed: 1917 (theological student years), 1937 (*Beyond Tragedy*), and finally 1943, the year of *The Nature and Destiny of Man,* vol. 2.

Niebuhr notes, the Resurrection, unbelievable to a modern generation in the literal terms of ascending bodily molecules, was discarded in favor of the doctrine of the immortality of the soul—a belief seemingly more plausible to modern minds. However, as Niebuhr also notes, an immortal, bodiless soul is, in fact, equally inconceivable considering the essential interrelatedness of organic, psychic, and spiritual power in each human person (ND 2:294–98).

As his own theological insights developed, however, Niebuhr came to understand these symbols *as* symbols, as pointing analogically and paradoxically to mysteries within human experience whose meaning could be affirmed by faith; these are mysteries of human nature, of history, of God, and so of the end and culmination of history. And at that point, the 'genius' of the symbol of the Resurrection became clear to him, as did that of the Creation and the Fall.

> The hope of the Resurrection nevertheless embodies the very genius of the Christian idea of the historical. On the one hand it implies that eternity will fulfill and not annul the richness and variety which the temporal process has elaborated. On the other it implies that the condition of finiteness and freedom, which lies at the basis of historical existence, is a problem for which there is no solution by any human power. Only God can solve this problem. From the human perspective it can only be solved by faith. (ND 2:295)

Niebuhr's discussion of the Resurrection sums up his entire view of human existence, human history, and the meaning of both. We can see within these passages how crucial a role his anthropology—his understanding of men and women as at once natural creatures bound by space and time and yet as self-transcendent and so related beyond history to eternity—plays in this culminating symbol of his theology (see esp. ND 2:312).

His acceptance of a modern scientific understanding of the human embeddedness in natural process is particularly clear in the long quotation above from *Beyond Tragedy*. Death here is, he says, a natural fact, a result therefore of creation and not of sin (FH 120; see also ND 1:167, 173–77), a position held by most liberal theologians since Schleiermacher.[13] But, as Niebuhr has also argued, this natural creature, subject to temporality and to death, transcends the nature and even the history in which she and he

---

13. Friedrich Schleiermacher, *The Christian Faith* (trans. of 2d German ed., edited by H. R. Macintosh and J. S. Stewart [Edinburgh: T. & T. Clark, 1948]), sec. 29, "The Original Perfection of the World," and sec. 76, "The Constitution of the World in Relation to Sin." See also Albrecht Ritschl, *Justification and Reconciliation,* vol. 3, chap. 5, sec. 42.

are embedded. Hence the meaning of historical existence—and Niebuhr always assumes it has a meaning—transcends the natural and the historic limits of life in eternity. Eternity, therefore, not only creates and upholds temporal process; it completes and fulfills it, embracing the richness and variety that historical process has helped to produce. The way this understanding follows for Niebuhr from the nature of human being (under God) is shown in the following:

> His creativity is directed towards the establishment, perpetuation and perfection of human communities. Therefore the meaning of his life is derived from his relation to the historical process. But the freedom which makes this creativity possible transcends all communal loyalties and even history itself. Each individual has a direct relation to eternity; for he seeks for the completion of the meaning of his life beyond the fragmentary realizations of meaning which can be discerned at any point in the process where an individual may happen to live and die. (ND 2:308)

> The hope of the resurrection reaffirms that ultimately finiteness will be emancipated from anxiety and the self will know itself as it is known. . . . The idea of the resurrection implies that the historical elaborations of the richness of creation, in all their variety, will participate in the consummation of history. It gives the struggles in which men are engaged to preserve civilizations, and to fulfill goodness in history, abiding significance and does not relegate them to a meaningless flux, of which there will be no echo in eternity. . . . The individual faces the eternal in every moment and in every action of his life; and he confronts the end of history in his death. The dimension of his freedom transcends all social realities. His spirit is not fulfilled in even the highest achievements of history; his conscience is not eased by even the most unequivocal approval of historical courts of judgment; nor need it be finally intimidated by historical condemnations. On the other hand the individual life is meaningful only in its organic relation to historical communities, tasks and obligations. (ND 2:312)

Niebuhr's entire understanding of human being thus leads inexorably to the symbol of fulfillment in eternity, and further to the particular symbol of the 'resurrection of the body'. Clearly, as this argument carefully scrutinized shows, there are grounds for this resurrection hope only if (*a*) the completion of meaning as human nature aspires to it is assumed to be fulfilled, as Niebuhr did so assume and as faith surely does, and (*b*) there is the power as well as the mercy of God to effect this fulfillment. As we have seen, Niebuhr assumes throughout an ultimate fulfillment of meaning whose precarious lodgment in historical life he so realistically describes;

and he ascribes that hope solely to God who completes what we cannot at all complete:

> Only God can solve this problem. From the human perspective it can only be solved by faith (ND 2:295)

> . . . the Christian faith knows it to be impossible for man or for any of man's historical achievements to transcend the unity and tension between the natural and the eternal in human existence. Yet it affirms the eternal significance of this historical existence from the standpoint of faith in a God who has the power to bring history to completeness. (ND 2:296)

The symbol of the Resurrection, therefore, expresses at once the unity of human existence as natural, organic, and temporal and yet as self-transcendent and related to eternity; and the hope of the fulfilled meaning of that existence is ascribed only to the power and mercy of God. As Niebuhr has already noted, this sums up almost all our discussion; for him the meaning of faith is precisely trust in that power and mercy.

Finally, it should be made clear that despite the hesitancy of Niebuhr to describe the content or character of this hope, there can be little doubt that he affirmed its validity. Perhaps surprisingly, he insists that the church was 'founded on this fact'—referring to the event of Christ's resurrection and the church's reception of it as 'fact' (FH 147–48). And in another place, despite our uncertainty about its detailed character, he refers to this hope as a certainty of the faith:

> It is therefore important to maintain a decent measure of restraint in expressing the Christian hope. Faith must admit 'that it doth not yet appear what we shall be'. But it is equally important not to confuse such restraint with uncertainty about the validity of the hope that 'when he shall appear, we shall be like him, for we shall see him as he is'. . . . It is an integral part of the whole Biblical conception of the meaning of life. Both the meaning and the fulfillment are ascribed to a center and source beyond themselves. (ND 2:298)

The eschatological conclusions, therefore, to Niebuhr's theology, although frustratingly brief and astoundingly short in descriptive adequacy, nonetheless are in the strictest continuity with all else he has said about nature, history, and human being, and especially about God on whom all meaning as well as all existence depends. Clearly if his preceding analysis of human existence and history is correct, there would be little meaning or completion in life without this eschatological fulfillment, nor would the power and mercy of God, on which faith depends, have any real relevance or hold any promise. For a faith that is at once realistic about the facts of historical experience, and yet certain of a secure meaning within the deep mystery of that existence, these symbols are neither extrinsic nor irrelevant but central. Unless the meaning of life is in the midst of its passage perfectly clear and fully secure—and he has surely shown that it is not—then the presence of the power and mercy of God at the Beginning and at the End, to complete what we cannot complete and to purge what we have corrupted, are the sole grounds for any real hope. And as all this shows, despite his realism, Niebuhr felt and expressed a very secure and well-grounded hope and a very great certainty about the promises of God.

CHAPTER 11

Reflections

In this book, I have sought to describe, to clarify, frequently to defend, and infrequently to criticize Niebuhr's theology from its beginnings in his political writings to its mature expression. I have tried to re-present this theology as he might have done. As the autobiographical note in the first chapter makes clear, and as probably most of the succeeding sentences reinforce, I am vastly indebted to this theology, and, as much as any person in another generation can agree with a thinker, I hold Niebuhr's theology to be amazingly profound and true to experience as I have known it—more so than any other viewpoint I have encountered. Hence its re-presentation to the theological world seems well worth this effort.

The explication of what I regard as the center of Niebuhr's theology having been completed, it is time to analyze its constituent parts, to see the central ideas and deeper assumptions that make it up—assumptions of which Niebuhr himself was probably only barely aware. Niebuhr well knew that our thinking reflects the most general notions characteristic of our cultural locus, and he probably knew that few of us are explicitly aware of these assumptions. Generally we think *from* them, not *about* them. Another generation has the opportunity to see this, partly because it no longer shares them in quite that form. Our children and grandchildren will tell us—and smile about—what we unconsciously assume.

Niebuhr sought in his preaching and his writing to present to us 'Biblical faith'. In this assurance Niebuhr was joined by almost all of his theological contemporaries—at least those of a 'Biblical' sort. Whether they did Biblical studies or systematics, almost all of these latter sought to express the 'Biblical viewpoint' in their work. And all of these assumed, as did Niebuhr, that there was in fact a common, unified, and coherent theme (I hesitate to say 'system') to the entire Scriptures that this contemporary theology expressed. All recognized, with differing degrees of tolerance, that there were alternative interpretations of this common thematic, ranging from Barth on the right through Brunner to Bultmann and perhaps Niebuhr on the left. But my point is that all believed that there was a *referent* in the Scriptures themselves to this theological viewpoint, that there was in fact a 'Biblical theology'.

As I have noted, moreover (p. 124 n. 16), these 'Biblical theologians' assumed as well—for some excellent reasons—that this theological viewpoint common to the Scriptures also represented the main, continuing framework of symbols within the most important tradition (for them) of Christian theological reflection. This is the tradition called the Pauline, Augustinian line culminating, for them all, in the Reformation. These theologians included in this line Irenaeus—but neither Justin nor Origen—and they excluded both medieval Catholic thinkers and the liberals—though the former, at least, used the same symbolic framework of creation, fall, revelation, Christology, atonement, ecclesia, and eschatology which the neo-orthodox did. More than anyone else, Niebuhr communicated this interpretation of Scripture and tradition to the American scene; and probably a good deal of his authority—besides that of his obvious brilliance—came from the weight of this commonly held interpretation of both Scripture and tradition. More than anything else, I believe, it has been the rather swift breakup of this massive Biblical and theological consensus that has accounted for the sharp reduction in the authority and prominence of Niebuhr's thought from the 1960s on.

Since roughly the end of the 1950s, that is to say, there has been an immense amount of questioning, skepticism, and counterargument as to whether these 'classical' symbols of creation, fall, redemption, incarnation, atonement, word, ecclesia, and eschatology together represent the major theme or message of Scripture, whether they can be found in Scripture at all, and even whether there is in fact any single major theological theme there. For example, there are the brilliant works of James Barr on this point, especially *The Semantics of Biblical Language* (Oxford University Press, 1961). For another aspect of this discussion, see Langdon Gilkey, "Cosmology, Ontology, and the Travail of Biblical Language" (*Journal of Religion* 41, no. 3 [July 1961]). Finally, I can remember Norman Perrin, my colleague at the University of Chicago Divinity School, saying to me in about 1970: "Well, Langdon, which one of my fifty-seven New Testament christologies do you want to use today?"

Nonetheless, it is, I think, true to say that during the period between the wars and shortly thereafter—say, 1918 to 1955—not many in the dominant centers of Protestant theology, from New York's Union Theological Seminary, to Basel, to Zurich, and even up to Upsala, questioned that this set of categories and symbols did in fact represent the major themes of both Testaments, and further that they accorded with the Pauline-Augustinian (as they interpreted Augustine), Reformation, and neo-orthodox line ('the classical line') of Christian tradition.[1]

In any case, Niebuhr was sure that this Biblical faith, as he reinterpreted it, represented the classical message of the historic Christian faith.[2] He understood himself as re-presenting that traditional viewpoint in our age, as one in that traditional line. And most of those who heard him so understood his thought, namely as in that sense 'neo-orthodox'. As he and we all knew, this was not the way the liberals—at least many later liberals—had seen themselves.[3]

My interpretation of Niebuhr's thought has sought to underscore the legitimacy of this self-consciousness, of re-presenting the tradition in that sense. He did recover and make central to his own thinking the classic symbols of the tradition; he gave them new life, relevance, and an astounding

---

1. For an excellent summary of this tumultuous period for the study of the Old Testament, see Brevard Childs, *Biblical Theology in Crisis* (Philadelphia: Westminster Press, 1970), and Walter Bruggeman, *Theology of the Old Testament* (Minneapolis: Fortress Press, 1997), chapters 1 and 2.

2. The word *classical* refers here to an essential and authentic characteristic of the entire authentic tradition—not unlike the word *orthodox* as that word is usually used, but without the latter's dogmatic connotations. It does not mean 'pertaining to classical culture' (Hellenic or Hellenistic), something that could well be said about early church theology. Nor does the word 'orthodox', to which I have likened it, refer in this context to the Greek-speaking church nor to Protestant orthodoxy of the seventeenth and eighteenth centuries. In this context both words seek to point to what is held to be the central and authentic line of Christian proclamation and theology; that is, for Niebuhr as for the other neo-orthodox, the Pauline-Augustinian-Reformation line.

3. When I was applying for my first teaching position, one of the posts to which I sent my résumé was at a small liberal arts college in Virginia. The head of the department there, clearly a devoted liberal, asked me to tell him my thesis topic and who were the main figures with which it dealt. I listed Bradley and Whitehead, and then mentioned I was defending the 'classical' Christian doctrine of *creatio ex nihilo,* depending especially on Irenaeus, Augustine, Luther, Calvin, Barth, Tillich, and Niebuhr. He wrote back asking me what on earth such thinkers as Irenaeus and Augustine, not to mention Luther and Calvin, had to say to us about the creation, now that science had developed so much further than in their day. For that, as for other reasons, I decided to go elsewhere. He did not see himself, as certainly Niebuhr and I did, as representing any 'classical' tradition in theology, although he certainly saw himself as a member of the modern Christian community.

persuasive power. As I have argued, central to these symbols, what makes them *these* symbols or *this* set of symbols, is their emphasis on transcendence, the way each of them points beyond history and culture and their limits and expresses not just our common cultural assumptions but the presence and activity of God in relation to nature, history, community, and the individual self. As he interpreted creation, fall, revelation, incarnation/atonement, and grace, each of these symbols mediated something from beyond creaturely reality, cultural assumptions, and general human experience to that reality and experience. And this, it can fairly be argued, was characteristic of the entire tradition—Biblical and theological—to which he appealed. If anyone in the twentieth century could validly claim membership in that line, he could—and this is one reason neither his liberal nor his secular contemporaries liked or welcomed his theology.

Nonetheless, as is also obvious, Niebuhr set these classical symbols in the modern context. This recontextualizing is, of course, neither new nor an illegitimate enterprise for a theologian. All examples of theology interpret their tradition in terms of their own time and place, that is, in terms of the deep presuppositions of the cultural locus in which each thinker finds herself. The liberals were acutely aware of their dependence on this modern context; and perhaps they alone—for reasons I have explored—welcomed this dependence. After all, they did believe in progress, and to depend on the latest cultural thought presented little problem to them. Certainly Niebuhr was aware of much of his own dependence; as noted, he saw valid theology (and so his own) as a synthesis of Reformation and Renaissance, and he would not at all have denied any of the elements of the following analysis. But he was, like many of his colleagues, intent on an act of *recovery*, a recovery of the Biblical tradition over against what he thought of as modern culture. And he was confident he was fairly stating 'the Biblical faith' or 'Biblical religion'.

Tillich was, I think, at this point more methodologically self-aware. He described valid theology, and so his own theological principles, as an interpretation of traditional symbols in the terms of a modern ontology, and such an interpretation is what 'correlation' meant to him. Correlation to Niebuhr, on the contrary, meant exhibiting the relevance of a Biblical symbol to contemporary experience and thus, by correlating it with present experience, helping both to understand and to validate that symbol. How conscious he was of the ways that contemporary experience—along with its ontological presuppositions—had refashioned those symbols is hard to say. It is, however, unwise to state too positively the limits of Niebuhr's awareness. In any case, the task now is to draw out what seem to be the most important of these assumptions of modern culture—

'modernity'—that Niebuhr presupposed and that helped to shape, at the most fundamental level, his theological interpretation.

My aim, therefore, is to repeat and now examine in some detail the question I raised earlier, one that has been interwoven with this whole analysis: What of 'modernity' did Niebuhr challenge (a challenge of which he and his hearers were very much aware) and what of 'modernity' did Niebuhr accept, and not only accept but make an intrinsic and essential part of the entire 'Biblical' and 'classical' viewpoint for which he so persuasively argued? I shall list these presuppositions of modernity in Niebuhr's theology roughly in the order of their appearance in modern culture. It is my view that they also informed all of relevant modern theology contemporary to Niebuhr, not least that of those 'Biblical' scholars and theologians who liked to speak of the opposition of their Biblical theology to the modern world. It is also my view that they inform most of what in our day calls itself 'postmodern' thought—which, often like Niebuhr, seems happily to forget that at many crucial points it, too, is 'modern'. Though I am not equipped to accomplish it, an interesting volume could be written on the similarities and the differences between the 'modernities' that Niebuhr and postmodernism respectively rejected.

The Concentration on Historical Life

Beginning with the Renaissance and vastly expanding during the Enlightenment (1650–1750), a remarkable shift in the concentration of Christian reflection and theology occurred, following, one may be sure, a parallel or even prior shift in the concerns of ordinary European life. This shift was from a concentration on the question of one's destiny in the next life, one's 'supernatural destiny', to a new concern with the importance of relations to others in this life, with one's experiences in this life of anguish or of joy, and one's experiences of suffering or of well-being. Historical life, both individual and social, gradually took center stage in the thought of writers, philosophers, and theologians alike, so that by the end of the Enlightenment in the mid–eighteenth century the 'salvation of the soul in eternity', while still certainly an important issue, had given central place to the gifts of grace enabling character and creating community in this life. By the end of the eighteenth century and into the nineteenth, the concentration on human experience and human community dominated philosophical and theological reflection, and by the close of the nineteenth century, the point of the gospel was for many the creation on earth of the social kingdom of God.

As this study of his theology shows, Niebuhr completely agrees with the "this-worldly" emphasis of modernity generally. Christianity, as he views it, is above all concerned with history and its meaning. The obligations that faith entails are those that mainly involve the creation of justice and love in our own historical communities, and the gifts of grace, besides those of the hope for a new possibility of love, are those of a forgiveness that quiets our deep anxieties and continuing remorse. And let us recall that for Niebuhr the central result of our sins against God—pride, unbelief, and inordinate self-love—is not any longer exclusion from God and eternal damnation, but injustice toward the neighbor in historical time. As perhaps the most important sign of that shift, this change in the understanding of the category of "guilt," which we rehearsed in chapter 6, signals this characteristic of 'modernity' as crucial to Niebuhr's Biblical understanding. To him "guilt" meant the responsibility of the sinner for the injustice against the neighbor that his or her sins have encouraged. Guilt here is not, as in the entire earlier tradition, 'before God', in and for eternity, a defacement or dismantling of our relation to God that results in eternal divine punishment or damnation and that has been taken away once and for all by the atoning work of Christ. Guilt is now the evil historical consequence of our acts against our neighbor, and hence it is entirely historical and not transhistorical in its character, although sin retains a transhistorical dimension concerned with the vertical relation to God. And let us not forget, eschatological hopes remain here even if vastly muted. This change in the meaning of guilt is, as I noted, consistent with Niebuhr's whole theology, and this shift, therefore, shows the tremendous influence of the modern concentration on history rather than on suprahistory as one of his most fundamental assumptions.

The Change and Relativity of the Forms of Life

The second element of this new sense of history is what has been termed "historical consciousness." This is the conviction that the forms of cultural life, and so back of that the forms of human consciousness, are importantly different in different spaces and times, in different periods of history: culture and consciousness alike change as history changes. This consciousness of fundamental historical change, that is, in the *forms* of historical life, is surprisingly modern. Even seventeenth- and eighteenth-century paintings of classical and Biblical times pictured their subjects dressed in the fashions and surrounded by the architecture of the painter's own time. As its political and religious writings (e.g., Deism) show, moreover, the Enlightenment assumed a universal consciousness common to all humans, a consciousness quite similar to their own consciousness. It was only with the appearance of the new science that awareness of the possibility of the really new (in this case, the new in knowledge) in history arose. As a consequence, it was during the course of the eighteenth century that it was seen that the consciousness that characterizes historical communities radically shifts from age to age.[4]

By the historical consciousness, then, I mean the awareness of historical change in the forms of communal consciousness: namely their forms of understanding and of self-understanding, their interpretation of their world and of themselves in it, their norms for action, and their expectations for life. These basic modes of understanding, our most fundamental presuppositions, are, after the eighteenth century (in 'modernity'), no longer accepted as universal and timeless but thought to differ from one community to another and from one age to another. One finds Herder speaking in 1783 of a "Hebrew consciousness," a "Greek consciousness," a "Hellenistic consciousness," and so on. One important result of this new awareness that consciousness itself changes its forms (and so is, so to speak, itself immersed in historical change) is a quite new sense of the *relativity* of our own most fundamental ideas and norms. As a result, all expressions of both in religion, in philosophy, and in morals—in texts—reflect a difference of outlook from our own. Hence the ideas embodied in ancient texts are strange to our own modes of consciousness. Each form of life and thought (Egyptian, Hebrew, Roman, European medieval) is located in space and time and is, therefore, not universal; hence each is particular, that is, relevant to its own situation, but often irrelevant and frequently obscure to another situation. Here arises what has been called the 'hermeneutical problem', the problem of *how* one can understand texts from another age. There is, further, for speculative philosophy, now a history of spirit (e.g., Hegel), and for later, more empirical philosophy, a history of ideas (e.g., Arthur Lovejoy). Probably the first example of this in theology was Schleiermacher's statement that in writing systematic theology he is interpreting Christian experience "for his time." Nothing, therefore, in history is absolute; all in history, every human expression, is relative to its own time.

This consciousness of the changeableness and so of the relativity of fundamental forms of life and of thought (individuals had always been regarded as changeable) appeared first in relation to historical change (e.g., "moderns"

---

4. A fuller discussion of the historical consciousness and its implications is found in Langdon Gilkey, *Reaping the Whirlwind* (New York: Seabury Press, 1976), pt. 2, chap. 8.

are different and even better than "ancients"). Then later (say, 1790–1830) this awareness surfaces in relation to the forms of the earth (geology), then with regard to forms of life in biology with Darwin (species as well as individuals change), and finally, in the twentieth century, in the entities that make up the wider astronomical cosmos.

This new sense of the rise and fall, appearance and disappearance, of the most fundamental forms of life—social, political, religious, biological, even cosmic—might be expected to raise at the deepest level the question of meaning. What is of worth if even the most permanent and treasured forms vanish? If every form, and so all value, ultimately vanishes, what possible meaning can there be in the passage of things? This 'modern' anxiety about relativity amidst transience was 'for the moment' assuaged in the later eighteenth, nineteenth, and the early twentieth centuries by confidence in the concept of temporal progress. Even if forms of life and of history are not permanent but constitute, in their coming and their going, a changing temporal sequence, that sequence of temporary forms is in itself progressive and represents a steady development of greater and greater value. This is one of the things Niebuhr meant when he said that the myth of progress represents the major article of faith of modernity, and that its demise raised the most urgent questions of meaning for our age.

This historical consciousness—consciousness, that is, of fundamental change in history and of our immersion in that change—represents a most important background of Niebuhr's thought. He accepts it without question and builds his theology on it throughout. In fact, it is for him one of the most significant aspects of our 'creatureliness'. He assumes that all of our human ideas and norms—scientific, social, philosophical, religious— represent particular perspectives relative to their time and place; none is absolute, and surely none are unequivocally divine. Church statements, Biblical interpretations, moral standards and ideals, however important and relevant in their time, are nonetheless for Niebuhr partial, located in time and place, shaped by their cultural assumptions, and generated out of class, racial, national, and (later) gender interests. They are and remain *creaturely,* and that means relative and transient.

Three concepts crucial to Niebuhr's thought arise from this new historical consciousness. (1) All historical authorities are relative, even religious and moral authorities. Hence scriptural texts, theological dogmas, church pronouncements, and any given theology (including, of course, his own), represent the partial perspectives of their time, place, class, and cultures. Their relevance and hence their authority thus recede as one moves into other times, places, and cultures. (2) This relativity of all ideas, norms, and beliefs is the source in creatureliness for the anxiety of transience and of meaninglessness. If all we hold to be valid will someday shift and even die, as we do, what do our efforts, and our life itself, mean in history? This is the anxiety of the intellect and its truth on the one hand and of the conscience and its norms on the other that correspond to the anxiety of the contingency and the mortality of one's existence. Each mode of anxiety tempts us to its own appropriate form of pride, pride of power, of intellect, and of virtue. Correspondingly, each mode of anxiety, and perhaps especially this one, raises pointedly the theological question of meaning—to which, as we have seen, the Divine Sovereignty and especially eschatology were for Niebuhr the answers.

(3) Finally, the concept of idolatry, making the relative absolute, claiming divine status for the creature, depends on the sharp sense of the relativity of all that is creaturely to which reference is here made. To name as 'pride' and 'idolatry', and so sin, all our efforts to make our merely relative truths, values, and creatures absolute, assumes that all of these are in fact relative and not absolute at all. It assumes this vision of historical process as a sequence of shifting, transient, and so relative forms of life.

One might argue, therefore, that very central to Niebuhr's interpretation of the tradition is this assumption of the relativity amid inevitable change of all creaturely forms, of the anxiety which this relativity creates, and the human answer of pride, of making absolute what is merely relative, as well as the divine answers of sovereignty and eschatology. What Niebuhr has in effect done is to accept this modern concept of the inevitable and continual change in the forms of history and then to accentuate in a thoroughly twentieth-century way the relativity of all forms implied in that Renaissance concept. To this he has explicitly added the appearance of the novel, and then this entire combination he has termed the Renaissance.

From this body of modern notions, which he accepts, he has then abstracted out and rejected the 'liberal' interpretation of this changing process, an interpretation characteristic alike of secular as of religious modernity, namely that which gave this changing process meaning. This was, of course, the conception of the progress of these developing forms, their role as leading through change to a culmination or fulfillment. Progress was, in other words, the 'religious' side of modern culture, secular and religious, its ground and source of meaning for most of modern life. In its place Niebuhr has given, first of all, that now uneasy and radically relative process a typically twentieth-century tone: change and relativity, far from leading to progress and increased well-being (an 'increment of value', as Whitehead put it), generate anxiety and thus pride; as a consequence there results the continuing return of injustice, cruelty, violence, and suffering. Second, he has tried to interweave into this modern worldview the Biblical vision of the turmoil and the meaning of history. The first aspect of Niebuhr's antimodernity he surely shares with the postmodern world, where apparently the sense of relativity has vastly increased. It is also true, however, that Niebuhr's sense of meaning in history 'by faith' has in large part evaporated from the postmodern perspective.

With the awareness that forms of social life change in history, that none is absolute, God ordained, or universally sacred, the correlate consciousness became possible in the modern understanding that human intentions and efforts, and human intervention in the course of history, could effect changes in the structure of society, that from our actions in the world new social forms could arise. Paradoxically, the sense of human freedom to create new forms in history expanded in modernity along with the sense of the immersion of human consciousness, the embeddedness of the human, in history just described. And with this awareness of the possibility of creating new forms of life appeared as a consequence a new sense of obligation: the obligation to effect such changes that were now seen to be possible. Freedom to create new forms carries with it new possibilities undreamed of before; it also implies, therefore, new obligations unfelt before. A new revolutionary consciousness in the seventeenth and eighteenth centuries thus accompanied the new sense of novel possibilities in history, and a new sense of social obligation accompanied both. Niebuhr, needless to say, accepts this point as well and builds his theology firmly upon it.

The change of fundamental forms in historical and, later, in natural life, represented a new *ontology*, one peculiar to the developing modern world. Correspondingly, this consciousness of the possibility of change in the forms of historical life represented the *ontological* root, the root in ontological consciousness, of the social gospel, namely the interpretation of Christian obligation as involving the changing of social structures in order to bring more justice into an unjust world. To several generations of liberals after 1850 or so, this is what 'faith' according to the prophets, to Jesus, and to the tradition really meant. On these assumptions, Walter Rauschenbusch proclaimed his stirring 'social gospel'; and, as we have noted, Niebuhr thoroughly agrees that social justice represents the true obligation of Biblical faith. Although, as we have also seen, he articulates a very different, nonprogressivist understanding of changing history than did Rauschenbusch, nevertheless he had no doubt to the end of his career that true Biblical faith impells us into effective action for structural change in social history. And he shared that extremely modern conviction with the liberals that preceded him.

In effect, then, a very great deal of Niebuhr's important theological contribution itself resulted from his assumption, learned as a modern person, that forms of life, including the institutional structures as well as the ideas and ideals of history, change in developing time. As we have seen, he means all this, perhaps most of it, when he seeks to synthesize 'Reformation and Renaissance', identifying, as I noted, Renaissance with the concept of history as characterized by dynamic change and the possibility of the new. Latent in this conception are the relativity of forms, new modes of anxiety, the peril of idolatry, and the obligation to create and establish new and more just forms. My point is that, while the Reformation side of Niebuhr's synthesis is clear enough, the importance of the Renaissance side, as he called it, must, I suspect, be spelled out.

The Influence of Science on Theology

Like most of his neo-orthodox colleagues, Niebuhr seemed quite unaware of the great influence of modern science on his theological understanding. By that influence I refer, in the first instance, to the effect that the new vision of nature and of ancient history had on their theological understanding of nature, of nature's past, and of the past of human history. This new vision of the past had been slowly established since the middle of the eighteenth century by the sciences of geology, biology, and astronomy and then later by anthropology, archaeology, and ancient history. Gradually there had unfolded an entirely different vision of the earth's past and of the human past than the picture universally accepted before, say, 1750. According to that picture, the universe had begun with a creation about six thousand years earlier, complete with its present astronomical structure intact, with its present species created within the first week, and with humans created on the sixth day—and falling from grace and becoming subject to death shortly thereafter. According to the new picture, the human past stretched almost endlessly back into a long prehistory of a slowly developing humanity; back of that lay an even longer evolutionary past replete with changing species of animal and marine life; back of both of those had been the slow development of life on earth, of earth itself, of the galaxies and of the physical universe itself—in all, some 13–15 billion years. Every important theologian in the twentieth century accepted this scientific, evolutionary understanding of the past without question, however much most of them studiously avoided referring to it. Clearly Schleiermacher had already seen some of this 'out of the corner of his eye' when, in 1825, he stated that creation was a speculative and not a Christian doctrine, and hence to be replaced by what we can experience now and be sure of, namely the symbol of providence. Nineteenth-century liberal theology heeded Schleiermacher's advice and ceased almost entirely—until Niebuhr's time—to refer theologically to the Biblical story of creation.

If, therefore, one wishes to know why Niebuhr states that the original Biblical myths are no longer credible if understood as literal truth, why primitive myth is now impossible for us, why Adam is a symbol and not a cause, and why death is a part of creation and not an effect of the historical fall—clearly the major reasons lie in Niebuhr's acceptance of these developing scientific concepts of our human past. One sees the effect of this new concept of nature not only on the content of theology but even more on its method: as Schleiermacher said, theology no longer makes scientific statements, and the Scriptures, whenever they make such statements, reflect the worldview of a much earlier time. Niebuhr is right (as was Kierkegaard) that there are excellent theological reasons for discarding a literal interpretation of the myths of creation and fall. But he seems (to me) sublimely unaware (or perhaps loathe to recognize) that the fundamental ground of this new 'symbolic' rather than 'literal' hermeneutic of the Scriptures was the influence of the new scientific understanding of nature and the new historical understanding of the ancient world. Again the quite valid effort to base theology on Biblical revelation rather than on modern 'cultural wisdom', especially on science and philosophy, has obscured the dependence of this theology—as of Barth's and of Brunner's and even of the later eschatological theologians—on important modern assumptions generated largely out of the natural and historical sciences.

It is, then, largely because of the new understanding by geological and biological science of nature's evolutionary past and by archaeology and anthropology of the human past that Biblical narratives about origins were transformed from narrations about particular historical events, about our 'first ancestors', into narrations containing theologically important symbolic content: the good creation, the temptation and fall, the expulsion and subsequent suffering. We have seen how Niebuhr has brilliantly taken these symbols to illumine our human situation: our created nature, our gifts and powers, our obligations, and our sinfulness. The transmutation of the fall from the historical *cause* of all of this to a *symbol* of it has, however, left one important aspect unexplained, even perhaps unintelligible. And to this new problem I now briefly turn.

The question that is now left quite unanswered is why each of us, and all of us together, fall. Why is our situation dominated by a lack of trust, a surfeit of pride, and subsequent injustice? And why is it universal, characteristic of us all, as both experience and doctrine alike amply verify? This universality is quite intelligible in terms of the literal myth. After all, Adam and Eve were the ancestors of us all; thus what they did could be conceived as the cause of the evident 'taint' that we have inherited from them. But if historical cause has become symbol, no explanation at all has been offered. A symbol at best *discloses* our situation to us; it does not provide for us an *explanation* of what the symbol discloses. Clearly the 'ground' in this case has to do with our freedom since sin is not a natural necessity. But why does our freedom so consistently and universally fall? Was there a pre-temporal fall as Origen held? Are we forced back to biological, to genetic explanations? In the first case the question of freedom's fall is merely put off; in the second all responsibility—and with that all humanity, including that of the geneticist and her husband—is sacrificed. The mystery of the origin of sin remains—softened perhaps by the very persuasive arguments of Niebuhr that any other categories fail much more thoroughly to enlighten this issue.

I would like to add a final note on the influence of science. With the advent of the new science in the post-Renaissance world of Galileo and then of Newton—and the Enlightenment culture that reflected that rise—came a deeper and more universal sense of the 'rule of law' in all the events of nature and history. Of course since the Greeks and Romans—and in their own way the Hebrews, too—nature had been seen to manifest a universal regularity, or order. Contingency still appeared for the Greeks via irrational matter, and especially in historical affairs; but on the whole, the order pervading all things could be understood by the mind and counted on, largely, by human action.

With the new science, however, this faith in order deepened and changed its character. This new order of material events seemed now to many to determine human and historical as well as 'natural' events; it characterized primarily the material realm, and it was intelligible through and through by the power of mathematics. By the eighteenth and nineteenth centuries, therefore, most members of the intellectual classes shared this sense of the 'rule of law' in material events; and, it was only by means of a 'dualism' of matter or 'extension' (Descartes) and of mind and will, that any concept of 'freedom' or responsibility on the part of mind or spirit was maintained. Miracles became a more and more difficult concept, almost disappearing in liberal theology and barely appearing (at least on the plane of observable historical events) in any examples of neo-orthodoxy. Niebuhr inherits this tradition of a rule of law in nature and writes his theology more or less assuming it.

Niebuhr calls nature 'a realm of necessity', indicating that he continued to think (so I believe) largely in terms of classical physics and the dualism it seemed to imply. History is for him of course a realm where "necessity" unites with spontaneity and human freedom in forming the novelty familiar to our experience, a point that leads him (rightly) several times to emphasize the "mystery" of natural life with its novelty and in its union under God's providence of causality with our freedom.

The main result of this tradition of law in his thought, however, is found, it seems to me, in what we can hesitantly call his 'naturalistic' understanding of the sequences of history. By that I clearly do not mean either the absence in those sequences of divine activity or of human freedom; obviously he thought both were effective in historical changes and their resulting events. I mean rather that for him only *finite* (secondary) *causes*—natural or human (free)—effect these changes; hence historical developments are the result of *historical* causes alone, be they natural, organic, psychological, or directly intentional. No supernatural interventions into the scheme of finite occurrences are to be expected. When God works in history—and for Niebuhr God does so work—it is *through* these finite causes, cajoling or luring them, limiting them, recombining them. God may even create new syntheses and help discourage harmful ones. The course of the world thus has assignable historical causes: political, economic, psychological, intentional; and both creativity and sin work through these causes—and providence continues to work with and against both. The vertical is ever present, but it works *through* the horizontal and so through the order (and novelty) characteristic of that process.[5]

---

5. Niebuhr, and the other neo–orthodox who agreed with him on this, were thus more dependent on Schleiermacher than they thought or admitted. When Schleiermacher said that he "wrote theology for his time," they seconded this view of the historical relativity of theological concepts. They also agreed when he said that the sense of absolute dependence upon God, the religious consciousness, is communicated to us *through* the order of nature (rather than outside it or against it) which order science studies but which each culture interprets differently. All of this was assumed but hardly, if ever, mentioned. See Friedrich Schleiermacher, *The Christian Faith,* sec. 1, no. 34; sec. 2, nos. 50, 51. Niebuhr thus also agreed with Troeltsch when the latter specified that every understanding of a historical event must understand that event entirely as the result of its historical context; that is, as the effect of all the various finite (natural and historical) causes (causes thus both inner and outer) that helped to bring that event to pass. See, e.g., Ernst Troeltsch, "Historical and Dogmatic Method in Theology" (1898; reprinted in *Religion in History,* by Ernst Troeltsch [Minneapolis: Fortress Press, 1991]).

The Critique of Religion

The final issue illustrative of Niebuhr's 'modernity' is the critique of religion. I have noted how pervasive this theme is in his earlier works; somewhat surprisingly this critique has become, I think, even more radical as the theological components to his understanding have increased. As I demonstrated, pride of religion is for him the worst sort of pride: in absolutist religion the creaturely and wayward self identifies itself with God, claims to be God's representative and voice, claims God's authority for its own truth, and God's virtue for the dubious virtues of the saints. This is, Niebuhr says, unbearably self-righteous; the self, its interests, and its community have here become quite explicitly the universal center, and new and deeper forms of scorn for the opponents and cruelty to them inevitably arise.

> For this reason religion is not simply as is generally supposed [in liberalism] an inherently human quest for God. It is merely a final battleground between God and man's self-esteem. (ND 1:200)

> Religion, by whatever name, is the inevitable fruit of the spiritual stature of man; and religious intolerance and pride is [sic] the final expression of his sinfulness. (ND 1:203)

Niebuhr's discussion of Christian history—Catholic, Protestant, and sectarian—moreover, shows that Niebuhr finds God losing that battle in religion over and over again. In fact, he seems to say that sin appears in its worst forms in Christianity—in prophetic Christianity and especially in the profoundest points of Protestant piety (ND 1:217–18). Modern secular criticisms of religion generally and of Christianity in particular could hardly be more radical than this. How are we to understand this in a theology based on the theological symbols and the faith of a *religious* community?

There are, I think, two complementary explanations of this puzzle, one theological and the other the new historical consciousness of modernity. The theological explanation is fundamental to Niebuhr's retrieval of the classical categories of Christian faith and to his entire understanding of human nature. This theological ground for the criticism of religion he shares with his other neo-orthodox contemporaries; Barth is even more critical of religion than Niebuhr, naming religion the quintessence of the human rebellion against God.[6] Briefly, authentic Christian faith—and so authentic religion—is for them based on God's revelation. 'Religion' is the

---

6. Karl Barth, *The Doctrine of the Word of God*, vol. I, 2, chap. 2, pt. 3.

human response to that revelation, and is, for Niebuhr, as ambiguous and creaturely as are all other creative human responses, especially spiritual ones. It is in and through revelation that this ambiguity of religion is challenged, judged, transformed, and purified, not through more religion; and this challenge to false religion in the name of the true God is for him the main theme of the tradition of prophetic religion. In turn, 'the means of grace'—Word, sacrament, and piety—can be channels of revelation, of judgment on religion's participation in sin, and of the gift of grace. Of themselves, however, shorn of revelation, these religious means are useless and dangerous, always in danger of being (like reason) instruments of sin rather than of redemption. And for Niebuhr the permanent criteria of God's Word in religion as against the human word in religion are the presence of critical judgment on our religious pretensions, repentant recognition of our own sin, and the hope alone for grace. Thus does religion represent the final contest between grace and pride. And thus are the structures, the authorities, the promise, and even the virtues of religion, when they are not the means of judgment and of grace, the greatest temptations to pride and injustice.[7]

> A religion of revelation is grounded in the faith that God speaks to man from beyond the highest pinnacle of the human spirit; and that this voice of God will discover man's highest not only to be short of the highest but involved in the dishonesty of claiming that it is the highest. (ND 1:203)

As Niebuhr and his contemporaries were well aware, this radical critique of religion in the name of a revelation of judgment and of grace represents theologically the precise opposite to the liberalism, especially the later liberalism, of the nineteenth and early twentieth centuries. Liberalism was grounded on the conception of the immanence of God in history; hence for liberalism God's action appeared precisely in and through "man's highest," especially religion. While liberalism, being itself modern, shared the Enlightenment and nineteenth-century critique of the dogmatic, authoritarian, intolerant, persecuting, and imperialist religions of the past, it possessed no standpoint from which such a general critique of religion, even of liberal religion, as Niebuhr's could be broached without losing all basis for liberalism's idealism and its hope for the future. If man's highest was itself under judgment for sin, what possible hope was there, what dike against cynicism could there be? This is, I think, one very fundamental reason for the deep antipathy of many liberals to Niebuhr: with him all their

---

7. See T. S. Eliot's masterful (and contemporary) portrayal of this theme in *Murder in the Cathedral*.

grounds for virtue and for hope seem now to be gone. On the other hand, Niebuhr and his contemporaries were so conscious of this break with liberal immanence and optimism that they failed to see the other important 'modern' ground for their radical critique. It is to this ground I now turn.

However 'Biblical' this critique of religion seemed to the neo-orthodox, there was, I believe, nothing like this critique of all religion in the name of revelation in the many forms of orthodoxy, Protestant or Catholic, or even in the forms of consciousness that produced the Scriptures. For all of these communities, of course, false religion is blasphemous, destructive, useless, and frequently dangerous; and for all of them God is against false religion. But over against them there is the possibility of "true religion": that is, revelation on the one hand and the authentic reception of revelation on the other. Together, revelation and its valid and proper reception represent "true religion," as Calvin put it. Perhaps this true recipient is the authentic covenant community, or the Roman church and its authentic ministry, or the true community of the Word, where the Word is truly preached and the sacraments truly administered. In all of these, transcendent revelation is combined with some authentic, valid, and God-given response: true sacraments, true religious doctrine and law, true faith. And, as can be expected, this union of revelation and reception constitutes an 'absolute', a divinely ordained and inspired form of religion incumbent on everyone to embody, to defend, and to practice.

Hence all of these forms are implicitly theocratic. The Enlightenment and the liberal criticism of all of these religious "absolutes," not least because of the wars based on fidelity to one or the other of them, severed this tie between revelation and certain forms of religion. One can see this very clearly in the change in the relations of 'faith' and of 'love' as requirements of Christian obedience, a change that took place between the Reformation and the end of the nineteenth century. The first requirement of Christian obedience was 'faith' for Calvin, namely a defense of God's true doctrine and law. The second and subordinate requirement was love for the neighbor. By the end of the nineteenth century this order had become inconceivable for liberals and neo-orthodox alike. Dogmatic faith is now seen not as the defense of God but as the source of intolerance, cruelty, and persecution—as precisely what Niebuhr called 'spiritual pride'.

This liberal sense of the danger of dogmatic religion to peace and freedom has, in Niebuhr, joined with the growing historical consciousness to create the radical critique explicated in this volume. For Niebuhr, no human word or action, institution or doctrine is absolute; all remain creaturely, finite, relative, and partial; none, therefore, unequivocally represent or could represent God. If such a claim is made, it is, in Niebuhr's words, an arrogant pretension, the ultimate "self-deification." It is, therefore, because of the modern sense of the relativity and partiality of everything in history, including the highest forms of religion and even contemporary forms of religion, that this radical critique of religious pretension becomes possible. Correspondingly, this inheritance of relativity from modernity now unites with the dependence in early twentieth-century theology on revelation and grace, even within the most valid forms of faith, to create this new understanding of the media of faith. The media of faith—all of them—can now also become vehicles of pride unless, as Tillich put it, the media point beyond themselves and deny themselves. Only then are they true media. Here again we see how it is that the intricate union of the traditional emphasis on revelation and grace with the very modern historical consciousness makes Niebuhr's (and Tillich's) understanding of religion and their radical criticism of it intelligible. And possibly the union of these elements reveals why again Niebuhr seemed quite unaware of the 'liberal' components of his own theology.

∽

Since Niebuhr's time two new issues have come to prominence in theological reflection and religious concern. These issues for a number of historical reasons were not at all on the theological horizon of his generation. The first is the question of nature and its survival—an issue that broke into the consciousness of the theological world (as it did other worlds) only in the 1960s and the early 1970s.[8] The second is the question of the relation of Christianity to other religions, an issue upon which also Niebuhr reflected theologically relatively little and certainly did not see as central to constructive Christian theology.[9]

8. It was in the 1960s that Rachel Carson and Barry Commoner began to warn us about the threats to nature, a point that *The Limits to Growth* made quite definitively in 1972, the year following Niebuhr's death (see Donella H. Meadows et al., *The Limits to Growth* [New York: Universe Books, 1972]). Hence this issue became central for most of the intellectual community and for contemporary theologians well after Niebuhr wrote his major works.

9. As the following comments will make clear, Niebuhr was on the one hand extremely tolerant of other religions; he knew their ethics well and taught them in his classes; and he took a leading, perhaps 'crusading' role in establishing close relations of all kinds with Conservative and Reform Judaism. As he once was reported to have said in the 1930s: "If a Jewish person comes to me to hear about the Christian faith, I will certainly speak to them of it. But I will not seek to convert any Jew—they have

This latter issue also came slowly to the fore in the second half of the twentieth century. It was initiated, I believe, by the break-up of the European empires following the end of World War II. Two results of that break-up, a vastly important historical and cultural event, were, first, the withdrawal of Western military and political rule from what we now term the Third World (it was not called that then) and the diminution of Western political authority over the rest of the world. Africa, India, Southeast Asia, and East Asia were now, for the first time in more than a century, free of outside rule. Second, as a result of this freedom, a new global vitality (as well as a new global unease and instability) appeared as non-Western cultures found a new relative autonomy. This is the deepest root of the present prominence of non-Western religions everywhere one looks. One can see this very clearly illustrated in the worlds of Islam, of Hinduism, and of Buddhism—all of which are now vibrant and active on a world scale. It is not too much to say that in the decades since Niebuhr's death the flow of mission work and influence has been reversed, flowing now from East to West.

As a final consequence, the theological as well as the purely practical problem of the relation of religions to one another, the issue of pluralism, rose rather suddenly to prominence. This occurred only in the late 1970s and the 1980s, instigated certainly by the beginnings of dialogue between major religions, and signaled, as a theological problem, by the publication of John Hick's seminal works, *God and the Universe of Faiths* (1977), and *God Has Many Names* (1980, 1982). While almost no working theologian dealt with either of these issues (nature or pluralism) in the first half of the century, it is a rare theologian in the past two decades that has not found herself or himself writing on each of these two problems.

Having dealt briefly with Niebuhr's relation (or lack of it) to the issue of nature, let us now turn to the other issue of pluralism and ask, What relevance, if any, does Niebuhr's critique of religion have for this new problem?[10] How does what he said about religion and the relation of

---

the same God, and theirs was the original covenant." On the other hand, as the text that follows seeks to show, a perusal of contemporary essays on pluralism shows that the theological problem of pluralism represents a quite different sort of theological issue, and one, to my knowledge, over which neither he, nor any of his "Biblical" contemporaries, puzzled theologically, as we have had to do.

10. For the issue of pluralism, see Langdon Gilkey, "Plurality and Its Theological Implications," in *The Myth of Christian Uniqueness,* edited by J. Hick and P. Knitter (Maryknoll, N.Y.: Orbis Press, 1987), and "The Mystery of Being and Non-Being," in *Society and the Sacred* (New York: Crossroad Press, 1981).

Christianity to religion, help or hinder our reflection on the new relations between religions that have appeared and established themselves at the end of the twentieth century? For many contemporaries find themselves engaging in dialogue with representatives of other religions, listening in new ways to what these representatives have, in both criticism and affirmation, to say to us, and in new ways reassessing our own faith and tradition in the light of these new viewpoints. Arguments between religions are not new; dialogue and listening with an open mind are. And such a practice seems to imply a kind of an assumption of parity, which is certainly new.

In the first place there were several elements of the cultural and theological world that Niebuhr inherited in the early part of the twentieth century that militated against a positive theological interest in other religions or dialogue with them. Certainly for all the 'neo-orthodox' their confidence and faith in revelation—and that meant to all of them special revelation in the covenant with the Hebrews and in Jesus Christ—and their distrust of religion generally, Christian or otherwise, were among the causes of their almost universal disinterest in dialogue or closer relations to other religions (except in many cases, and especially for Niebuhr and Tillich, to Judaism). For various theological reasons already mentioned, moreover, most of them rejected a 'mystical' understanding of humanity and God; certainly, as I have demonstrated, they had little interest in religions that saw no meaning in history or in social reconstruction in history. Thus, almost a priori, they were not attracted at all to either Hinduism or Buddhism. The mystical practice of religion, for example Yoga or Zazen, had nothing like its present almost universal appeal in roughly the first half of the twentieth century.

Most important, however, is, I believe, their emphasis on special revelation as the essential source of Christian faith, and so on the uniqueness and decisiveness of the Christ Event, of the Word, and of faith in that Word. As we have seen, Niebuhr recognized a general revelation of God that was both true and healing and that was the source in God's disclosure of the truth and vitality of other religions. But for him this revelation remained in significant ways obscure and unclarified, and so it failed (though he did not say this) to counteract the universal human problem of idolatry. In this sense the clear emphasis on the uniqueness and decisiveness of the Christ Event, of the atonement, and of the gospel message about both certainly made difficult any recognition of the 'parity' of Christian faith to other religions that were unrelated to that event.

I think, finally, that the point I have made in other connections is important here. The fundamental cause, in my mind, of the new relations among religions is the loss of the total dominance in world affairs—military, political, and cultural—of the West. There is dominance by the United States and by Europe today, of course, but it pales in scope and depth with that which was characteristic of the pre–World War II world. In that world, all the European empires were still intact, and so almost all of Asia, Africa, and the Middle East were not merely influenced by the West but ruled by them. The result was an assumed sense of the superiority of the West that almost every member of Western society, including its theologians, accepted almost without question. I assumed it when, as a recent college graduate, I traveled to China in 1940, and I do not think the great minds of the 1920s and 1930s felt very differently. Most disturbing of all, this sense of superiority was shared and resented by many of those thus looked down upon—which in part explains their reactions to the West since. In any case, the shift, subtle as it is, in the balance of cultural and spiritual power that resulted from these changes of rule came slowly, after the war and in the subsequent decades. Among that generation only Tillich, to my knowledge, felt the shift deeply, and that in large part at the close of his life. Niebuhr certainly disapproved of Europe's empires as thoroughly as any twentieth-century liberal figure; but the deeper results of their disappearance probably came too late for him to feel them.

On the other hand, there is much in Niebuhr to approve of and much that supports the present situation of relative parity, puzzling theologically as it certainly is to all of us. There is the strong Niebuhrian point that all religion, even religion with the most faithful proclamation of the Word and the most loyal kind of obedience of faith, is relative, human, and neither divine nor absolute, and probably itself in many ways corrupted. This view has almost certainly helped immensely to soften and to weaken the claims of superiority by one religion over others. In his own life, this deep humility meant a constant tolerance of other religions and of persons representing them; and of course, it meant also his remarkable and pioneering work in developing new and thoroughly equal relations with Judaism.

This whole complex of attitudes, I am sure, helped the subsequent generation bring the various religions somewhat closer together. If none has an absolute truth, doctrine, moral law, authority, or virtue, then all can associate and even share dialogue about their admittedly relative beliefs and ideals. Criticism of every aspect of the sacred tradition comes naturally to such a mind-set, and the possibility to hear some word of judgment or of grace from outside one's own tradition is now a real possibility. For God and God's truth transcend them all. Furthermore, the Niebuhrian emphasis on the symbolic character of theological truth was very important. In both Hinduism and Buddhism a somewhat similar sense of transcendence and of the symbolic character of all human speech and religious rites concerning the divine had led to a greater tolerance of other faiths than was characterized by Christian history. Correspondingly, the new Christian sense of the symbolic and relative character of its affirmations helped immensely to make close interrelations between denominations (the Ecumenical Movement) and later between religions (pluralism) possible.

Thus it is precisely this common, modern sense of the relativity of all forms of religious institution and religious faith—inherited from liberalism but made more radical in Niebuhr's thought by the insight into the sin in each tradition—that now made possible the growth of the Ecumenical Movement among Christian denominations, first in liberalism, and then, as a surprise, continued on its own principles in twentieth-century Biblical theology. And the same denial of absolute forms has in the latter half of the century helped to encourage dialogue among religions; in dialogue each community seeks to learn from another on the important assumption that none is absolute. In this sense, on one level at least, a universal tolerance within religion or religions has apparently grown apace in our own time.

One might suggest, however, that another emphasis of neo-orthodox understanding—not its emphasis on the unique event of Christ, nor its insight into the relativity of all faith, but its radical criticism of the potential sins of religion—is now, unhappily, even more relevant than it was in Niebuhr's time. It was Niebuhr above all who reminded us that religion can also become the primary vehicle of the demonic; that has also been validated more by the second half of the twentieth century than by the first half. In that first half, it was *secular* ideology and possibly *secularism* that seemed to represent the worst threats to authentic humanity and authentic community. In our present, however, it is religion—rampant religious orthodoxy and fanaticism—that in each corner of the globe seems to pose the gravest danger to peace and justice. Two Niebuhrian principles, the need for a nonabsolutist toleration of other faiths juxtaposed to a self-critical judgment on our own form of faith, seem perhaps even more necessary now than in his own turbulent time.

∞

Our reflections on Niebuhr's achievement and in part on his legacy are coming to an end. Can we summarize this complex set of notions in some brief but important fashion? What kind of synthesis in the end was this—was it really of Renaissance and Reformation, of Biblical theology and the modern categories, and how did it work?

Let me suggest that Niebuhr's own analysis of culture and its relation to religion helps to provide an answer. Every culture, so he said, has a religious 'faith' at its center, a myth or vision of the entire scheme of things that gives meaning as well as structure or order to the community's individual and common life, that provides its norms and standards, its goals and its assessment of success or failure—and that gives that community grounds for confidence and hope. The most creative of these examples of 'religious substance' are those that are both religious and historical, that is, that find the meaning of life intertwined with, and dependent on, a transcendent, divine principle on the one hand and supportive of an affirmed meaning to the community's life in the course of history on the other. Then the community is neither drawn away from concern for their common communal existence—that is, for justice—nor in despair about it. Such, of course, was the 'Biblical view' that Niebuhr formulated and for which he argued.

Another historical principle of meaning, also a 'faith', was the confidence in progress that had dominated, invigorated, and comforted modern (Western) communities since the Renaissance (or at least since the Enlightenment). It provided that crucial scheme of meaning without which every culture withers. And I should note that this "religious" sense of developing progress was itself associated with another important ontological element in the modern vision of the structure of things, namely the new understanding of cosmos and of history as representing a sequence of changing essential forms, a developing evolutionary process.

The other important ingredient of any culture besides its religious substance, therefore, is constituted by those general assumptions about process, about nature and history, about society and the individual, which characterize that culture—in short, what we have called its 'ontology'. These two always in the end go together in some fashion, that is, they complete and reinforce one another, as evolutionary development and progress completed and reinforced one another. Niebuhr would of course have recognized the importance of ontology as well, and like most other moderns, he would have added at once that the assumptions that constitute this modern 'ontology' (or, as Whitehead called them, 'these metaphysical presuppositions') are themselves relative, transient, and partial.

In modern (Western) life these assumptions have taken a particular and unique form. In discussing the ontological assumptions that lie back of Niebuhr's thought, we have described a good number of them: the reality and goodness of this world; the radical change or development—even of fundamental forms—that characterize that world; the consequent relativity to one another of all of these forms and their embeddedness in their context or their 'contextuality'; the resulting contingency of everything in our experience, that the natural or historical process might have taken a different course and can therefore be shaped in new ways; and the transience or mortality of all things in nature and in history. Corresponding to this dynamic developmental vision of the natural and historical worlds around us is the 'historical consciousness' that sees ourselves and our modes of consciousness as results of this contingent, changing, and relative process; the sense of the rule of law or of order even amidst novelty in this process; and finally the optimistic confidence that we are autonomous and so able to refashion an unfinished world.[11]

For vast numbers of thoughtful modern people this dynamic, changing, and fluid process so understood was considered to be "all there is." Any transcendent factor in relation to it, or any transcendent dimension to it, was regarded as quite superfluous and unwarranted; a transcendence that is unobserved and unobservable and so for an empirical age a 'nonentity'. Because of the belief in progress, Niebuhr once remarked, modern intellectuals find religion, and especially a transcendent God, even more *irrelevant* than they find the doctrines about that God *incredible*. Thus this ontological vision of a developing, progressive process seems to drive in a 'secular' or secularistic, a naturalistic, direction, even when (perhaps unaccountably) this process is seen as essentially progressive. Needless to say, Niebuhr disputes this secular interpretation of our general experience throughout his work. He seeks to show that, insofar as we can understand at all natural and historical sequence, and the existence of the human individual and community, in this modern way, then we are impelled to understand them as related to a transcendent dimension if we are to understand them at all. This relation to a transcendent dimension is essential if we are to make sense of the puzzling and paradoxical character of our actual experience of existence and of ourselves. A secular interpretation of reality so understood falsifies ordinary and common experience and so cannot be valid.

In any case, all this is—especially after the discussion in this volume—fairly obvious. But it does give us a clue to what Niebuhr's major enterprise in his work came to, what he was about intellectually—and, ncidently, what his synthesis of Renaissance and Reformation really

11. I have attempted with much more care and specificity to spell out these assumptions that make up 'modernity' in Langdon Gilkey, *Naming the Whirlwind* (Indianapolis: Bobbs-Merrill, 1969), chap. 2, and to describe the historical consciousness in *Reaping the Whirlwind* (New York: Seabury Press, 1976), chap. 8.

represented. It seems to me we can say that Niebuhr accepted and so used the major ontological assumptions of his modern context about nature and history—about finitude or what he would call the 'creaturely world'. As I have shown, these assumptions represent not only the fundamental presuppositions of his analysis of finite nature, of human being, and of communal history; it is, generally speaking, in terms of these assumptions that he defines his important theological category 'the human as creature'. More than this, however, these ontological assumptions provide the basis for most of his entire subsequent *theological* interpretation of creaturely existence, its creativity and goodness, its anxiety and temptations, its characteristic sins, and its consequent evil. Modern ontology is, moreover, not only present to his understanding of creatureliness, of anxiety, of idolatry, and of injustice; it is even more, as I have tried to show, an essential *ingredient* in his own interpretation of each of these theological categories. It is because we are (as modern culture saw) transient, relative, and contingent, and our ideas are therefore partial and vulnerable to criticism, that we are anxious, that we seek to make our ideas and ourselves absolute, and that we sin against our neighbor. A modern ontology is thus essential to all Niebuhr says; in fact it is essential to each of the elements of his interpretation of Biblical faith—just as is, of course, the transcendent dimension that a secular interpretation drops out.

Is, then, what Niebuhr did merely to put a religious gloss on modern ontology, thereby adding a dimension that a secular view omitted? If this were so, then his achievement would have been simply another example of Biblical theology, and any claim to have created a new synthesis of Renaissance and Reformation would have been misleading. Hence the most important element in Niebuhr's synthesis concerns what he did with the *religious* dimension of modernity's liberal and secular ontological vision— for Niebuhr was sure that, despite its denials, modernity had a religious center. And in this he was quite right. It was, as we have seen, not just Christian liberal theology that gave to the dynamic process characteristic of modern ontology a 'religious' interpretation, an interpretation in terms of the immanent God and God's purposes. On the contrary, for Niebuhr—and he showed this insistence to be quite correct—even the secular interpretations of modern process (evolutionary, naturalistic, liberal, or communistic) had at their essential core a principle of meaning. This "religious" category, or "religious substance," gave spiritual power and communal efficacy to their understanding of reality. These secular visions too, therefore, were 'myths', myths of meaning and hence deeply religious in character.

As I have demonstrated, this religious core was represented by the two myths of progress, modern liberalism on the one hand and communism on the other. A different interpretation of progress is inherent in each myth, but for both the religious heart of their visions of reality is evident. It was, therefore, in terms of this myth of progress at the center of modernity's ontological vision that this vision became meaningful, a source for communal norms and goals, and an inspiration for communal hope. It was also this religious element of modernity that, Niebuhr saw, was vulnerable to empirical criticism and so to falsification. Hence his enterprise was to abstract this 'modern' religious core, the vision or myth of progress with all its consequences (and among them "the easy conscience of modern man") from the ontology he accepted. And then, having abstracted via criticism that religious core of progress, he sought to re-present that ontology via an examination of experience in the terms of the transcendence and yet the relatedness of God, of a reinterpretation of Biblical faith or of classical Christian faith (the Reformation).

Both the ontology and the Biblical faith, both the Renaissance and the Reformation, are hereby reinterpreted. The synthesis reshapes and redefines them both. The modern ontology of radical temporality, of change of fundamental forms, of contingency, relativity, transience, and autonomy is now viewed in the light of creation, sin, and grace, of creativity, anxiety, self-concern, and self-deception, and rescued by divine judgment and mercy. And in turn, as we have seen, Creation, Fall, Revelation, Incarnation, Atonement, and Eschatology are each interpreted in the terms of modern ontology. To Niebuhr, furthermore, the modern religion of progress is not only partial, prejudiced toward Western and middle-class values; it is also empty of empirical validity, of spiritual vitality, and, most important, of redemptive power in the face of the tragic character of life.

Niebuhr's most fundamental argument was that human existence so viewed (i.e., in modern terms) must be viewed Biblically, in relation to the transcendent God who is continually related in judgment and in grace to our world; and that modern life must in turn be lived in faith, love, and hope if it is to escape self-destruction and despair. Niebuhr's theology represents, therefore, a correlation, if ever there was one, between a modern ontology and Biblical symbols, a correlation in which each side reshapes the other—and makes possible a Christian existence within the precarious terms of modern life. Augustine had used the ontology of the late classical world, of Hellenistic culture, to reinterpret human existence as upheld, illumined, and centered on the transcendent Divine Light, but still as (paradoxically) radically transient, dominated by *cupiditas,* and driven toward death, a synthesis of Biblical tradition and Hellenistic ontology. So Augustine's descendant, Niebuhr, has used the modern ontology of radical change, relativity, contingency, and autonomy—and dropped out the religious element in modernity, progress—to reinterpret for our age the same tradition and to create a new synthesis of the modern sense of change, development, and autonomy on the one hand with the Augustinian and Reformation sense of sin and the coming of grace on the other.

Index